THE EFFECTS OF THE EGYPTIAN FOOD RATION AND SUBSIDY SYSTEM ON INCOME DISTRIBUTION AND CONSUMPTION

Harold Alderman
Joachim von Braun

Research Report 45
International Food Policy Research Institute
July 1984

Library of Congress Cataloging
in Publication Data

Alderman, Harold, 1948-
   The effects of the Egyptian food ration and
subsidy system on income distribution and consumption.

   (Research report / International Food Policy
Research Institute ; 45)
   Includes bibliographical references.
   1. Consumers–Egypt. 2. Income distribution–
Egypt. 3. Food supply–Government policy–Egypt.
4. Food relief–Government policy– Egypt. I. Von
Braun, Joachim, 1950- . II. Title. III. Series: Re-
search report (International Food Policy Research
Institute) ; 45.

HC830.Z9C612 1984   339.2′2′0962   84-15700

CONTENTS

TABLES

ILLUSTRATIONS

FOREWORD

Subsidies aimed at keeping food prices low for consumers are found in many developing countries. These subsidies may be costly to governments and cause distortions in the economy. They may also help the poor meet their food and nutrition requirements. The nature of existing subsidy programs and their costs and benefits vary among countries. In order to assist governments in their deliberations regarding food price policies in general and subsidies in particular, IFPRI undertakes studies of food price subsidies existing in various countries. Several such studies have been published, including studies of policies in Brazil, Bangladesh, Sri Lanka, and Kerala State in India (Gray, *Food Consumption Parameters for Brazil and their Application to Food Policy*, Research Report 32; Ahmed, *Foodgrain Supply, Distribution, and Consumption Policies within a Dual Pricing Mechanism: A Case Study of Bangladesh*, Research Report 8; Gavan and Chandrasekera, *The Impact of Public Foodgrain Distribution on Food Consumption and Welfare in Sri Lanka*, Research Report 13; George, *Public Distribution of Foodgrains in Kerala—Income Distribution Implications and Effectiveness*, Research Report 7; and Kumar, *Impact of Subsidized Rice on Food Consumption and Nutrition in Kerala*, Research Report 5).

A comprehensive study of the food ration and subsidy system in Egypt is near completion. A thorough description of the system and analyses of implications for domestic agriculture, fiscal cost, foreign trade, and several macroeconomic aspects have been published (Alderman, von Braun, and Sakr, *Egypt's Food Subsidy and Rationing System: A Description*, Research Report 34; Scobie, *Food Subsidies in Egypt: Their Impact on Foreign Exchange and Trade*, Research Report 40; and von Braun and de Haen, *The Effects of Food Price and Subsidy Policies on Egyptian Agriculture*, Research Report 42). In this report, Harold Alderman and Joachim von Braun present the results of analyses of the effects the system has on income distribution and nutrition.

This study was financed at a level that allowed a comprehensive analysis of many aspects of the complex issues of food subsidies. An overview report is planned. It is the comprehensiveness of the study that is its strength and that provides the basis for a major improvement in knowledge of public policy toward food subsidies. Such a large coordinated effort would not be possible without many participants. Per Pinstrup-Andersen is the coordinator of this large multifaceted effort. The substantial financing was supplied by the United States Agency for International Development (AID), Bureau for Science and Technology, Office of Nutrition, with the technical supervision of the Nutrition Economics Group, Office of International Cooperation and Development, of the United States Department of Agriculture. We are grateful to Roberta van Haeften, Martin Forman, and Nicolaas Luykx for their understanding, cooperation, and thoughtful input in this complex effort. The help of several other people at AID, Washington and at USAID, Egypt and the Ford Foundation's Cairo office is also gratefully acknowledged. Essential to this study was the collaboration of many people in several Egyptian institutes, in particular the Institute of National Planning and the Ministry of Economy, the Ministry of Supply and Home Trade, the Ministry of Agriculture, and the Ministry of Investment and Economic Cooperation. This collaboration is gratefully acknowledged.

John W. Mellor

Washington, D.C.
July 1984

ACKNOWLEDGMENTS

The authors gratefully acknowledge the encouragement and support of Per Pinstrup-Andersen, Ahmed Abdel Ghaffar, and Ismail Badawy. Sakr Ahmed Sakr and the staff of the Institute of National Planning were also essential pillars on which this research rests. The patience and guidance of Mohammed Abdel Alim who directed the field work is also gratefully acknowledged. Roberta van Haeften and Nicolaas Luykx provided useful insights. Richard Wallman provided assistance with the computations. The research was funded by the U.S. Agency for International Development, Bureau for Science and Technology, Office of Nutrition, under the technical supervision of the Nutrition Economics Group, Office of International Cooperation and Development of the United States Department of Agriculture.

1

SUMMARY

The Egyptian government controls the distribution of a number of basic food commodities, including bread, flour, pulses, sugar, and oil. The government handles the major share of the total marketed quantity of those commodities. Commodities are distributed in rationed quantities at low prices and made available at higher, but still subsidized, prices through cooperatives, flour stores, and bakeries. The regulations of this system vary by governorates and by urban or rural locale, and access to subsidized foods is affected by the distribution of outlets and other factors. These complexities make it difficult to determine who benefits from the system and by how much. But in order to be able to design future policy, it is important to understand both the distribution of the benefits and the likely effects that changes in current policies will have.

Provided that changes in the system would be aimed at allowing it to improve the nutrition of the poor more effectively and at a lower cost, the effects of the system should be evaluated not only by region and income group, but also by commodity and outlet. A new household budget survey specifically designed to make this possible was conducted between December 1981 and June 1982.

According to this survey, most of the population uses the system: 93.1 percent of the urban population and 91.9 percent of the rural population have ration cards. More than 95 percent of these cardholders reported that in each of the three months preceding the survey they obtained the rationed commodities—sugar, oil, tea, and rice—that they were eligible for.

A significant share of the population consumed more of each commodity than was available from either the basic or additional ration. For example, 77.2 percent of rural and 81.9 percent of urban consumers obtained sugar outside the ration shop. Comparable percentages of consumers did the same for tea and rice. Urban consumers are more likely than rural consumers to obtain their above-ration quantities from cooperatives. Nevertheless, more than 25 percent of the urban population purchased rice and sugar on the open market.

Only 25 percent of the villagers reported regular access to subsidized bread, but 75 percent in the cities did. Flour from government shops was available locally to 75 percent of rural families, which somewhat made up for their lack of access to subsidized bread. Because flour was rationed and scarce, however, only half the rural population claimed to have regular unlimited local access to either subsidized flour or bread. Rural residents purchased half of their flour on the open market. The majority of this flour was purchased by individuals from the government and then resold in smaller quantities or in neighboring villages. Although this flour generally cost the final consumer more than flour from government shops, its price was still far less than the world market price.

Less than 3 percent of the rural population purchased frozen meat or chicken and only 11 percent purchased frozen fish. In the urban areas less than a third of the families obtained these subsidized commodities, with no sharp differences between income groups. The quantity of frozen meat and chicken purchased, however, did increase as income did, which indicates that monthly quotas were not universally enforced. It also indicates that the subsidies on these goods benefited the poor less than those better off.

Rice was unavailable at least once to 17.5 percent of the cardholders in the rural sample during the time of the survey. Beans and lentils, which are not strictly assured in the ration system, were usually available in the winter months but not in the spring. There was little variation in the average size of purchases by expenditure group, but urban consumers obtained higher oil and rice rations.

The system contributes a sizable share of the budgets of Egyptian households, especially those of the rural and urban poor.

An income transfer is defined as the difference between the border price with local transport costs subtracted and the reported purchase price times the quantity purchased. Calculated that way, explicit or implicit transfers from all outlets directly controlled by the government (rations, cooperatives, bakeries, and government flour shops) totaled LE 29.59 per capita in urban areas (LE 1 = U.S. $1.22). Transfers decreased as income increased. But since many open market purchases, including fresh meat, cost the consumer more than their equivalent in international prices, the net income transfer implicit in current pricing policies differed from the transfer through government channels.

An urban dweller obtained LE 8.73 annually from the ration system. Urban consumers, on the average, spent more than rural consumers on meat, the price of which was considerably higher in Egypt than in the international market. When such implicit losses are considered along with the gains from direct subsidies, the net per capita consumer transfer in urban areas falls to LE 13.32. The transfer for the poorest quartile in urban areas was equivalent to 12.7 percent of expenditures.

Under the subsidy system, farm households with less than 3 feddan purchased more subsidized cereals (including bread) than they delivered to the procurement system. In addition, the presence of a bakery in a village reduced grain production significantly, on the average. Availability of subsidized cereals in farm households mainly increases consumption and, to a lesser extent, increases sales of a household's own produce or reduces production of cereals.

The demand for most food commodities increased with income. Income elasticities were highest for fresh meat, chicken, fish, eggs, fruit, and milk. Demand for bread varied little by income, whereas flour purchases increased. The elasticity for *fino* flour was higher than for *balady* flour in both urban and rural areas. Expenditure elasticities for other commodities distributed through government channels were moderate, usually positive but less than one. In general, expenditure elasticities declined with income.

Rural residents gained an average LE 6.67 per capita annually from the ration system, and LE 19.68 from all government outlets. Their net consumer transfer was LE 21.90, because they gained appreciably from low prices on open market purchases of flour and cereals. The poorest quartile in rural areas received a net consumer transfer equivalent to 18 percent of their total expenditures.

The system of subsidies and consumer prices favors the poorer groups of the population more than the upper-income groups when both government outlets and the open market are taken into account. The ration system and the subsidies on *balady* (coarse) flour and bread are especially beneficial for the poor. Some parts of the system favor the rich. These include the subsidies on commodities sold by the cooperative, and to a lesser extent, the subsidy on *fino* (fine) flour and bread. On the whole, the subsidies transferred through the government outlets— leaving the open market out of consideration—favor the urban population and are slightly regressive.

As many rural residents are producers as well as consumers, the net effects of food pricing should include the effects of farmgate prices and input subsidies, although the prices of agricultural outputs are not directly linked with government food subsidies. The average net production transfer to rural areas was LE −3.14 per capita, indicating an implicit tax. This was only LE −1.10 for the lowest expenditure quartile and LE −6.80 for the highest, largely because the protected livestock sector is concentrated on small farms (and with landless rural residents) and because the higher shares of implicitly taxed cotton, sugar, and rice in the upper expenditure groups increased losses. The protection of livestock, then, transfers income from the urban middle class chiefly to small farmers.

The largest estimated price elasticities were associated with the commodities that had high expenditure elasticities. The price elasticities for flour, however, are exceptionally high. This reflects the willingness of consumers to shift between purchasing bread and baking it, as well as the quantity discounts of bulk purchases that influence the statistical relationship. Even accounting for shifting between bread and flour, consumers appear to respond significantly to changes in the prices of flour products.

The report concludes that the use consumers make of the system is affected by the time required to acquire food. Urban consumers were willing to buy higher priced open market goods or to forgo purchases when lines at cooperatives increased or when the low probability of obtaining the good made repeat visits necessary. Workers having access to cooperatives at their place of work were more likely to wait in line than those purchasing their food from neighborhood cooperatives. Similarly, if consumers had to wait at bakeries, they bought bread less often and flour more often.

Low-income consumers appeared to be at least as unwilling to wait in line or to be subject to other search costs as the rest of the population. This reflects the opportunity costs of time but not wage costs. Furthermore, as higher income consumers purchased more per visit than the poor, and the costs of queuing are calculated for each visit and not for each unit purchased, queuing contributed to the middle class bias of the cooperatives.

Assessment of the nutritional implications of the system reveals that there was no evidence that a protein gap exists that would require a change in the system to upgrade the quality of the diet. But the absence of this gap is not a product of the subsidies on frozen meat and chicken, which contribute little to the amount of protein households consume. They contribute less to the amount of calories consumed, which makes the need for such subsidies questionable.

Calorie consumption was high, on average, but it was low for approximately 17 percent of both the urban and rural populations.

The probability that a family would consume less than household energy requirements was negatively correlated with income. It is likely that the current system contributes to nutritional adequacy. It is also an important instrument for a broad-based nutritional policy, though it is not an optimal tool for fine tuning one.

This report's assessment of the effects of the system on the distribution of food provides a basis for analyzing policies that attempt to increase the effectiveness of the system in improving nutrition while reducing the system's cost. It also provides a basis for determining how to reduce the fiscal costs of the system without having an adverse effect on income distribution. Changes in parts of the system that have a regressive effect on distribution, such as the cooperative system (frozen chicken, for example) and the subsidies on refined flour and its products, might be considered if that were the goal.

2

INTRODUCTION

Throughout history, Egyptian governments have taken upon themselves the task of making the supply of food secure, both by increasing the ability to regulate the flow of the Nile and by increasing their involvement in consumer-oriented food policies. Since the mid-1970s the burden the government has taken up has increased, as the increasing share of total public expenditures spent on food subsidies makes evident. This share was less than 1 percent at the beginning of the seventies and has ranged between 10 and 17 percent since 1974, although total public expenditures during this period grew.

The fiscal and economic costs of the system are an issue of concern in Egypt. If the system is to be changed to reduce costs, the key question to begin with is where to start. And a good place to start is with the segments of the system that are least effective in improving nutrition or are regressive or the least progressive in their effects on income distribution. This report attempts to identify these.

In the system of subsidies and food marketing that has developed since the middle 1970s, the Egyptian government dominates marketing of all basic food items.

The assumption by the government of a portion of the burden of providing food security may contribute significantly to household welfare, at least in the short run. It may also be a factor in household investment and production allocation. At the same time, it is a cost to society as a whole, not only because of public expenditures, which are easily measured, but also because of the opportunity costs of commodities that are procured and distributed by the government. In addition, the large government allotment to consumption may affect the performance of the national economy, either through the deficit or through investment planning. Furthermore, all sectors may be affected by the commitment of foreign exchange needed to maintain a high and regular supply of food. Agriculture, in particular, may be affected by the links between pricing policies and consumption policies.

This report uses household survey data to investigate the effects of the system on income distribution and consumption. Inasmuch as the costs of the system were covered in the earlier reports, this report concentrates on the distribution of its benefits.

Chapter 3 discusses how the system is used, while Chapter 4 reports on the size of expenditures and food purchases from various outlets. The intake of calories and protein by households is described next. The following chapter analyzes the transfer of income to and from households, which is implicit in the multitiered pricing system. It reports on the welfare gains and losses to producers as well as consumers and evaluates the major determinants and distribution of these gains and losses. Following that, the interaction of the subsidy system with farm production cropping systems and marketing is analyzed.

Chapter 8 presents estimates of income and price parameters derived from the household survey. Chapter 9 begins a discussion of the implications time allocation has for purchasing food. Chapter 10 continues that discussion with a statistical analysis of how time affects consumption.

The report ends with a summary of the implications that the conclusions of this report have for the subsidy system.

3

HOW HOUSEHOLDS USE THE SYSTEM

System Overview

Subsidized wheat flour and bread are available, in principle, to all consumers without restriction. Monthly quotas of rice, tea, cooking oil, and sugar, the goods in the "basic ration," are provided at low, subsidized prices to the population through ration cards. These quotas vary by region and are distributed through registered grocers. A second tier of quotas is for goods that are part of the "additional ration." Prices on these goods are also subsidized, but are higher. They are also marketed through cooperatives and government retail stores, but their availability is less assured. Beans and lentils are sold at quota prices but are not always available.

Frozen meat and poultry are distributed through government stores and cooperatives with monthly limits on purchases. The per capita quantities of the goods in the basic ration have changed little, but the quantities of goods in the additional ration have grown faster than population, as have sales of frozen meat and chicken. Per capita consumption of wheat flour products has also risen.

Some of the increase in consumption is the result of numerous changes in regional quotas authorized by the Ministry of Supply and Home Trade. Local quotas are based on ration guarantees and regional supply. However, because keeping the supplies and prices of basic foods stable is given high priority, the system is not responsive to international price fluctuations in the short run. Official prices do not rise when local demand exceeds the quotas, but waiting lines and other costs of food acquisition influence consumer purchases. There also is open market trading in scarce commodities.

Data Source

The analysis of the effects of subsidies on consumption and production is based on data collected in household interviews.[1] Although household surveys have been undertaken by the Central Agency for Public Mobilization and Statistics (CAPMAS) regularly, the larger breadth of those surveys precludes the detail on market channels included here. The survey used for this report not only allows for disaggregation by households but also for disaggregation of commodities and prices by source of purchase—ration store, cooperative, or open market—or production by the household itself.

The main rural survey was conducted between December 1981 and March 1982 and included 1,389 households in 77 villages throughout the country (see Appendix 1). Two questionnaires were included for each household. A production and income schedule was given to the male head of household, and a food purchase and consumption questionnaire was directed to the female head of household. This latter questionnaire included a recall of foods eaten by the household in the preceding 24 hours. Each head of household was interviewed by someone of the same sex. In addition, a village background questionnaire was used to gather information from the mayor, miller, and merchants on the village as a whole.

The urban survey consisted of 980 interviews conducted between April and June 1982 in 50 census tracts. Although a few questions pertained to land ownership and foods received directly from agricultural sources, the questionnaire was modeled on the consumption questionnaire of the rural survey.

---

[1] This chapter and the two following present details of the food distribution system. A reader mainly interested in an analysis of the welfare impact is advised to jump to Chapter 6 and subsequent chapters.

Selections in both samples were chosen to cover as many areas as possible given the constraints of sample size and logistics. For example, as villages in Egypt are administrative units consisting of four or more satellite villages, the sample was selected from a subsection of census tracts within the entire administrative unit. The emphasis on spatial diversity was motivated by two concerns. First, as preliminary studies indicated that prices vary appreciably even within a small geographic area, selecting from many areas would increase the variability of observed prices, hence the likelihood of determining price responses.[2] Second, in order to ascertain whether a portion of the population was excluded from access to subsidized goods because of poor transportation or administrative oversight, it was desirable to sample every governorate (frontier areas excluded) and to include as many neighborhoods as practical. These two guidelines were used to make the sample of urban areas as well, since earlier case studies indicated that the variability in the availability of commodities in the cooperatives and open markets was noteworthy.

In order to gain some information on seasonal patterns in rural areas and to augment the data from the sample, a subsample from the first rural round was reinterviewed. This sample consisted of 453 households from 26 of the villages. This second round was undertaken at the same time as the urban round and, whenever possible, by the individual who conducted the first interview.

Coverage of Rural Households

In a number of developing countries having food subsidy systems with government-controlled food outlets, rural areas are not completely covered by the distribution network. But in Egypt, they are. Out of the 77 survey villages, 76 had ration shops, 59 had flour shops selling subsidized flour, 11 had a bakery selling subsidized bread, and 39 had a cooperative shop selling subsidized food items.

Tables 1 and 2 show that even small villages are reasonably well served by the outlets, and significant regional discrepancies only appear in the distribution of flour shops.

Ration System

The Egyptian ration system is broad-based rather than targeted by administrative measures. Few households are excluded from the ration distribution: 6.9 percent of urban and 8.1 percent of rural households reported that they did not possess a ration card. In both population groups the percentage of households without cards is highest in the highest income quartile (see Table 3). The percentage of persons registered as ration recipients is higher than the percentage of registered households (95.5 percent urban, 93.0 percent rural).

Households with more than 10 feddan are legally restricted from receiving the full ration.[3] However, this regulation is not strictly enforced. Five out of the 10 households reporting ownership of more than 10 feddan still had a ration card. According to landownership statistics, however, there are about 70,000 owners with more than 10 feddan in the country. This represents only about 1 percent of all households. Stricter enforcement of this regulation could hardly affect targeting in the overall system significantly.

Another regulation restricting access to the ration system is the exclusion of households whose head is working abroad. 15.1 percent of the urban and 8.8 percent of the rural households having no card, that is, 1.0 percent of all urban households and 0.7 percent of all rural households, gave this as the reason why they were excluded. Given the high number of foreign workers (about 1.2 million in 1982) and the ease with which card holdership for those traveling could be controlled, this group seems to have potential for targeting.

---

[2] For documentation of such variations see Diana de Treville, "Food Processing and Distribution Systems in Rural Egypt: The Case of Grain and Bread," working paper written for the International Food Policy Research Institute, Washington, D.C., n.d. (mimeographed).

[3] Harold Alderman, Joachim von Braun, and Sakr Ahmed Sakr, *Egypt's Food Subsidy and Rationing System: A Description*, Research Report 34 (Washington, D.C.: International Food Policy Research Institute, 1982), pp. 19-23. One feddan is equal to 1.038 acres.

Table 1—Survey villages with food outlets, by size of villages

| | Size of Villages (Number of Inhabitants) | | | | | | | | | |
| Outlets | Less than 4,000 | | 4,000 – 8,000 | | 8,000 – 15,000 | | More than 15,000 | | Total | |
	Number	Percent	Number	Percent	Number	Percent	Number	Percent	Number	Percent
Ration shops										
1 – 4	20	91	17	59	7	44	0	0	44	57
More than 4	1	5	12	41	9	56	10	100	32	42
Flour shops	15	68	24	83	11	69	9	90	59	77
Bakeries										
1	3	14	4	14	3	19	1	10	11	14
More than 1	0	0	3	10	1	6	4	40	8	10
Flour mills	7	32	16	55	9	56	9	90	45	58
Cooperatives	11	50	12	41	9	56	6	60	39	51
Cooperatives with subsidized meat or fish	6	27	6	21	3	19	2	20	17	22
Total	22	100	29	100	16	100	10	100	77	100

Source: Data from the household survey made by the International Food Policy Research Institute and the Institute of National Planning, Cairo, 1981/82.

Lack of eligibility is only one reason for not holding a card. Households of recently married couples frequently go without cards for several years. It is considered impolite if they apply for their own card immediately after leaving the parents' household. This accounts for about 25 percent of households without cards. Also, transferring people to newly issued ration books is difficult and involves checking the ration book of the families.

The ration card has space for recording purchases over a decade. It is up to the card holder to report changes in family size to the local supply bureau. A card holder is more likely to record additions to the household than death or emigration. But comparison of the number of persons registered to actual

Table 2—Survey villages with food outlets, by region

| Outlets | Upper Egypt | | Middle Egypt | | South Delta | | North Delta | | Total | |
	Number	Percent	Number	Percent	Number	Percent	Number	Percent	Number	Percent
Ration shops										
1 – 4	7	50	9	56	10	59	18	60	44	57
More than 4	7	50	7	44	6	35	12	40	32	42
Flour shops										
1 – 4	9	64	7	44	12	70	19	63	47	61
More than 4	5	36	3	19	2	12	2	7	12	16
Bakeries										
None	10	71	11	69	12	71	25	83	58	75
1	2	14	4	25	2	12	3	10	11	14
More than 1	2	14	1	6	3	18	2	7	8	10
Flour mills	7	50	11	69	8	47	19	63	45	58
Cooperatives	8	57	5	31	15	88	11	37	39	51
Cooperatives with subsidized meat or fish	1	7	1	6	12	71	3	10	17	22
Total	14	100	16	100	17	100	30	100	77	100

Source: Data from the household survey made by the International Food Policy Research Institute and the Institute of National Planning, Cairo, 1981/82.
Note: Eighteen percent of the survey villages were in Upper Egypt, 21 percent in Middle Egypt, 22 percent in the South Delta, and 39 percent in the North Delta.

Table 3—Households with ration books and registered persons, by expenditure quartile

Location/Household or Person	Expenditure Quartile				Total
	1st	2nd	3rd	4th	
	(percent)				
Urban					
Households with ration books	96.7	95.5	92.3	87.8	93.0
Registered persons	96.4	97.6	96.3	95.5	96.5
Rural					
Households with ration books	94.0	93.1	91.9	88.5	91.9
Registered persons	93.2	93.6	92.8	92.9	93.1

Source: Data from the household survey made by the International Food Policy Research Institute and the Institute of National Planning, Cairo, 1981/82.

Notes: Expenditure quartiles were determined by ranking rural and urban households independently according to total reported expenditures per capita. The 1st quartile had the smallest expenditures; the 4th, the largest.

members of households indicates that over-reporting is only a small problem.

Frequently the regulations of a ration system provide fertile ground for abuse by individual shopkeepers. In Egypt, however, consumers can often choose between ration shops, which probably helps maintain the efficiency of the distribution system. The survey reveals that almost all households indicated that transfer of registration from one shop to another is possible (94.6 percent of rural households, 96.2 percent of urban households). In fact, 23 percent of the rural households and 42.7 percent of the urban households had transferred their cards. The lower density of shops in rural areas certainly makes it harder to change registration. About one-fifth of all reallocations of registration from rural households result from problems with the shopkeeper. Measured against the total sample, the share is similar in urban areas, where registrations are changed more frequently. Payment of tips to the shopkeeper for the sales of the rationed food is not common.

In each of the three surveys, households were asked to indicate whether during any of the three preceding months the actual rations they received were less than they felt they were entitled to. This makes it possible to determine how regular the supply of ration commodities is. In general, deviations between official allowances and actually received rations are small for the highly subsidized goods in the basic ration (sugar, oil, tea, rice). Depending on commodities and location, 1.2 to 4.2 percent of the households did not receive the other commodities at least once in the previous three months

(see Table 4). Rice in rural areas is an exception: 17.5 percent of rural households said that they had not received their full basic rice ration during the preceding three months, while only 4.8 percent of the urban households did so.

While the supply of basic rationed food is fairly stable and assured, distinct differences appear for the foods of the additional ration. Supplies of these commodities were less regular. This is in accord with the official policy. As opposed to the basic ration, rice is less frequently available to urban ration-book holders at the higher prices than it is to rural households. The availability of the additional ration of oil and tea supplies for the rural population is erratic. A remarkable seasonal pattern is shown in the availability of pulses: far fewer beans and lentils were supplied on subsidized and rationed terms during the spring of 1982 than in the preceding winter. The shortage in subsidized distribution was similar in rural and urban areas. The seasonality of distribution is shown by comparison of the first and second rounds of the rural survey (see Table 4). The ration system does more to stabilize the consumer prices of pulses through the seasons than to transfer permanent income. (It does not do this for the prices of other commodities.) Withdrawal of pulses from the scheme during the domestic harvest period is attractive as a way of increasing incentives to produce. Beyond the seasonal pattern, pulses are in shorter supply in the ration system in general than other commodities.

There are scarcities of rationed commodities and differences in the way the system is managed in rural and urban areas.

Table 4—Average rations per capita by expenditure quartile and the share of eligible households not receiving them

| Ration/ Commodity | Urban Expenditure Quartile | | | | All Urban House-holds | Rural Expenditure Quartile | | | | All Rural Households | | Share of Eligible Households Not Receiving Ration | | |
| | | | | | | | | | | | | | Rural | |
	1st	2nd	3rd	4th		1st	2nd	3rd	4th	1st Round	2nd Round	Urban	1st Round	2nd Round
					(grams)								(percent)	
Basic ration														
Sugar	728	721	707	680	712	682	691	684	691	687	687	1.8	1.3	1.6
Oil	355	378	371	347	364	173	184	175	185	179	171	2.8	1.7	2.3
Tea	39	38	38	37	38	38	37	37	37	37	37	2.0	1.2	4.2
Rice	807	788	823	716	788	347	376	407	386	378	399	4.8	15.3	17.5
Beans	60	72	67	64	66	106	97	110	127	108	61	59.2	36.5	63.4
Lentils	19	19	23	31	22	146	146	145	168	150	21	85.3	32.8	92.1
Additional ration														
Sugar	686	697	697	642	683	673	672	641	662	662	662	4.6	4.5	7.2
Oil	83	88	88	81	85	104	131	118	140	122	117	4.9	6.5	13.1
Tea	37	39	37	36	37	36	36	35	35	35	35	2.5	2.2	22.3
Rice	334	411	401	440	391	84	104	120	121	106	90	26.2	9.3	6.7

Source: Data from the household survey made by the International Food Policy Research Institute and the Institute of National Planning, Cairo, 1981/82.

Notes: Expenditure quartiles were determined by ranking rural and urban households independently according to total reported expenditures per capita. The 1st quartile had the smallest expenditures; the 4th, the largest. The first round of the survey took place during the winter of 1981/82. The second round took place at the same time as the urban survey, in the spring of 1982, which makes it more comparable with the latter. There was no additional ration of beans and lentils.

Ninety-two percent of ration-book holders in urban areas indicated that they could pick up their basic ration throughout the month, whereas only about 74 percent of rural households said that they could. Most of the remaining households stated that the ration was usually available only during the first half of the month. With the exception of beans, only a small proportion of ration-book holders do not take the rations available to them.

Cooperative Shops

Cooperative shops are government-controlled outlets for subsidized food established throughout Egypt. All cities and about half of the villages have such shops. In rural areas, they are more highly concentrated in the Southern Delta than in Middle Egypt and the Northern Delta (see Table 2). About 37 percent of the rural and 44 percent of the urban households are registered at cooperative shops. Out of the three different types of cooperative shops (workplace, neighborhood, government) the workplace cooperative is found much less frequently in rural areas.[4] Fifteen percent of rural households are registered at such a cooperative whereas 36 percent of the urban households are. However, being a member of a cooperative does not necessarily mean access to subsidized food, especially in rural areas.[5]

Apart from those subsidized basic food commodities mentioned above, subsidized frozen poultry, meat, and fish are distributed through the cooperative network. Shortages of cold storage and transportation facilities

---

[4] For a description of the cooperative network and related companies see Alderman, von Braun, and Sakr, *Egypt's Food Subsidy and Rationing System*, pp. 23-24.

[5] Households not purchasing at cooperative shops in rural areas mentioned the following reasons: shop too far away (27.2 percent), shop too crowded and long waiting time (9.3 percent), shopkeeper not fair (6.2 percent), available goods too few or undesirable (9.3 percent), not permitted to buy (13.4 percent), others (34.5 percent).

were mentioned frequently as reasons that these commodities are so seldom distributed in rural areas. So it is not surprising that the commodities are available mainly in villages of the Southern Delta along the major traffic lines, which imposes a distinct regional bias on the subsidized food system for these products (see Table 2). Thirty percent of all rural households mentioned that these commodities were sometimes available in their village but only 21.6 percent actually purchase them.

Subsidized Flour

The wheat distribution network is well developed even in rural areas. Seventy-seven percent of all survey villages have a flour shop selling the fixed price flour, and 25 percent of the villages have at least one bakery (see Table 1). Although small villages are not excluded from access to flour shops, there is a positive relationship between size of village and availability of bakeries.

Subsidized flour is, in principle, available at the specialized flour shops and—less importantly—at government cooperative shops. According to the households interviewed, however, subsidized flour is not always available. In rural areas, 44 percent of the households mentioned that they had been at the flour shop and did not find flour at least one time during the previous three months. Flour is frequently only available on some fixed days during the month (see Table 5). Some ad hoc rationing rules are commonly applied to distribute subsidized flour to the governorates when it is in short supply. No country-wide policy is formulated for this. Permanent or occasional rationing of flour is left to the governorates' supply authorities. Thus in rural Egypt there is a wide range of ration regulations that change by location and over time.

An attempt was made in the rural household survey to get an idea about how prevalent flour rationing was. About one-fourth of all rural households—which corresponds to about 60 percent of rural households purchasing flour—mentioned that subsidized flour was available only in rationed quantities during some months in the preceding year. This varies somewhat by month. While *balady* flour (coarse flour) was usually rationed per person, most *fino* flour (fine flour) was rationed per family. Rationing of *fino* flour showed a peak in June-August, which was the period of Ramadan in 1981. The ration book is usually used to record the flour rations received. In some districts, households that wanted to receive subsidized flour had to apply for it at the local Supply Authority Office. In others, it was reported that during Ramadan special shipments of flour were sold directly from a truck on a first-come-first-served basis of one bag per customer in the village.

The coarse flour from government sources is usually not used directly to bake bread in the households, but is sifted to a lower extraction rate before baking. Eighty-eight percent of the households indicated they sifted the flour. Some of the bran was used to cover the bread while it baked, some was fed to animals, and some was sold. In a few locations private flour mills sift flour mechanically but this is an exception. Most sifting is done by hand with simple tools, a process that is quite time consuming.[6] It is done exclusively by women. Sifting the flour is only one step in processing the homemade bread. The production of bread is analyzed in its relation to subsidized flour and bread availability below.

The flour sifting habit has interesting implications for targeting food subsidies. First, it is important to note that the commodity distributed is not readily used for processing the final bread product. A significant share of calories is sifted out and used partly as animal feed. Second, sifting requires that female labor be available in the household at low opportunity costs. Households with shortages of female labor might purchase more baked bread at the subsidized bakeries if they have this option at their location. Households with abundant female labor might be able to do the sifting work for others, in the extended family, for example. Final distribution of the subsidy on fixed price flour is thus influenced by the economics of processing activities at the household level and by the "market" for these services.

---

[6] According to villagers, sifting an *ardeb* (150 kilograms) of milled wheat requires about 9 hours, and sifting the same quantity of coarse flour takes about 4 hours. Thus time spent sifting adds up to 72,000 full-year work-place equivalents (300 work days per year).

Table 5—Availability of fixed price flour and households purchasing it

| | Households that Purchase Fixed Price Flour | | | Availability of Fixed Price Flour in Preceding Three Months | | | |
| | Share of All House-holds | Share that Purchase from Flour Shops | Share that Purchase from Cooperatives | Not Available | Occasionally Available | Available on Fixed Days | Usually Available |
Area/Type of Flour							
	(percent)			(percent of purchasing households)			
Urban	65.2	77.7	22.3	14.1	14.0	13.7	58.3
Rural							
All flours	49.0	89.8	10.2	...	...	...	...
Balady flour	...	...	...	0.6	5.0	42.5	51.9
Fino flour	...	...	...	13.0	26.1	32.6	28.3

Source: Data from the household survey made by the International Food Policy Research Institute and the Institute of National Planning, Cairo, 1981/82.

Bread baking is still common in rural households; nor has it yet been given up by many urban households. Most rural households (96.7 percent of them) regularly bake their own bread, but fewer do it and they do it less frequently in villages where subsidized bread is available. One out of four urban households (25.4 percent) reported baking bread, but most of these only do it occasionally.

Subsidized Bread

Subsidized bread is available to a majority of the urban population. 78.3 percent of the urban households surveyed said that bread was available in their neighborhood and 75.9 percent of the households said that they could obtain the amount of bread they wanted without restrictions (see Table 6). The latter figure compares to 25.3 percent of rural households, which was as expected as only 25 percent of the villages have a bakery (see Table 7). At locations with a bakery in rural areas and even in urban areas, however, subsidized bread was not always supplied without restriction; about every fourth rural household purchasing at a bakery noted limitations in bread supplies and about every fifth of all urban households mentioned that they had shortages in their location. This has important implications for the demand of bread substitutes (flour, rice,

noodles), which are addressed in the demand analysis below. But neither the absence of a bakery nor shortages of availability necessarily precluded the purchase of bread.

The cross tabulation for availability of flour by availability of bread shows that only 2.9 percent of all urban households could get neither bread nor flour at their location (Table 6). This means that virtually all urban households were reached by at least one branch of the subsidized wheat distribution system. The biggest group in the matrix represents the households that affirmed that bread and fixed price flour were always available (41.1 percent of all households, Table 6).

The pattern in rural areas was different from that in urban areas: in those villages where bread was available in principle, only 1.6 percent of all households stated that neither bread nor fixed price flour was available to them in desired quantities. However, 12.2 percent of the households were in villages where no bread was available and too little flour was reported to be available. A total of 46.6 percent of all rural households were directly and sufficiently reached by at least one branch of the subsidized wheat distribution system—as compared to 95.0 percent in urban areas (Tables 6 and 7). Of course these quantitative groupings do not tell what proportions of rural and urban households participated in the system. This will be further analyzed in a following chapter.

Table 6—Availability of subsidized bread and flour to urban households

Availability of Flour	Availability of Bread			
	Does Get Desired Quantity	Does Not Get Desired Quantity	No Purchase	Total
	(percent of all households)			
Usually not available	10.0	2.9	0.0	12.9
Available 1 – 3 days each month or on fixed days	18.1	6.8	0.2	25.1
Always available	41.1	11.4	0.7	53.2
No purchase	6.8	1.1	0.9	8.8
Total	75.9	22.2	1.9	100.0

Source: Data from the household survey made by the International Food Policy Research Institute and the Institute of National Planning, Cairo, 1981/82.

Waste

An issue frequently debated in Egypt is whether highly subsidized bread is being wasted, especially when it is used to feed animals. The perception that it is and that the use of bread for animal feed is as immoral as it is wasteful may reduce the use of wheat and wheat products for animal feed even if distorted prices might work in favor of using wheat as feed instead of, say, maize. The grain equivalent price of balady bread, the most subsidized wheat commodity (selling for 1 piaster per loaf), is about LE 97 per ton.[7] The farm-gate price of maize, which is the most important feedgrain, was about LE 70 to 80 per ton during 1978 and 1980 but about LE 100 during the survey periods in 1981/82, with significant regional differences. As bread is not available in bulk at bakeries, the collection costs to be added to the imputed grain-equivalent price mentioned above are large, which reduces the incentive to use bread as feed in bigger enterprises. This is not true for small backyard and "urban" agriculture, where excess bread may be used for feed in households where animals are produced for home consumption. A set of detailed questions in the survey was addressed to this touchy issue.

As bread from bakeries does not keep long, a supply and disappearance balance for subsidized bread was put together for

Table 7—Availability of subsidized bread and flour to rural households

Availability of Flour	Bread Available in Village		Bread Not Available in Village	Total
	Does Get Desired Quantity	Does Not Get Desired Quantity		
	(percent of all rural households)			
Does get desired quantity	8.6	2.8	18.5	29.9
Does not get desired quantity	5.7	1.6	12.2	19.5
No purchase	11.0	5.3	34.3	50.6
Total	25.3	9.7	65.0	100.0

Source: Data from the household survey made by the International Food Policy Research Institute and the Institute of National Planning, Cairo, 1981/82.

---

[7] In this report, all tons are metric tons. One Egyptian pound (LE) equaled U.S. $1.22 in July 1982.

the two days preceding the interview. In urban households about 10.3 percent of the *balady* bread purchased during the preceding two days had not been consumed by household members by the third day—the day of the interview. A little less than half of this, 4.6 percent, was reportedly given to animals, and 3.9 percent was still stored "for later consumption." Small amounts (1.2 percent) were given to others outside the household, and marginal amounts (0.5 percent) were thrown in the garbage, where they usually ended up as animal feed (see Table 8). Rural households gave somewhat higher shares of bread to animals (6.6 percent). At least in urban areas, the percentage of bread fed to animals is clearly lower for the more expensive types of bread baked from *fino* flour (*fino* bread and *shami*).

Taking the quoted shares of bread fed to animals and thrown away yields a total of 165,000 tons of wheat (grain equivalent).[8] The equivalent sum of subsidies spent on this amount of wheat (about LE 20 million) equals about 4 percent of the wheat subsidy bill. However, the total value of the quantity fed to animals and wasted is not equal to the loss to the economy from "waste." Therefore the processing costs of bread should be added and the animal produce resulting from the bread input (at shadow values)

should be deducted, which would result in a net loss to the economy that is less than the gross value given above. A similar calculation could be done for the share of bran that is sifted from the flour and fed to animals. Neither calculation is made here. One may argue that the figures reported by the households understate the waste of bread because of its perceived immorality. To check for this, the aggregate figures for the disappearance of wheat and wheat products reported by the households were compared with the national disappearance figures reported by the Ministries of Agriculture and Supply. A comparison shows that total disappearances (food plus feed) are even 6 percent higher in the survey than in the national statistics. Therefore, the households' reporting on wheat consumption and use for feed seems to be accurate on these grounds. This may also be checked by comparing the aggregated disappearance reported in the family budget survey of CAPMAS with the national disappearance figures. The latest CAPMAS data available are from 1974/75. Since then, per capita wheat consumption has certainly gone up, as income and price elasticities indicate. However, just comparing per capita wheat disappearance on the unadjusted basis used in the 1974/75 data with the 1981 national data yields a difference of 15

Table 8—Purchases and use of subsidized bread

	Urban			Rural		
Use	Balady	Fino	Shami	Balady	Fino	Shami
			(percent of purchases)			
Human consumption	89.7	92.4	86.1	94.1	91.6	93.0
Animals	4.6	1.7	3.2	6.6	6.9	3.2
Given to others	1.2	0.5	1.9	1.1	0.0	0.0
Garbage	0.6	0.7	0.0	0.1	0.3	0.5
Stored	3.9	4.9	7.7	0.8	0.0	3.2
Average number of loaves purchased per day per household[a]	11.4	2.2	1.1	4.5	0.7	0.2

Source: Data from the household survey made by the International Food Policy Research Institute and the Institute of National Planning, Cairo, 1981/82.

[a] These are mean values for households in the urban or the rural sample.

---

[8] The number of loaves purchased and the shares reported as "fed to animals" and "thrown away" by type of bread converted into wheat-grain equivalent yield 5.7 kilograms per capita per year in urban areas and 2.5 kilograms per capita per year in rural ones. This corresponds to the aggregate reported.

percent. This includes the increase in human consumption caused by income growth and by relative price changes. Thus, also on these grounds, there is no strong evidence for assuming that the use of wheat for animal feed exceeds the share reported.

Households were also asked to report how much wheat grain from their own production and from purchases they used for animal feed. The reported quantities add up to 4.1 percent of total domestic production of wheat.

4

EXPENDITURE PATTERNS

In both rural and urban areas the majority of the population reported spending over half their total expenditure on food, with people in rural areas, who are generally poorer, spending a greater percentage on food than those in urban areas. This share may be considered fairly high, but it reflects, in part, the low costs of rent and utilities. Fuels are heavily subsidized and rents are fixed at the rate of two decades ago, though "key money" (money needed to gain access to rent-controlled apartments) and other unreported housing expenditures might make this expenditure share higher. Besides indicating the income and food budget shares of the quartiles, Table 9 also provides a consistency check with GNP statistics. Weighting the rural sample at 55 percent of total population (it was 56.1 in the 1976 census), the average annual expenditure per capita is LE 334.

Household Expenditures

A regression of budget shares of food indicates that the average expenditure elasticity for food is 0.78:

$$BF = -0.48 + 0.355LTX - 0.0289\,LTX2$$
$$(4.3)(5.7)$$

$$+\,0.04\,NUM - 0.0066\,NUM \times LTX$$
$$(2.6)(3.3)$$

$$+\,0.04\,RURAL - 0.04\,UPPER;$$
$$(4.7)(4.1)$$

$$R^2 = 0.20;\ 1{,}389\ \text{observations};$$

where

BF   = the budget share of food,

LTX   = the log of monthly expenditures per capita in piasters,

LTX2 = the square of LTX,

NUM = the total household size,

RURAL = a dummy variable defined as 1 if the family lives in a village and 0 otherwise, and

UPPER = a variable defined as 1 if the family is in Upper Egypt and 0 otherwise.

The regression also indicates that families in rural areas spend a greater proportion on food than families in urban areas do, even after controlling for their smaller incomes, and that families in Upper Egypt allot smaller shares of their budgets to food than families in Lower Egypt. Furthermore, for any family with expenditures greater than LE 4.5 per capita per month (virtually the entire sample), budget shares allotted to food decrease as family size increases. As Deaton argues, smaller budget shares allotted to food can be considered an indicator of a higher standard of living.[9] This implies that with the same expenditures per capita, larger families have higher standards of living in Egypt—showing economies of scale in household budgets. A similar inference that rural families have lower standards of living, however, is not warranted as prices and expenditure opportunities as well as tastes differ between rural and urban areas.

In general, urban consumers purchase a greater proportion of their food through outlets at which the food prices are fixed. These purchases include ration allotments and goods from cooperatives and from government flour shops and licensed bakers. The highest share, for the urban poor, was a quarter of the food budget and 15 percent of total expenditures. This declined to only 7 percent of food expenditures from such outlets, or 3 percent of total expenditures, for the highest income consumers in rural areas.

As indicated in Table 4, there is little variation by quartile in the quantities obtained from either tier of the ration system in rural or urban areas. The only category in which

---

[9] Angus Deaton, "Inequality and Needs: Some Experimental Results from Sri Lanka," *Population and Development Review* 9 (1983): 35-49.

Table 9—Characteristics of households and their expenditures, by expenditure quartile

Category	Urban Expenditure Quartile				All Urban House-holds	Rural Expenditure Quartile				All Rural House-holds
	1st	2nd	3rd	4th	holds	1st	2nd	3rd	4th	holds
Number of households	245	245	245	245	980	347	348	347	347	1,389
Number of individuals	1,578	1,435	1,317	1,037	5,367	2,472	2,539	2,340	1,792	9,143
Percent of sample	29.4	26.7	24.5	19.3	99.9	27.0	27.8	25.6	19.6	100.0
Average household size (number of people)	6.44	5.86	5.38	4.23	5.48	7.12	7.30	6.74	5.16	6.58
Total monthly expenditures (LE/capita)	14.48	25.35	38.11	82.52	36.33	9.37	15.08	22.09	43.62	20.92
Percent of rural or urban expenditures	11.7	18.7	25.7	43.9	100.0	12.1	20.0	27.0	40.9	100.0
Percent of food expenditures spent through government channels[a]	25.7	19.2	14.7	10.1	15.8	17.9	12.1	8.6	6.8	10.1
Budget shares										
Home-consumed food	0.63	0.56	0.51	0.39	0.48	0.68	0.65	0.61	0.48	0.57
Electricity and fuels	0.033	0.031	0.026	0.033	0.031	0.035	0.025	0.025	0.021	0.025
Rent	0.027	0.019	0.018	0.015	0.018	0.001	0.002	0.001	0.002	0.001
Clothing	0.087	0.089	0.087	0.071	0.089	0.068	0.067	0.063	0.065	0.066
Durables[b]	0.028	0.045	0.049	0.089	0.049	0.010	0.014	0.020	0.027	0.017
Medical	0.041	0.044	0.043	0.048	0.044	0.036	0.047	0.040	0.053	0.043

Source: Data from the household survey made by the International Food Policy Research Institute and the Institute of National Planning, Cairo, 1981/82.

Notes: Expenditure quartiles were determined by ranking rural and urban households independently according to total reported expenditures per capita. The 1st quartile had the smallest expenditures; the 4th, the largest.

[a] Includes rations, purchases at cooperatives, government flour shops, and licensed bakeries.

[b] Excludes furniture purchased for marriages.

the highest quartile consumes noticeably more than the lowest is the extra quota of rice (at 14 piasters). This may indicate that this rice is not always strictly rationed. Distribution of sugar and tea is the same in both rural and urban areas, although rice and oil distribution is higher in the cities. The apparently greater distribution of beans and lentils in rural areas is the handiwork of the season; pulse distribution diminishes in the summer. In the second rural round, per capita monthly distribution of beans was only 61 grams and distribution of lentils was only 21 grams.

Ration distributions, however, are seldom the only source of these commodities for a household. Because of this, the marginal price at which a household determines its budget allocation is the price in the open market or the cooperative. Rations are, in general, inframarginal. Since most consumers purchase either on the open market or at the cooperative, rations at subsidized prices can be considered to be income transfers. In theory, a consumer reallocates less following an inframarginal price change than following a marginal change. For at least 75.8 percent of urban families and 73.5 percent of rural families, rationed sugar (both tiers) is inframarginal (see Table 10). The percentages for tea are similar and only slightly less for oil or rice. As also indicated in the table, not only do appreciable numbers of families purchase beyond ration levels but the quantities obtained often exceed those distributed through the ration system.

In urban areas, where the cooperatives are more important, sugar, oil, and lentils are more commonly obtained from them. Rice, tea, and beans are more likely to be purchased on the open market. In contrast, in rural areas purchases from cooperatives are smaller than purchases from the open market. In both areas, it was seldom observed that a family purchased the same commodity from both cooperatives and the open market in the month of the survey. Inasmuch as open market prices are, on the average, greater than those in the cooperatives (see Table 11), the different purchasing patterns probably reflect differences in access and have distributional implications.

Table 10—Monthly purchases of commodities on open markets and in cooperatives, by expenditure quartile

Product/Place of Purchase	Urban Expenditure Quartile				All Urban House-holds	Rural Expenditure Quartile				All Rural House-holds
	1st	2nd	3rd	4th		1st	2nd	3rd	4th	
					(percent)[a]					
Sugar										
Cooperatives	52.6	60.0	54.7	58.4	55.4	15.6	16.7	15.0	18.7	16.5
Open market	24.1	22.9	29.0	30.8	26.5	46.1	56.0	69.7	70.9	60.7
Both	4.9	7.3	4.5	7.8	6.1	1.7	2.6	5.2	5.5	3.7
Share of total purchase from cooperatives	16.1	21.9	22.2	30.9	22.5	4.2	4.3	5.1	7.3	5.2
Share of total purchase from open market	7.9	8.8	11.9	15.3	10.8	15.5	21.7	29.2	36.8	25.9
Oil										
Cooperatives	22.4	24.9	32.2	35.5	28.8	7.8	10.3	6.3	10.9	8.9
Open market	14.3	16.3	20.0	23.7	17.6	23.0	30.2	44.4	46.1	35.9
Both	0.8	2.0	2.4	2.0	1.8	0.3	0.6	0.9	1.4	0.8
Share of total purchase from cooperatives	14.3	17.3	21.2	27.9	20.0	5.9	8.1	3.3	8.9	6.6
Share of total purchase from open market	9.1	9.9	12.3	17.9	12.2	18.1	23.6	37.1	41.0	30.6
Tea										
Cooperatives	5.7	8.2	9.6	9.2	8.2	6.9	7.8	6.3	5.8	6.7
Open market	55.9	64.5	69.0	69.8	64.8	56.5	68.7	72.9	77.5	68.9
Both	0.4	3.3	2.9	2.4	2.2	1.7	2.0	1.1	2.3	1.8
Share of total purchase from cooperatives	1.8	2.3	3.7	2.9	2.7	2.2	1.9	2.3	6.1	3.1
Share of total purchase from open market	22.7	34.5	36.6	48.6	35.5	20.6	27.6	37.0	43.1	32.2
Rice										
Cooperatives	21.2	25.3	28.2	31.4	26.5	6.6	6.9	4.6	6.9	6.3
Open market	24.1	29.8	34.7	35.1	30.5	33.7	45.1	50.7	52.4	45.5
Both	2.0	2.9	3.7	4.1	3.2	1.1	2.3	0.6	0.3	1.1
Share of total purchase from cooperatives	8.7	12.5	14.8	18.6	13.7	4.4	2.4	2.3	2.8	2.8
Share of total purchase from open market	22.9	34.0	33.8	37.6	32.3	60.1	68.9	78.8	83.5	75.4
Beans										
Cooperatives	6.9	9.4	6.5	7.3	7.6	1.1	1.4	2.9	1.4	1.7
Open market	13.5	18.8	18.0	20.8	17.8	17.3	25.9	29.7	31.4	26.0
Both	0.4	0.4	0.8	0.4	0.5	0.3	0.3	0.3	0.3	0.3
Share of total purchase from cooperatives	13.9	13.8	13.2	10.5	12.8	2.2	1.6	3.6	2.8	2.5
Share of total purchase from open market	45.8	60.8	61.5	72.8	63.3	50.7	58.1	61.7	61.3	58.5
Lentils										
Cooperatives	15.5	22.0	22.0	20.2	20.3	1.4	2.9	4.3	3.7	3.1
Open market	10.6	11.8	11.0	13.1	11.6	18.7	28.2	38.0	41.5	31.6
Both	0.0	0.8	0.8	0.4	0.5	1.7	0.3	0.6	0.6	0.4
Share of total purchase from cooperatives	55.2	54.3	49.8	53.5	53.1	1.9	2.5	4.9	4.8	3.7
Share of total purchase from open market	26.9	32.2	35.7	31.2	31.7	30.3	44.4	50.8	54.0	46.1
Per capita purchases					(grams)					
Sugar	1,860	2,047	2,130	2,457	2,092	1,687	1,840	2,022	2,422	1,959
Oil	572	640	690	790	661	365	463	491	651	480
Tea	101	122	126	150	121	96	103	119	142	111
Rice	1,669	2,240	2,379	2,502	2,183	1,202	1,857	2,462	3,834	2,224
Beans	205	287	265	381	276	234	242	316	356	270
Lentils	106	146	157	204	148	215	277	328	407	299

Source: Data from the household survey made by the International Food Policy Research Institute and the Institute of National Planning, Cairo, 1981/82.

Notes: Expenditure quartiles were determined by ranking rural and urban households independently according to total reported expenditures per capita. The 1st quartile had the smallest expenditures; the 4th, the largest.

[a] The percentage of households not purchasing in either market would be 100 minus the percentages of households purchasing at cooperatives or on the open market, plus the percentage purchasing at both. This avoids double counting.

Table 11—Average open market and cooperative prices for selected commodities

Commodity/Outlet	Rural Areas		Urban Areas			
	Delta	Upper Egypt	Alexandria	Delta	Cairo	Upper Egypt
			(LE/kilogram)			
Sugar						
Cooperatives	31	29	30	30	31	30
Open market	60	54	32	41	37	52
Oil						
Cooperatives	32	27	33	33	34	33
Open market	49	38	34	51	50	46
Tea						
Cooperatives	384	477	560	451	506	503
Open market	515	503	515	514	598	523
Rice						
Cooperatives	14	16	14	14	14	14
Open market	25	19	17	26	18	20
Beans						
Cooperatives	18	24	15	18	19	13
Open market	37	35	31	33	39	32
Lentils						
Cooperatives	26	36	34	30	34	33
Open market	66	56	40	63	62	53

Source: Data from the household survey made by the International Food Policy Research Institute and the Institute of National Planning, Cairo, 1981/82.

The size of the rural open market purchases was partially affected by the cropping season. In the second round, the average open market purchase of rice declined.

Frozen meats, poultry, and fish were rarely available in rural areas, while approximately one-third of the urban sample consumed these commodities (see Table 12). The number of consumers of frozen beef and fish in the higher expenditure brackets declined although the average size of a purchase did not. Equal numbers of families from each group purchased frozen chicken, but the average purchase by the highest expenditure group was far larger than that of the lowest. Rationing of these commodities does not appear to be strictly binding at all locations; families report purchasing up to 20 kilograms per month. The sizes of the purchases of those few rural families who obtained frozen commodities are comparable to those in urban areas.

While fewer than half of either sample consumed frozen meat, more than 80 percent of both samples consumed fresh meat during the survey period. Frozen meat cost between 80 piasters and LE 1 per kilogram while at the time of the survey fresh meat frequently cost three times as much. Frozen chicken generally cost LE 1.05 while the fresh commodity cost about 25 percent

more. On the average, fresh fish cost three times the 40 piasters the frozen product cost, although this average includes several species. With fewer constraints on availability and access, a pattern by expenditure groups is evident. Somewhat less chicken was purchased than meat, although it cost roughly one-third as much. In rural areas, however, consumption of home-produced poultry (including pigeons, rabbits, and guinea pigs) averaged 728 grams per capita per month, more than was purchased. Consumption of other meat from a household's stock of animals was reported as only 75 grams per capita per month. Purchases of fresh fish were roughly half those of chicken. In urban areas, frozen fish purchases from cooperatives appreciably augmented purchases on the open market and, for the poorest quartile, exceeded those of fresh fish.

The average egg purchases reported in the urban areas were 6.3 per capita per month, nearly five times greater than those in the rural regions. They were augmented by eggs from home production, 1.1 in urban areas and 0.7 in rural. Reported milk purchases averaged 2.2 kilograms per capita in urban areas and only 0.2 in the villages, reflecting the fact that 82 percent of the urban families purchased milk, while only 18 percent of the villagers did. Another 24 percent con-

Table 12—Per capita purchases of frozen and fresh beef, poultry, and fish by expenditure quartile

Commodity/Category	Urban Expenditure Quartile				All Urban House-holds	Rural Expenditure Quartile				All Rural House-holds
	1st	2nd	3rd	4th		1st	2nd	3rd	4th	
Frozen beef										
Average monthly purchase (grams)	183	177	178	109	166	5	11	28	16	14
Share of total purchase (percent)	32.4	28.5	26.4	12.7	100.0	8.8	21.3	48.3	21.6	100.0
Share of quartile that purchased (percent)	31.0	24.1	25.7	14.7	23.9	1.7	2.9	3.2	2.6	2.6
Average purchase of share purchasing (grams)	590	734	694	741	695	289	395	882	630	538
Frozen chicken										
Average monthly purchase (grams)	209	282	322	469	306	11	9	13	46	18
Share of total purchases (percent)	20.0	24.6	25.8	29.5	100.0	16.2	14.5	18.9	50.4	100.0
Share of quartile that purchased (percent)	33.5	32.2	31.0	29.4	31.5	1.7	2.9	2.3	4.0	2.8
Average purchase of share purchasing (grams)	624	876	1,039	1,594	973	637	328	565	1,150	654
Frozen fish										
Average monthly purchase (grams)	249	303	288	206	265	32	90	88	129	81
Share of total purchases (percent)	27.7	30.6	26.7	15.0	100.0	10.5	30.8	27.7	31.0	100.0
Share of quartile that purchased (percent)	35.5	38.8	35.5	22.0	33.0	6.3	12.1	12.7	13.2	11.0
Average purchase of share purchasing (percent)	701	782	812	935	802	500	749	695	973	734
Average monthly purchases (grams)										
Fresh beef	412	810	1,135	2,057	1,014	381	491	759	1,088	646
Fresh chicken	379	673	881	1,029	706	262	549	704	1,212	639
Fresh fish	202	472	681	810	487	166	244	395	653	340

Source: Data from the household survey made by the International Food Policy Research Institute and the Institute of National Planning, Cairo, 1981/82.

Notes: Expenditure quartiles were determined by ranking rural and urban households independently according to total reported expenditures per capita. The 1st quartile had the smallest expenditures; the 4th, the largest.

sumed home-produced milk. The 1.3 kilograms per capita of home-produced milk consumed brought average rural fluid milk consumption to 70 percent of that of urban families. The disparity of consumption of dairy products is removed when cheese is considered. While both samples reported 315 grams per capita of white cheese purchased, the rural sample reported an additional 565 grams of cheese consumed from family production.

The pattern of bread and flour consumption differed between samples (see Table 13). More bread was consumed in urban areas, and more flour was purchased in rural areas. The total of 336 grams of *balady* flour consumed daily per capita in rural areas included bread, and flour purchases from the flour shops, cooperatives, and the open market. The latter is frequently flour resold by flour shops either from another village or in smaller units. In terms of grain equivalents, rural consumers purchased more than their urban counterparts, the difference being mainly wheat purchased as unmilled grain.

Aggregate Consumption Indicated by the Sample

The consumption figures produced by the survey can be compared with figures for aggregate national consumption by weighting the rural sample at 55 percent of the

Table 13—Per capita bread and flour purchases by expenditure quartile

Type of Bread or Flour	Urban Expenditure Quartile				All Urban House-holds	Rural Expenditure Quartile				All Rural House-holds
	1st	2nd	3rd	4th	holds	1st	2nd	3rd	4th	holds
Balady										
Loaves per day	2.00	2.21	2.12	1.95	2.06	0.37	0.40	0.40	0.33	0.38
Percent of total	28.1	28.5	25.1	18.2	100.0	26.5	29.0	27.3	17.1	100.0
Fino										
Loaves per day	0.23	0.41	0.50	0.44	0.39	0.02	0.03	0.04	0.11	0.04
Percent of total	18.6	28.6	31.5	22.2	100.0	9.2	19.2	22.0	49.6	100.0
Shami										
Loaves per day	0.12	0.14	0.24	0.40	0.21	0.01	0.01	0.04	0.04	0.03
Percent of total	16.6	17.7	28.5	37.1	100.0	7.1	15.7	43.0	34.2	100.0
Balady										
Flour (grams/day)	84	52	55	67	65	267	290	268	336	288
Purchased on the open market	...	...	...	...	...	93	139	157	193	141
Percent of total	37.9	21.4	20.8	19.9	100.0	25.1	28.0	23.9	22.9	100.0
Fino										
Flour (grams/day)	22	40	31	40	32	19	27	32	67	35
Percent of total	20.0	32.9	22.9	23.9	100.0	15.4	22.1	24.1	38.3	100.0
Balady										
Flour and flour in bread (grams/day)	288	280	274	268	278	306	331	310	370	326
Fino										
Flour and flour in bread (grams/day)	52	88	94	113	84	21	30	39	74	38
Grain wheat (kilograms/month)	0.28	0.37	0.15	0.86	0.38	1.49	1.60	2.04	2.26	1.81
Total purchased wheat in grain equivalents (kilograms/month)	12.98	14.28	14.09	15.37	14.05	13.56	14.96	15.04	18.88	15.37
Grain maize purchases (kilograms/month)[a]	0.35	0.65	0.25	0.42	0.42	1.61	2.01	2.93	3.52	2.43

Source: Data from the household survey made by the International Food Policy Research Institute and the Institute of National Planning, Cairo, 1981/82.

Notes: Expenditure quartiles were determined by ranking rural and urban households independently according to total reported expenditures per capita. The 1st quartile had the smallest expenditures; the 4th, the largest.

[a] This was used for human consumption.

population, and assuming that the population of Egypt at the time of the survey was 41.8 million (this extrapolates from the 1976 census using an annual growth rate of 2.5 percent). The Gini coefficient for per capita expenditures in urban areas is 0.371 and in rural areas, 0.348. When transfers from government distribution are excluded, they show a slight move away from equality, becoming 0.391 and 0.367.

In general, the amounts consumed reported in the survey, including the amounts of home-produced commodities, are similar to figures for national aggregate availability.[10] While the figures for marketed beans and lentils are smaller than the national figures, a significant portion of these commodities is used to make prepared foods by commercial enterprises not included in the survey. Using reported expenditures on these prepared foods, *fuul* and *tamiya,* with the assumption that 10 piasters purchase 147 grams of beans as *tamiya* (180 piasters cooked), the prepared foods indicated in the survey include 180,000 tons of beans. This brings reported total consumption to 340,000 tons compared to imports and production of 300,000. Similar data were not available for *koshari,* another prepared food, but the amount of lentils used in that product is probably significant.

Figures of the Ministry of Agriculture

---

[10] These figures are from the Egyptian Ministry of Supply as quoted in Alderman, von Braun, and Sakr, *Egypt's Food Subsidy and Rationing System;* and U.S. Department of Agriculture, Office of the Agricultural Attaché, Cairo, *Annual Agricultural Situation Report* (Cairo: U.S. Embassy, Office of the Agricultural Attaché, 1983).

indicate that 3.31 million tons of maize were produced. In addition, 1.39 million tons of yellow maize were imported. These are largely used to prepare animal feed and starch. The survey indicates that human consumption of own-produced white maize was 0.6 million tons and that an additional 0.7 million tons were purchased for human consumption. Furthermore, 0.19 million tons were fed to animals. This leaves 1.8 million tons unaccounted for. It is unlikely that this was for human consumption, as the 1.3 million tons from the survey compares reasonably well with figures in the 1974/75 household budget survey, which aggregate to 1.27 million tons for the 1981 population. If per capita maize consumption is aggregated and a trend line is drawn through the figures from the 1958, 1964/65, and 1974/75 surveys, the expected consumption of maize in 1981 would be only 0.94 million tons. In addition, the intake of calories calculated from the current survey is sufficiently high to make a major underestimation of human consumption unlikely. The survey was targeted at households and was not conducted on commercial poultry and livestock operations. It is likely that the bulk of the maize not accounted for was consumed by animals.

The smaller purchases of frozen meat shown by the survey may reflect, in part, the increase in the distribution of this commodity during the holy month of Ramadan. There is a major discrepancy between the survey data for chicken and the national figures, even when the amount produced at home—a third of the total—is discounted since it may not have been entered into national accounts. Aggregation of the urban fresh and frozen chicken purchases alone, which are in accord with means calculated from what families recalled eating in a 24-hour period (see Chapter 5), accounts for 0.23 million tons. It is likely, then, that national accounts record only imports plus commercial production and that they neglect a sizable amount of family production and trade between neighbors.

The survey indicates that the budget shares allotted to food declined after the 1974/75 expenditure survey. In the earlier survey rural families allotted 63.9 percent of their expenditures to food while urban families allotted 53.1 percent. The decline in the budget share allotted to food is indicative of rising real incomes, although the decline exceeds what the cross-section regression reported above predicted.

5

NUTRITIONAL CONSIDERATIONS

Surveys of nutritional indicators reveal that malnutrition does exist in Egypt, but to a lesser extent than might be expected looking at per capita income and cross-country studies.[11] These indicators and the high infant mortality in the country, which are frequent correlates of malnutrition, show that an improved health policy is needed, but their implications for food policy are less clear.

This chapter focuses on family food consumption. This is not the only determinant of malnutrition. Just as aggregate statistics on food intake may mask low consumption by selected groups, family food intake data may mask inequalities within the family. And they do not show how the body's use of food is affected by disease, parasites, and sanitation. But family food consumption is the determinant of nutrition that is most influenced, either positively or negatively, by changes in income and pricing policies, and it is the one most directly related to the food subsidy system.

Aggregate food consumption in Egypt is high. Table 14 shows average per capita daily calorie availability by income group. It was calculated by two methods, each using different information from the questionnaire. In one, monthly food acquisition was recorded and multiplied by the appropriate calorie contents of the foods; in the other, food reported eaten in the preceding 24 hours was converted to calories.[12] In the former method, per capita intake was obtained by dividing consumption by the number of family members. In the latter method the total consumption at each meal was divided by the number of people present, including guests. If a family member was not present,

the intake of that member outside the home was recorded when available and included in the mealtime total. Particular care was taken to record between-meal snacks, which are common, especially in households with young children. Although only a part of the family may have consumed such a snack, the calories in it were divided by the total number of family members. Not to have done so would have been to assume implicitly that other family members obtained the same calories as those eating the snack from another source and would have biased family intakes upward.

Each method of estimating calorie consumption has its advantages and disadvantages.[13] Food purchase data do not record drawdown of stocks, although in this study farm consumption was estimated as a linear drawdown of retained produce. Similarly, the method may overestimate consumption when stocks are built up. The 24-hour recall method is subject to random fluctuations of daily intakes and to patterns specific to Thursday nights and Friday afternoons. On the average, however, both methods can be expected to reliably indicate consumption by specific groups of families.

For the urban sample, the figures for average intake by expenditure groups produced by the two methods vary by only a few percent, although the correlations of individual observations were moderate. Average meat, fish, and poultry consumption from the 24-hour recall method was higher, while the oil and sugar consumption given by the purchase method was nearly twice as high as that given by the recall method. The latter gap may reflect the difficulty in remembering the quantity of oil used in frying and the

---

[11] Egypt, Ministry of Health, Nutrition Institute, *Arab Republic of Egypt National Survey, 1978* (Washington, D.C.: U.S. Agency for International Development, 1978); and Mohammed el-Lozy, J. Field, G. Roper, and R. Burkhardt, *Childhood Malnutrition in Rural Egypt,* Health Care Delivery System Project Monograph 4 (Cambridge, Mass.: Massachusetts Institute of Technology, 1980).

[12] Coefficients were derived from P. Pellett and S. Shaderevian, *Food Composition Table for Use in the Middle East* (Beirut: American University, 1970).

[13] See, for example, M. Pekkasinen, "Methodology in the Collection of Food Consumption Data," *World Review of Nutrition and Dietetics* 12 (1970); and Aaron Lechtig et al., "The One-Day Recall Dietary Survey: A Review," *Archivos Latinoamericanos de Nutrición* 26 (1976).

Table 14—Average daily calorie consumption by expenditure quartile

Method/Source	Urban Expenditure Quartile				All Urban House-holds	Rural Expenditure Quartile				All Rural House-holds
	1st	2nd	3rd	4th	holds	1st	2nd	3rd	4th	holds
					(calories)					
Calorie consumption										
24-hour recall	2,343	2,761	2,915	3,174	2,798	2,357	2,574	2,716	3,149	2,654
Food purchase	2,420	2,850	3,072	3,731	3,016	2,273	2,892	3,409	4,571	3,274
					(percent)					
Source of calories										
Ration system[a]	19	17	15	12	16	15	12	10	8	11
Cooperatives[b]	5	6	6	7	6	1	1	1	2	1
Flour and bread[c]	49	45	42	35	42	34	25	19	19	23
Additional share of open market flour	...	...	...	...	...	14	16	15	15	15
Sugar[d]	10	9	9	9	9	10	8	8	7	8
Rice[d]	8	8	9	8	8	9	13	12	16	13
Meat[d]	2	2	3	4	3	1	1	1	1	1
Chicken[d]	1	1	1	1	1	1	1	2	1	1
Fish[d]	1	1	1	1	1	<1	<1	<1	<1	<1
Production by household	...	...	...	...	...	8	13	13	14	12

Source: Data from the household survey made by the International Food Policy Research Institute and the Institute of National Planning, Cairo, 1981/82.

Notes: Expenditure quartiles were determined by ranking rural and urban households independently according to total reported expenditures per capita. The 1st quartile had the smallest expenditures; the 4th, the largest. Calorie consumption recorded by 24-hour recall is the food reported eaten in the preceding 24 hours converted to calories. The "food purchase method" of recording calorie consumption uses the calorie content of the food purchased in one month by a household.

[a] These include both basic and additional rations.

[b] These figures include frozen meat.

[c] These figures are for bakeries and government flour shops only.

[d] These include all sources, including production by a household.

amount of sugar used in tea in a 24-hour period.

There is greater divergence between the recall methodology and the recorded food acquisition in the rural sample, especially for the highest expenditure group. This difference occurs because larger portions of both farm production and cereals obtained on the open market are stored, not because purchases of directly subsidized foods are higher. In many households, farm production that is retained and even grains purchased locally are for consumption by an extended family unit. This extended family has branches in different dwellings and, frequently, in different towns. It is larger than the unit used in the study, which means that there is a potential for an upward bias. The bias cannot be major, as aggregate food availability is in accord with other food balance data for Egypt. This is true even though the highest income group acquired more calories than its members could reasonably consume. Food acquisition may exceed consumption because of wastage, storage loss, and milling, although the by-products of milling have a value in animal nutrition.

Because oil quotas in urban areas are high, the ration system provides a greater share of total calories. And the cooperatives are more important as a source of food. Overall, 64 percent of urban caloric consumption, by purchase, is obtained directly from government-controlled outlets, compared to only 35 percent in rural areas. As mentioned elsewhere, rural consumers purchase much of their flour from the open market and mill grain themselves more often than urban dwellers do. For this reason, government-controlled bread and flour distribution provides a smaller share of total calories than it does in urban areas. Sugar provides a significant share of total calories in both rural and urban areas.

Protein Consumption and Protein Score

The nutritional goals of the food subsidy system are frequently expressed in terms of the need to increase consumption of protein, especially of "animal" protein. Table 15 shows the average per capita protein consumption by expenditure quartile. In addition, protein consumption, corrected for the amount of amino acids that could not be used, is recorded, using the information available in the 24-hour recall section of the survey. There is no human need for animal protein per se. In fact, the body cannot absorb proteins of any kind. During digestion, the protein ingested from any source is broken into the amino acids that it is composed of. The notion about the importance of animal proteins arises because the amino acid composition of animal proteins more closely resembles that of human proteins than does the composition of most proteins from vegetable sources. But since most meals contain a variety of foods and each has a unique amino acid pattern, a proper measurement of the protein value of a meal must evaluate the entire food composition.

To compare the implications of methods, the amino-acid-corrected quantity of protein consumed in the Egyptian diet was derived using the following methodology. The amino acid content of a given meal was determined. Then the limiting amino acid was determined (generally, but not always, lysine). It was assumed that any quantity of amino acids in excess of what is needed to combine with lysine in the proper human ratio was used as an energy source, regardless of what was consumed in another meal. The proportions of amino acids were lysine:tryptophan, 5.23:1, lysine:sulphur-containing amino acids, 2.125:1, lysine:threnonine, 1.36:1. These represent the biological needs of children

Table 15—Average daily protein consumption by expenditure quartile

Method/Source	Urban Expenditure Quartile				All Urban House-holds	Rural Expenditure Quartile				All Rural House-holds
	1st	2nd	3rd	4th		1st	2nd	3rd	4th	
					(calories)					
Protein consumption										
Purchase	72	88	96	114	91	70	90	107	125	95
24-hour recall	81	92	104	118	99	71	78	83	97	80
Amino-acid corrected	63	73	90	108	83	45	55	61	76	57
					(percent)					
Source of protein										
Ration system[a]	5	4	4	3	4	5	3	3	3	3
Cooperatives[b]	6	6	6	5	6	<1	1	1	1	1
Flour and bread[c]	58	51	47	41	49	41	31	23	22	28
Additional share of open market flour	...	...	...	...	...	17	20	18	17	18
Rice[d]	5	6	6	6	6	6	10	7	12	9
Beans and lentils[d]	3	4	3	4	3	4	2	4	4	4
Meat[d]	4	6	7	11	7	3	4	4	4	4
Chicken[d]	4	5	6	7	6	3	5	6	10	7
Fish[d]	3	4	7	5	5	1	2	3	3	2
Production by household	...	...	...	...	...	11	16	17	23	17

Source: Data from the household survey made by the International Food Policy Research Institute and the Institute of National Planning, Cairo, 1981/82.

Notes: Expenditure quartiles were determined by ranking rural and urban households independently according to total reported expenditures per capita. The 1st quartile had the smallest expenditures; the 4th, the largest. Calorie consumption recorded by 24-hour recall is the food reported eaten in the preceding 24 hours converted to calories. The "food purchase method" of recording calorie consumption uses the calorie content of the food purchased in one month by a household.

[a] These include both basic and additional rations.

[b] These figures include frozen meat.

[c] These figures are for bakeries and government flour shops only.

[d] These include all sources, including production by a household.

and consequently are more stringent than adult requirements.

It is not surprising that although fresh meat and chicken provide few calories they are moderately important sources of protein. The cooperative system sells rice, beans and lentils, frozen meat, fish, and poultry, but it has little importance in providing protein. Neither has the ration system, whose calorie contribution, even in urban areas, is predominantly from sugar and oil. On the other hand, flour and bread provide nearly half of total protein in both urban and rural areas. Farm production provides a greater share of protein than of calories because of the milk and cheese produced at home.

Even the consumption of amino-acid-corrected protein by the urban poor is high, on the average. Given the low share of the cooperative in providing protein, this cannot be due to the subsidized sales of meat, fish, and chicken. Although the rural poor consume less than the urban poor, the average percent of calories provided by protein is 12 percent (7.6 percent using the amino-acid-corrected protein figures), which is adequate if calorie consumption is also adequate although, as mentioned, the requirements will depend on the composition of the household. For example, a household composed of one adult male (35 years, 70 kilograms), one adult female (30 years, 55 kilograms, pregnant), and three children (males, 10 and 4 years; female, 8 years) would have a per capita requirement of 35.7 grams per day. It appears, then, that nutritional needs do not justify the subsidy on frozen products, either to meet a need not currently met or to maintain current consumption.

Implications for Nutritional Adequacy

There are, essentially, three reasons why consumption often falls below protein and calorie requirements. The most obvious one is that a family, for reasons of both economics and preferences, may not obtain enough food to meet its requirements.

Another may be error in measurement. In any survey there is some sampling "noise" stemming from errors by both the respondents and the recorders. In addition, neither stock changes, changes in family composition in the period preceding the survey, nor a variety of other events that reflect the complexity of the real world can always be captured in an hour-long interview. They may make the real consumption of a family different from the consumption measured. If the error is random and normally distributed with its mean at zero, this type of error will not affect averages. Depending on the distribution of the sample, however, it may affect either the number of individuals below a given cutoff point or the characteristics observed as correlates with the group of individuals below the cutoff point.

Finally, the distribution of the deficiencies observed may be affected by the nature of the requirements themselves. Protein requirements are determined by clinical observation of intakes and bodily losses and are given per kilogram of body weight. While the use of protein is affected by a variety of environmental factors, the body has no mechanism to adapt intakes to requirements. In a probabilistic sense, then, no correlation is expected between intakes and requirements. This means that one can make a meaningful probability statement about the expected adequacy of an observed intake. Average requirements of individuals do vary because individuals differ by age, size, sex, and other biological factors. But it can be assumed that the variability of these factors is randomly distributed about its mean so that, for example, the probability that an intake two standard deviations below average requirements will be adequate is 0.025. The protein intakes that are generally recommended are two standard deviations above average requirements to cover individual variations.

The situation with energy (calories) is more complicated. Here, again, there is natural biological variation in requirements due to age, size, sex, and whether the individual is pregnant or lactating. There is also variation because of the amounts of activity. All these factors can help determine requirements. So can additional variations in basal metabolism (the basic use of energy). But because individuals can, and usually do, adjust requirements to intakes within certain limits, the probabilistic approach used to evaluate protein inadequacy is not applicable to the adequacy of calories. An observed low calorie intake may reflect a normal adjustment to modest physical requirements, or it may represent reduced activity (or growth) because too few calories are available. That is, intakes and requirements are correlated in a manner that links any discussion of dietary adequacy to a standard for the amount of activity that is socially desired. Without some assessment of the amount of activity that would be pursued if calories were available without budget constraints, it is not possible to fully assess the implications of an observed intake of calories.[14] One relies as much on a normative judgment as on a probabilistic statement.[15]

The cutoff points used in Table 16 were established taking into account the points mentioned above. The estimated requirement for protein was based on the age and sex of each member. This was adjusted upward by two standard deviations (assumed to be 12.5 percent). If a family's intake was greater than this and distribution within the family was proportional to requirements, the probability that the family's protein intake was inadequate is 0.025. Consumption, however, needs to be adjusted for digestibility. Accordingly, observed consumption was reduced by 15 percent in keeping with average digestibility of protein in the Egyptian diet.[16]

Calorie requirements were treated in a different manner. In order to take into account the correlation of intakes and requirements, the minimum amount of calories defined as adequate was set 15 percent below average requirements based on family composition, age, sex, and the assumption that activity was moderate. The 15 percent figure is somewhat arbitrary and may in fact be an overcompensation. In both calculations the requirements for adult females under 45 were increased in accord with the assumption that there was a 10 percent probability of lactation and a 10 percent probability of being in the second half of pregnancy.[17]

The study does not deal with overconsumption and the health problems associated with it, although they are a concern for part of the population.

The third line of Table 16 indicates that there is no protein problem per se. That is, there is no evidence that families obtaining enough calories need more protein in their diet. About one-sixth of both samples report

Table 16—Share of households below calorie and protein cutoffs by expenditure quartile

	Urban Expenditure Quartile				All Urban House-holds	Rural Expenditure Quartile				All Rural House-holds
Position of Household	1st	2nd	3rd	4th		1st	2nd	3rd	4th	
					(calories)					
Below both calorie and protein cutoff	10.6	4.9	1.2	0.8	4.3	20.3	6.0	3.2	2.0	7.9
Below calorie cutoff only	20.8	15.5	9.8	6.2	13.1	17.4	8.9	4.3	2.9	8.4
Below protein cutoff only	0.4	0.8	0.2	0.0	0.4	0.3	0.0	0.0	0.0	0.1

Source: Data from the household survey made by the International Food Policy Research Institute and the Institute of National Planning, Cairo, 1981/82.

Notes: Expenditure quartiles were determined by ranking rural and urban households independently according to total reported expenditures per capita. The 1st quartile had the smallest expenditures; the 4th, the largest.

The calorie cutoff point was set 15 percent below average requirements, which are based on family composition, age, sex, and the assumption that activity was moderate. The protein cutoff was based on the estimated requirement for protein, which depends on the age and sex of each member of a household. This was raised two standard deviations (assumed to be 12 percent). Observed consumption was reduced 15 percent to account for the average digestibility of protein in the Egyptian diet.

---

[14] Healthy children's activities vary less than adults', but there is debate over optimal growth patterns.

[15] For a discussion of the use of requirements for assessing population status see George H. Beaton, "Energy in Human Nutrition: Perspectives and Problems," *Nutrition Review* 41 (1983): 325-340.

[16] Mohamed Amr Hussein, "Protein Requirements of Egyptian Women," paper presented at a symposium on protein requirements, University of California, Berkeley, Cal., 1981.

[17] Requirements are based on 1973 WHO guidelines while the methodology of their use has been modified in conformity with the new guidelines of the Food and Agriculture Organization of the United Nations, the World Health Organization, and the United Nations University. No adjustment was made for intraindividual homeostatic variations of requirements as such regulatory mechanisms are still unknown and controversial.

household calorie consumption lower than the cutoff point used in this sample. Considering the variations in monthly purchases of food and in individual requirements, is this alarming? If the variation of requirements were truly a random process then there should be no correlation between being under the calorie cutoff point and other measured family characteristics. Clearly Table 16 shows that there is some relationship between calorie inadequacy and consumption. Even if one assumes that the 5-7.5 percent underconsumption of the upper-income groups represents the basic sampling and methodological error of the technique used here, apparently 30 percent of the rural low-income families are below requirements. A probit analysis shows how income helps determine underconsumption (see Table 17).

Income is highly significant in explaining the family calorie and protein deficits observed, with increases in income more likely to decrease the probability of a deficit in rural areas than in urban. The income elasticities for the probability of a calorie or protein deficit are 0.48 and 0.43 in urban areas. They are 0.99 and 1.19 in rural areas.

From another perspective, an increase of LE 5 of monthly per capita income would reduce the probability of a calorie deficit by 0.01 (mean = 0.17) in urban areas, whereas LE 1.5 would achieve the same reduction in rural areas. Such a pattern is unlikely to be generated by random variations in requirements. It probably reflects pockets of undernutrition in Egypt that persist even though overall food consumption is high.

One notes that these pockets are more likely to occur in Cairo and Alexandria among urban areas and are most prevalent in Upper Egypt among rural areas. Households headed by women are less likely to have low calorie intakes in cities and the larger the proportion of children in a family, the less likely the family is to have a deficit. The family requirements were determined from the age distribution of the family. Therefore, families with high proportions of children have lower overall requirements. There is no way of determining whether the children themselves are more or less likely to consume as much as they require. Even after accounting for income, landholders have a

Table 17—Results of regressions for the probability of calorie and protein inadequacy

Independent Variable	Urban		Rural	
	Below Calorie Cutoff	Below Protein Cutoff	Below Calorie Cutoff	Below Protein Cutoff
Constant	−0.840	−0.159	−0.063	−0.094
TXN	−0.0082 (5.00)	−0.0052 (2.49)	−0.034 (7.83)	−0.064 (7.45)
SEX	−0.319 (2.17)	−0.149 (0.72)	−0.081 (0.64)	0.004 (0.03)
CITYGRT	0.259 (2.63)	−0.034 (0.27)	...	...
UPPER	...	...	0.156 (1.76)	−0.106 (0.91)
NORAT	0.471 (2.48)	0.348 (1.32)	−0.043 (0.26)	−0.058 (0.28)
CHL	−0.114 (2.05)	−0.089 (1.10)	−0.589 (2.17)	−0.599 (1.76)
LANPC	...	...	−0.801 (2.93)	−1.39 (3.25)

Source: Data from the household survey made by the International Food Policy Research Institute and the Institute of National Planning, Cairo, 1981/82.
Notes: The calorie cutoff point was set 15 percent below average requirements, which are based on family composition, age, sex, and the assumption that activity was moderate. The protein cutoff was based on the estimated requirement for protein, which depends on the age and sex of each member of a household. This was raised two standard deviations (assumed to be 12 percent). Observed consumption was reduced 15 percent to account for the average digestibility of protein in the Egyptian diet.
    The independent variables are defined in Appendix 2.

lower probability of underconsumption, although their average requirements may exceed those used in the study if cultivation takes more than moderate activity.

In the cities, those who hold ration cards are less likely to consume fewer calories than required than those who do not, whereas there is no statistical difference in rural areas. This is puzzling since the ration system provides only a moderate share of total calories and since families without a card can shop for the same goods at the cooperative or the open market. But as a number of families without cards had recently formed and since it is customary to give household staples to newlywed couples, this observation may reflect a drawdown of stocks that was not adequately covered in the interviews. The total number of families without ration cards is small and distributed throughout the range of expenditures.

A probit regression was also used to try to ascertain whether there was a relationship between the probability of having had a child under five years old die in the year before the interview and calorie and protein inadequacy. Although 7.5 percent of the rural families surveyed reported such an occurrence—which is alarming when one considers that many families had no children of this age—no statistical relationship with either income (which showed a negative correlation that was not significant) or dietary inadequacy was observed. The distribution of food within the family and the quality of health care delivery are probably more important predictors of child mortality than family food consumption.

6

INCOME TRANSFER EFFECTS OF FOOD SUBSIDIES AND PRICE DISTORTIONS

The food subsidy system transfers a significant amount of income, although it was not originally designed to do so. This has important effects on income distribution. To assess these effects completely, the financing of subsidies and its effect on incomes should be taken into account, and the actual recipients of subsidies should be defined.

A look at the tax system gives some insight into how subsidies are financed. In Egypt only about 4 percent of all tax revenues came from personal income taxes in the second half of the 1970s. About 60 percent of tax revenues came from commodity taxes; another 25 percent came from business income taxes.[18] Because they are only marginally important, personal income taxes are not included in the assessment that follows. Indirect taxation is taken into account insofar as it is combined with distorted farm producer prices, that is, prices of export commodities that are depressed below their international equivalents.

The distributional analysis is performed in a comparatively static fashion. The main issues addressed are:

- Who are the direct recipients of food subsidies?

- To what extent do food subsidies indirectly benefit consumer groups through depressed market prices?

- To what extent are producers affected by subsidized consumer prices and the distorted prices of their products?

- What is the net effect of food subsidies and distorted farm prices on income distribution?

Methodology of Evaluation

The theoretical approach is easily explained using Figure 1: a common feature of basic food markets in Egypt is that more than one price subsidy can apply to the same commodity. For consumers, this segregation of the market is enforced by quantity restrictions (rationing). The rice, sugar, oil, and, to some extent, wheat flour markets show the pattern described by Figure 1. The total subsidy that is received by a household is the difference between the equivalent international price and the domestic price. It is the sum of S^1, the subsidy on the basic ration (lower prices), S^2, the subsidy on the additional ration (higher prices), and S^3, the subsidy on open market purchases.

If all quantities of the commodity under consideration are imported, the sum of S^1, S^2, and S^3 multiplied by all households appears as "explicit subsidies" in the government's budget. Tea and lentils are such commodities, having no domestic supplies or only negligible ones. The other extreme would be a commodity produced domestically and not imported. The sum of S^1, S^2, and S^3 need not appear in the subsidy budget if the government procures it from domestic producers at prices below selling prices. Still, consumers would be heavily subsidized, as the comparison between domestic prices and international prices, which represents the opportunity costs of domestic consumption, suggests. Egypt's rice market is a case in point here. Such subsidies to the consumer are "implicit subsidies" and are financed by domestic producers. In the following analysis both types of subsidies—explicit and implicit—are taken into account.

---

[18] M. Reda A. el-Edel, "Impact of Taxation on Income Distribution: An Exploratory Attempt to Estimate Tax Incidence in Egypt," in *The Political Economy of Income Distribution in Egypt,* ed. Gouda Abdel-Khalek and Robert Tignor (New York: Holmes and Meier, 1982), pp. 140-141.

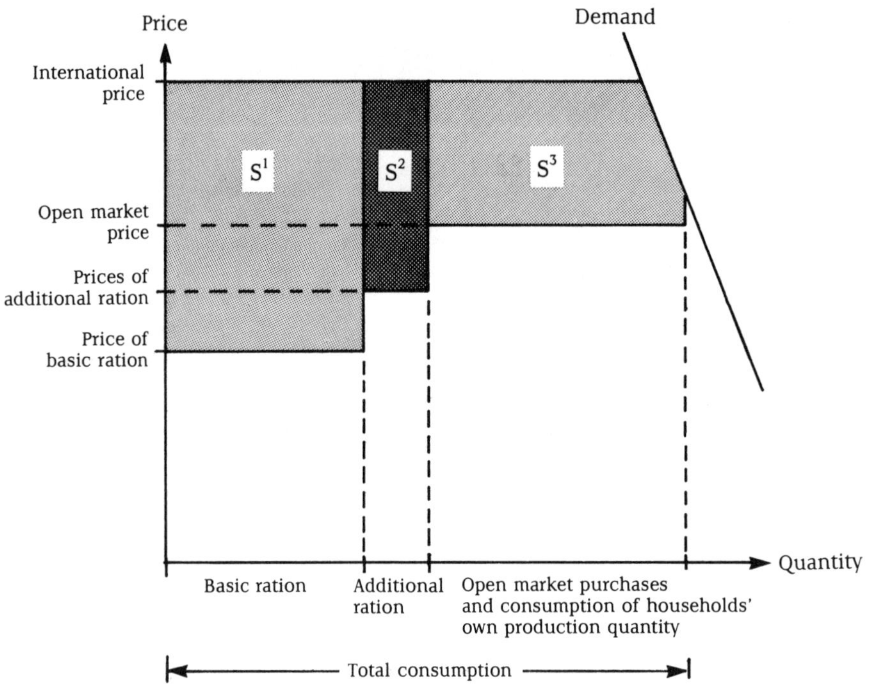

It is well known that international prices are not a stable point of reference. Their developments for Egypt during the 1960s and 1970s were recently assessed for the major food commodities at the farm-gate and for consumers by von Braun and de Haen.[19] It should be noted that most real international food prices in 1981 were close to their long-term averages. The income transfer effects caused by price distortions computed in the following framework, then, are not exaggerated or underestimated from a long-run perspective.

Insofar as households are farm producers, their incomes are affected by explicit food subsidies to the extent that they actually obtain them. On the other hand implicit food subsidies may reduce and support prices may increase the incomes of food producers, depending on whether the farm household produces surpluses of the commodity under consideration. The production side of a household is described by Figure 2. Gross losses of the farm household may stem from compulsory procurement by the government (L^1) or the losses due to depressed open market prices (L^2, L^3). In this geometric description the consumption by a farm household of its own produce evaluated at depressed prices is included in the gross losses (L^2), but these losses are reduced by the implicit subsidies that the farm household receives as a consumption unit (as a part of S^3).

If domestic prices were adjusted to international prices, the demand and supply response of households and farm producers could be elastic. This possibility, though certainly relevant for an assessment of the allocative efficiency of the system, is not taken into account here.[20] The probable size of any overestimation of the implicit subsi-

---

[19] See Joachim von Braun and Hartwig de Haen, *The Effects of Food Price and Subsidy Policies on Egyptian Agriculture*, Research Report 42 (Washington, D.C.: International Food Policy Research Institute, 1983).

[20] For an assessment for all of agriculture, see ibid., pp. 44-48.

38

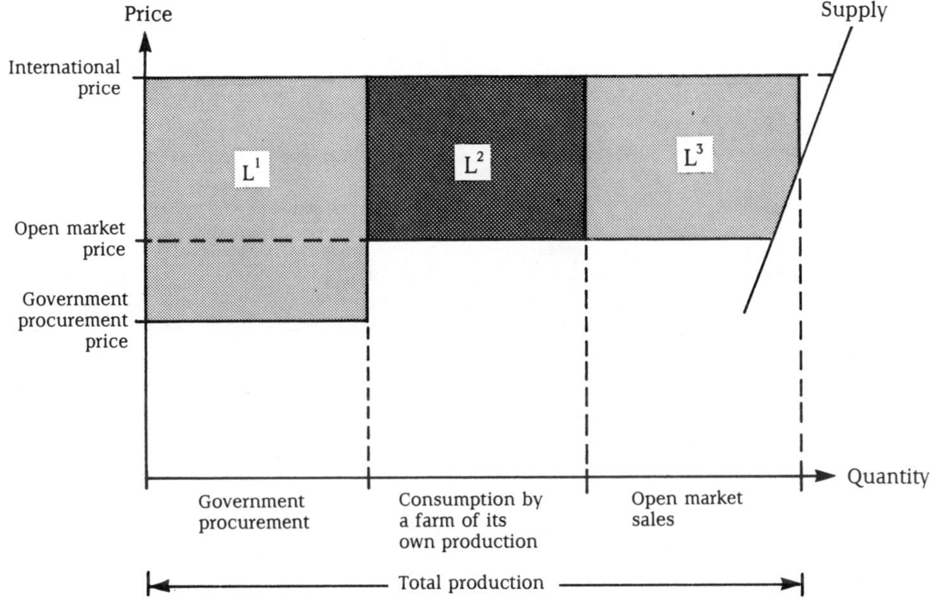

dies received by consumers or underestimation of producer losses—these are represented by the triangles above the households' demand curve (D) and the farmers' supply curve (S)—does little to affect the evaluation of the distributional effects of pricing.

Figures 1 and 2 depict a situation where domestic prices are below international prices. However, this is not the case on all Egyptian food commodity markets. Meat and dairy products were increasingly protected in the 1970s and 1980s.[21] The theoretical picture of this pricing and income transfer pattern is simply the reverse of the one shown and needs no further explanation. A second remark seems necessary to refine the simplified description of the approach: farm producers receive considerable benefits from subsidies on inputs, such as fertilizer and insecticides. These are actually included in the assessment of the income distribution effects of pricing but are neglected in the simplifying Figure 2.

The following accounting model was computed for each rural and urban household in the sample. (A complete list of the variables used in this report is given in Appendix 2.)

Transfers to and from households on the consumption side were given by

$$TC_i = \sum_s \sum_r Q_{i,r}^s \times (PIC_1^s - PDC_{1,r}^s), \quad (1)$$

where

TC_i = income transfers to or from household i on the consumption side in 1981/82; the result is in Egyptian pounds; i runs from 1 to 2,386;

$Q_{i,r}^s$ = quantity consumed in a year by household i of commodity s of price tier r;

PIC_1^s = the equivalent international consumer price of commodity s at applicable location 1; and

---

[21] Ibid.

$PDC^s_{1,r}$ = the domestic consumer price of commodity s at applicable location 1 and price tier r.

Transfers to and from households on the farm production side were given by

$$TP_i = \sum_s \sum_v Q^s_{i,v} \times (PDF^s_{1,r} + PIF^s_1)$$

$$+ \sum_k (I_{i,k} \times PS_k) \quad (2)$$

where

TP_i = income transfers to or from household i on the production side in a year; the result is in Egyptian pounds; for urban households, TP is assumed to be 0;

$Q^s_{i,v}$ = the quantity consumed in a year by household i of commodity s produced by farm households in quantity v;

PIF^s_1 = the domestic farm producer price of commodity s at applicable location 1 and procurement price tier r;

$PDF^s_{1,r}$ = the equivalent international farm-gate price of commodity s at applicable location 1;

$I_{i,k}$ = the input costs of farm household i for input k; and

PS_k = the subsidy rate on input k (this is calculated as the difference between the international and domestic prices of the input divided by its domestic price).

The total net income transfer (TN_1) was given by

$$TN_1 = TC_i + TP_i. \quad (3)$$

Transfers to households were shown by positive results; transfers from households were shown by negative results.

The effect of food subsidies and price distortions on income distribution can be assessed by relating the net income transfer per capita and its components to household income per capita. This yields a static comparison of per capita income with and without food subsidies and distorted domestic food prices:

$$IWS_i = (IC_i - TN_i)/NUM_i \quad (4)$$

where

IWS_i = per capita expenditure in household i in a hypothetical situation, without food subsidies or price distortions;

IC_i = expenditure in household i as actually observed (with subsidies).

The distribution of IWS may then be subjected to a conventional analysis of income distribution measures and compared to current actual distribution (IC/NUM). Relative changes by income quartile are computed for this purpose. Total expenditure rather than income is used for the evaluation because of the general problems of income assessment noted earlier.

Income Distribution Effects for the Urban and Rural Populations

The income transfer incorporated in the government-controlled food distribution is larger in urban areas than in rural. Explicit and implicit subsidies on the commodities of the basic ration, the additional ration, purchases from cooperatives, frozen meat, and government-supplied flour and bread have a mean of LE 29.6 per capita per year in urban areas and LE 19.7 in rural areas (see Tables 18 and 19). About half of the absolute difference (LE 4.7) in the subsidization of urban and rural households is due to the higher quantities of subsidized bread available to urban dwellers. Another part of the difference (LE 2.0) stems from higher subsidies transferred to households through basic and additional rations. This was not a result of differences between the rural and urban prices for the rationed commodities. Rather, it occurred because oil and rice rations were larger in the urban areas and the availability of rationed commodities was less stable in rural areas. Subsidies on commodities from cooperatives, including frozen meat, account for the remaining part of the difference (LE 2.2).

Although subsidies on food whose distribution is directly controlled by the govern-

Table 18—Income transfers to urban consumers from food subsidies and distorted prices, by expenditure quartile

Source of Transfer	Expenditure Quartile				All Urban Households
	1st	2nd	3rd	4th	
			(LE/capita/year)		
Government channels	27.55	29.90	29.72	31.22	29.59
Basic ration	7.45	7.30	7.30	6.75	7.20
Additional ration	1.40	1.54	1.52	1.66	1.53
Purchases from cooperatives	1.10	1.63	1.94	3.04	1.92
Frozen meat	2.14	1.94	2.20	1.62	1.97
Flour and bread	15.44	17.47	16.74	18.13	16.95
Open market	−5.20	−9.99	−14.67	−35.24	−16.27
Cereals	0.71	2.23	3.04	1.34	1.83
Sugar, oil, and tea	−0.06	−0.11	−0.05	−0.08	−0.07
Meat, fish, and poultry	−5.79	−12.03	−17.54	−36.35	−17.92
Beans and lentils	−0.06	−0.08	−0.11	−0.14	−0.10
Total transfer	22.34	19.90	15.04	−4.01	13.32
Total annual expenditures	173.76	304.20	457.33	990.20	435.92

Source: Data from the household survey made by the International Food Policy Research Institute and the Institute of National Planning, Cairo, 1981/82.

Notes: The figures for government channels and the open market do not always equal the sum of the categories beneath them because of rounding. Expenditure quartiles were determined by ranking urban households according to total reported expenditures per capita. The 1st quartile had the smallest expenditures; the 4th, the largest.

 Basic rations include sugar, oil, tea, and rice. Additional rations include those commodities, at higher prices, plus beans and lentils. Purchases from cooperatives include the same commodities included in additional rations. The category "flour and bread" includes only the flour and bread distributed through government channels. Flour sold on the open market is included in cereals.

ment were 33 percent less in rural areas than in urban, they reduce the difference between the rural and urban income distribution because the difference in incomes between rural and urban households was 43 percent (see Table 20). In both groups the absolute amount of subsidies received is more or less constant as income increases; therefore the subsidies reduce inequality within the rural and urban groups. These subsidies accounted for 16.9 percent of total per capita income in the lowest quartile of the rural population and 4.2 percent in the highest. In the urban group, the respective shares were 15.5 percent and 3.2 percent (see Table 20). Even though the absolute values of bread and flour subsidies were higher for urban consumers, the share of the subsidies of these commodities in income was larger in rural areas. This is mainly a result of the government's flour distribution scheme, which is more important than the bakery network in rural areas. There was, however, both an absolutely and a relatively larger income transfer to urban consumers from subsidized commodities from cooperatives (including frozen meat). These branches of the system were clearly oriented toward the urban population (see Table 20).

Not only do government-controlled prices differ from international prices, but open market prices differ from border prices. On the one hand, cereal prices are less than their international equivalent because imports of wheat and maize are subsidized and export of rice is controlled. On the other hand, prices of meat products exceed international prices because of import management and foreign exchange regulations.[22] These policies also affect income distribution.

Consumers having less access to subsidized cereals supplied directly by the government are reached by the system indirectly through depressed cereal prices. Meat consumers are losers in this system. As meat consumption usually increases as income does, groups with high income lose more, at least in absolute terms, because meat prices

---

[22] For a discussion of the general pricing regime, see ibid., pp. 63-70.

Table 19—Income transfers to rural producers and consumers from food subsidies and distorted prices, by expenditure quartile

Source of Transfer	Expenditure Quartile				All Rural Households
	1st	2nd	3rd	4th	
				(LE/capita/year)	
Cereal production	−1.24	−2.75	−4.27	−9.75	−4.47
Wheat	−0.23	−0.29	−0.97	−2.12	−0.89
Rice	−0.88	−2.21	−2.76	−6.53	−3.08
Maize, sorghum, and barley	−0.08	−0.18	−0.25	−0.74	−0.31
Beans and lentils	−0.03	−0.05	−0.28	−0.35	−0.18
Animal production	4.19	5.64	9.24	13.43	8.09
Livestock	4.12	5.47	9.36	14.62	8.36
Dairy	0.13	0.55	0.39	1.18	0.56
Poultry	−0.06	−0.38	−0.51	−2.37	−0.83
Sugar production	−1.62	−0.52	−0.09	−0.52	−0.69
Cotton production	−5.62	−8.81	−15.60	−24.08	−13.47
Inputs	3.19	5.30	7.11	14.12	7.40
Total transfer from production	−1.10	−1.13	−3.63	−6.80	−3.14
Government channels	18.76	18.92	17.43	23.66	19.68
Basic ration	5.44	5.53	5.66	5.98	5.65
Additional ration	0.93	1.04	0.97	1.13	1.02
Purchases from cooperatives	0.31	0.32	0.31	0.67	0.40
Frozen meat	0.13	0.38	0.35	0.66	0.38
Flour and bread	11.92	11.63	10.12	15.20	12.21
Open market	1.32	2.93	3.01	1.61	2.22
Cereals	6.58	9.86	13.53	19.30	12.28
Sugar, oil, and tea	−0.29	−0.26	−0.41	−0.37	−0.33
Meat, fish, and poultry	−4.80	−6.34	−9.65	−16.58	−9.31
Beans and lentils	−0.17	−0.33	−0.46	−0.74	−0.42
Total consumer transfer	20.08	21.86	20.44	25.27	21.90
Total transfer	18.98	20.72	16.81	18.47	18.76
Total annual expenditures	112.40	180.95	265.08	523.42	251.06

Source: Data from the household survey made by the International Food Policy Research Institute and the Institute of National Planning, Cairo, 1981/82.

Notes: The subtotals for cereal production, government channels, and so forth do not always equal the sum of their parts because of rounding. Expenditure quartiles were determined by ranking rural households according to total reported expenditures per capita. The 1st quartile had the smallest expenditures; the 4th, the largest.
   Inputs include fertilizers, insecticides, machinery, feed mix, cotton cake, maize, and berseem sales. Basic rations include sugar, oil, tea, and rice. Additional rations include those commodities, at higher prices, plus beans and lentils. Purchases from cooperatives include the same commodities included in additional rations. The category "flour and bread" includes only the flour and bread distributed through government channels. Flour sold on the open market is included in cereals.

are high. On the other hand, rural households benefit significantly from depressed cereal prices (see Table 20). For instance, the survey showed that the rural poor acquired an implicit subsidy from cereals equal to 6 percent of their income. For urban households this type of transfer was far less important (0.4 percent at the mean). The extent to which these gains of rural households were offset by losses on the production side because the prices for their marketable surplus were depressed will be determined later in this chapter.

Although meat consumption is much higher among the urban population, its share in total household expenditure is lower and hence the effect of meat prices on income is lower than on rural household income. To these negative transfers are added losses from purchases of rationed commodities on the open market. Rural households use this market more often than urban ones because the latter have greater access to the subsidized cooperative marketing system. Sugar and tea are major commodities that can be mentioned as part of this asymmetry in distribution. Still, the overall net effect of these positive and negative income transfers is an income loss for urban consumers and a slight gain for rural consumers. This adds to the favorable effect that directly government-controlled subsidized food marketing has on distribution for the rural population.

Table 20—Effects of income transfer from food subsidies and distorted prices on income distribution, by expenditure quartile

Source of Transfer	Urban Expenditure Quartile				All Urban Households	Rural Expenditure Quartile				All Rural Households
	1st	2nd	3rd	4th	holds	1st	2nd	3rd	4th	holds
	(percent of annual per capita expenditures)									
Government channels	15.5	9.7	6.4	3.2	6.0	16.9	10.3	6.6	4.2	7.0
Basic ration	4.2	2.4	1.6	0.7	1.5	4.9	3.0	2.1	1.1	2.0
Additional ration	0.8	0.5	0.3	0.2	0.3	0.8	0.5	0.4	0.2	0.4
Purchases from cooperatives	0.6	0.5	0.4	0.3	0.4	0.3	0.2	0.1	0.1	0.1
Frozen meat	1.2	0.6	0.5	0.2	0.4	0.1	0.2	0.2	0.1	0.1
Flour and bread	8.7	5.7	3.6	1.8	3.4	10.8	6.4	3.8	2.7	4.4
Open market	−2.8	−3.3	−3.1	−3.4	−3.2	1.1	1.6	1.1	0.3	0.8
Cereals	0.4	0.7	0.7	0.1	0.4	6.0	5.4	5.1	3.4	4.4
Sugar, oil, tea, and pulses	−0.1	−0.1	0.0	0.0	0.0	−0.5	−0.3	−0.3	−0.2	−0.3
Meat and poultry	−3.3	−3.9	−3.8	−3.5	−3.6	−4.4	−3.5	−3.7	−2.9	−3.3
Total net consumer transfer	12.7	6.4	3.3	−0.2	2.8	18.0	11.9	7.7	4.5	7.8
Total transfer	...	...	...	...	...	17.2	11.4	6.4	3.3	6.7
Quartile expenditures as share of urban or rural expenditures	35.8	61.7	93.0	209.6	100.0	39.4	65.0	94.4	203.1	100.0
Quartile expenditures as share of national expenditures	47.9	82.7	124.7	280.9	134.1	29.9	49.3	71.7	154.2	75.9

Source: Data from the household survey made by the International Food Policy Research Institute and the Institute of National Planning, Cairo, 1981/82.

Notes: Expenditure quartiles were determined by ranking urban and rural households independently according to total reported expenditures per capita. The 1st quartile had the smallest expenditures; the 4th, the largest. Basic rations include sugar, oil, tea, and rice. Additional rations include those commodities, at higher prices, plus beans and lentils. Purchases from cooperatives include the same commodities included in additional rations. The category "flour and bread" includes only the flour and bread distributed through government channels. Flour sold on the open market is included in cereals.

Distributional Implications for Selected Social Groups

Farmers

The income transfer effects discussed above pertain only to consumption. But the incomes of farm households are affected by price policy on the production side as well. In general, farm households lose from implicit taxation of basic food crops and cash crops (cereals, sugarcane, cotton) while they gain from protection of animal produce. Beyond that, they gain significantly from input subsidies. The computations show that the net effect of these components is a loss in the income in the rural population (Table 19). They also show that net losses increase with income.

This pattern may be further clarified by looking into how households, grouped by farm size, lose or gain from specific crops.

Patterns of losses and gains, and finally the size of the net loss or gain, are determined by the size and structure of price distortions, the structure of farm production (that is, the shares of protected crops compared to the shares of implicitly taxed crops), input intensity and productivity, and farm size. Production structures and input intensity are again heavily determined by input and output price ratios and levels, including the prices of such inputs as labor. If family labor is abundantly available at low opportunity costs to small farms, production intensity on those farms is usually higher. This may, all else being equal, result in higher yields or greater production of such labor-intensive goods as livestock.

These determinants establish a distinct pattern of gains and losses on farms as small farms concentrate more on the labor intensive and protected livestock sector while bigger farms actually lose disproportionately because they produce higher shares of implicitly taxed crops. Table 21 shows these patterns for three farm size classes.[23]

It should be mentioned that not all of the differences in allocation between farm size classes are a consequence of the incentive structure but that some were the result of government-enforced area allotments for cotton, sugarcane, and rice.[24] Small farmers (those farming less than 1 feddan) were net gainers as producers from the distorted price structure, which added to their gains (income transfers) as consumers. For this group, losses from cereals, sugarcane, and cotton were overcompensated for by gains from animal production and input subsidies (mainly those on feed). While medium-size farms (1 to 5 feddan) were net losers on the production side, these losses were less than their gains on the consumption side, which leaves the group with a net gain. This was not so for the bigger farms (more than 5 feddan). In this group the net losses on the income-generating production side greatly exceeded the income transfers on the consumption side.[25]

For the rural population as a whole, the combined effect of food subsidies and distorted agricultural prices on both the production and consumption sides was even more progressive than the income transfer effects on the consumption side alone (see Table 11). The breakdown by farm size showed a more distinct pattern than the breakdown by expenditures did because many of Egypt's rural households are either part-time farmers or landless. Judging by the reported main occupation of the head of household, only 42 percent of the rural households cultivated land and had the head of household call farming his main job. Only this group is shown in the first three columns of Table 21. A look at the remaining social groups in rural areas, however, reveals that each was involved in some farm production.

Landless Farm Laborers

Even landless farm workers (wage earners, 9 percent of the rural sample) engaged in some animal production activities. This group was the poorest of the 10 groups in the classification by employment: its mean per capita income was 32 percent less than the rural average and 62 percent less than the urban average. Transfers from the subsidies and price distortions accounted for 14 percent of their current nominal income, while the bigger farmers had a net loss of 18.8 percent (see Table 22).

In order to ascertain what implications for equity the different net transfers had for farm groupings and employment classes, two criteria are used. The first defines the share of food subsidies accrued by each of the groups as a proportion of its share in the total population:

$$EQPOP_i = [(TRANR_i / \sum_i TRANR_i) /$$

$$(POP_i / \sum_i POP_i)] \, 100, \quad (5)$$

where

$EQPOP_i$ = the equity share of group i on the basis of its share in the population; i runs from 1 to 10;

$TRANR_i$ = the income transfer received by group i from government subsidized food (that is, food from ration shops, cooperatives, flour shops, and bakeries); $TRANR_i$ is the per capita transfer multiplied by the number of people in group i; and

POP_i = the population of group i according to survey results, grouped by the main occupation of the heads of household.

The second criterion defines the share of food subsidies accrued by each of the groups as a proportion of its share in total income (calculated using expenditures):

$$EQEX_i = [(TRANR_i / \sum_i TRANR_i) /$$

$$(EXP_i / \sum_i EXP_i)] \, 100, \quad (6)$$

---

[23] In addition to these farms, there are large-scale commercial livestock and poultry operations not covered in the household survey.

[24] For a discussion of this policy, see von Braun and de Haen, *Effects of Food Price and Subsidy Policies.*

[25] It should be noted that on-farm consumption is excluded from the balancing of gains and losses in production and consumption because it does not affect net income transfers (see equations [1], [2], and [3]).

44

Table 21—Income transfers from food subsidies and distorted prices, by employment group

| | Rural Households | | | | | | | Urban Households | | |
| | Farm Households | | | Landless Farm Labor | Non-farm Wage Labor | Non-farm Self-Employed | Others | Self-Employed | Wage Labor | Others |
Source of Transfer	Small Farms	Medium-Size Farms	Large Farms							
					(LE/capita/year)					
Cereal production	−1.35	−9.41	−30.89	0.00	−1.46	−2.44	−2.97	...	...	...
Wheat	−0.39	−1.65	−8.86	0.00	−0.40	−0.40	−0.31	...	...	...
Rice	−0.69	−6.75	−17.75	0.00	−0.81	−1.83	−2.55	...	...	...
Maize, sorghum, and barley	−0.19	−0.59	−2.47	0.00	−0.23	−0.15	−0.04	...	...	...
Beans and lentils	−0.06	−0.41	−1.79	0.00	−0.01	−0.04	−0.07	...	...	...
Animal production	6.77	17.34	15.61	0.78	4.98	4.69	4.60	...	...	...
Livestock	6.80	16.71	17.18	1.34	5.43	5.31	5.51	...	...	...
Dairy	0.42	1.14	1.08	0.12	0.24	0.04	0.73	...	...	...
Poultry	−0.44	−0.51	−2.65	−0.69	−0.69	−0.66	−1.64	...	...	...
Sugar production	−0.36	−1.26	−7.84	0.00	−0.40	−0.04	−0.09	...	...	...
Cotton production	−5.66	−28.45	−88.09	0.00	−5.87	−3.26	−9.21	...	...	...
Inputs	6.73	12.85	30.57	1.61	4.14	4.14	5.55	...	...	...
Total transfer from production	6.13	−8.93	−80.65	2.38	1.37	3.08	−2.11	...	...	...
Government channels	21.20	15.60	13.68	19.57	21.48	19.98	23.03	27.14	29.52	32.13
Basic ration	5.83	5.51	4.90	5.10	5.68	5.81	6.01	6.61	7.23	7.70
Additional ration	1.19	0.85	0.79	0.84	1.01	0.90	1.34	1.18	1.47	1.99
Purchases from co-operatives	0.24	0.33	0.27	0.15	0.75	0.42	0.36	1.49	1.91	2.38
Frozen meat	0.23	0.21	0.16	0.03	0.87	0.21	0.48	1.20	2.22	2.21
Flour and bread	13.69	8.68	7.54	13.44	13.15	12.61	14.82	16.64	16.66	17.84
Open market	2.66	2.37	−6.20	4.59	−0.12	0.62	5.69	−20.93	−13.93	−16.58
Cereals	12.12	11.18	8.33	13.01	10.92	12.14	16.00	−0.04	2.35	2.58
Sugar, oil, and tea	−0.38	−0.32	−0.35	−0.58	−0.29	−0.27	−0.28	−0.17	−0.04	−0.05
Meat, fish, and poultry	−8.74	−8.06	−13.53	−7.48	−10.29	−10.89	−9.51	−20.60	−16.14	−19.01
Beans and lentils	−0.32	−0.43	−0.64	−0.35	−0.45	−0.35	−0.51	−0.10	−0.10	−0.09
Total consumer transfer	23.87	17.98	7.48	24.17	21.36	20.61	28.72	6.21	15.58	15.55
Total transfer	30.00	9.04	−73.16	26.56	22.74	23.69	26.61	6.21	15.58	15.55
Total annual expenditures	238.72	274.49	388.38	189.87	303.33	317.90	297.24	543.59	461.46	513.51
Share of survey households (percent)	8.0	14.5	1.6	5.4	12.2	6.8	10.0	10.0	21.2	10.3

Source: Data from the household survey made by the International Food Policy Research Institute and the Institute of National Planning, Cairo, 1981/82.

Notes: Households are classified by the main employment of the head of the household. Small farms have less than 1 feddan; medium size farms have between 1 and 5 feddan; large farms have more than 5 feddan.

The subtotals for cereal production, government channels, and so forth do not always equal the sum of their parts because of rounding.

Inputs include fertilizers, insecticides, machinery, feed mix, cotton cake, maize, and berseem sales. Basic rations include sugar, oil, tea, and rice. Additional rations include those commodities, at higher prices, plus beans and lentils. Purchases from cooperatives include the same commodities included in additional rations. The category "flour and bread" includes only the flour and bread distributed through government channels. Flour sold on the open market is included in cereals.

where $EQEX_i$ is the equity share of group i on the basis of its share of income (calculated as expenditures) and EXP_i is the expenditures of group i according to survey results, grouped by the main occupation of the heads of household.

The results of these computations are shown in the last two lines of Table 22. Based on the income criterion ($EQEX_i$), the landless farm workers gained the most: they received 157.1 percent of an equity share from food subsidies.

Table 22—Comparison of income effects of subsidies and distorted prices on selected employment groups

			Rural			Urban	
Category	Small Farms	Large Farms	Land-less Farm Labor	Non-farm Wage Labor	Nonfarm Self-Employed	Self-Employed	Wage Labor
					(percent)		
Per capita expenditure as share of average expenditures	64.8	105.4	51.3	82.3	86.3	147.5	125.2
Transfers (shares of the group's expenditures)							
Consumption							
Government food distribution[a]	8.9	3.5	10.3	7.1	7.7	5.0	6.4
Open markets	1.1	−1.5	2.4	−0.04	1.9	−3.9	−3.0
Total	10.0	1.9	12.7	7.0	9.7	1.1	3.4
Farm production							
Cereals	−0.6	−8.0	. . .	−0.5	−1.0	. . .	. . .
Meat and milk	2.8	4.0	0.4	1.6	1.5	. . .	. . .
Total (including sugarcane, cotton, and input subsidies)	2.6	−20.8	1.3	0.5	−0.7	. . .	. . .
Net transfers in consumption and production	12.6	−18.8	14.0	7.5	9.0	1.1	3.4
Equity of subsidies received[b]							
According to the group's population share	88.8	56.3	81.5	90.2	83.8	114.0	124.0
According to the group's income share	136.5	52.9	157.1	110.0	96.6	77.0	99.2

Source: Data from the household survey made by the International Food Policy Research Institute and the Institute of National Planning, Cairo, 1981/82.

Note: Small farms have less than 1 feddan and large farms have more than 5 feddan.

[a] This is distribution from rations, cooperatives, flour shops, and bakeries.

[b] A group gained from subsidies if its figure here exceeds 100 and lost if its figure is less.

On the other hand, they ranked among the most neglected groups if the distribution of subsidies is assessed on the grounds of per capita distribution (EQPOP$_i$): they received only 81.5 percent of a "fair" share of subsidies on this basis. Only the big farmers received less. This reflects the high proportion of subsidy in the value of the items purchased by the landless, which gives them a high relative subsidy. The total subsidies on many items increased with the size of the purchase, hence landless laborers, being poor, obtained a smaller absolute share of the subsidies.

Cereal prices were important for the households of landless farm laborers. It is particularly striking that this group benefits by the directly subsidized cereals available from government distribution (wheat flour and bread) to the same extent as from low open market prices of cereals. Each of these explicit and implicit subsidies transferred about LE 13 per capita per year, which represented 13.9 percent of the per capita expenditure of the group (see Table 21). Given the large share of basic food expenditures in the budgets of landless agricultural wage laborers, any reduction in subsidized food supplies to rural households would worsen this group's food situation. Unlike the farm households that produce cereals or can, landless laborers would not immediately benefit from compensatory measures focusing on output pricing if such instruments were applied parallel to a reduction of food subsidies. In the long run they may, however, benefit from increased demand for farm labor if that followed from a pricing policy change.

Nonagricultural Rural Wage Laborers and Self-Employment

In rural Egypt, 21 percent of the rural households are headed by nonfarm wage earners and 12 percent by nonfarm self-employed workers.[26] But farming is an important source of income and food supplies in many of these households. This is indicated by the effects income transfers have on the production side (see Table 21). The per capita income of the group was about 60 percent higher than that of landless farm workers. Based on the income criterion for equity of subsidies distribution ($EQEX_i$), these groups received close to or more than their equity shares (see Table 22).

Wage Earners and Self-Employed Workers in Urban Areas

The per capita income of wage earners and self-employed workers in urban areas exceeded the national average, the former by 25.2 percent and the latter by 47.5 percent. In absolute values the two gained larger income transfers through the government's food supply channels than any of the other groups distinguished (about LE 28 per capita per year). Because of their higher incomes, this represents only 5.0 to 6.4 percent of per capita expenditure, which is a smaller share than for most rural groups. Both of these urban groups incurred losses from the open market purchases of food (mainly meat), which significantly reduced their net transfers (see Table 22).

Recognizing that these urban groups received the highest absolute values of food subsidies per capita, it immediately follows that equity criterion EQPOP will indicate that both groups received preferential treatment. However, the other criterion, EQEX, indicates that the urban wage earners just received an equity share and that the urban self-employed, the richest group in this comparison, got only 77 percent of an equity share (see Table 22). These values refer only to subsidies received through government-controlled food marketing. If losses on open markets were included, the resulting net gain would have been smaller.

An Analytical Assessment of the Determinants of Distribution Effects

The assessment of the effects the subsidy system has on distribution by income groups or on a stratification by employment categories reveals that these effects may not fit easily into rural-urban or rich-poor dichotomies. Many components of the system and their related income-transfer effects worked in opposite directions for some population groups. Therefore major economic, structural, demographic, and locational variables are regressed on the transfers to test statistically for the effects of the transfers on income distribution. The variables identified as important in the explanation of the distribution of the benefits from some components of the subsidy system may not be so for others. So the analysis is to be understood as testing for the distribution of benefits from components of the system as well as from the system as a whole. Essentially this means that the analysis will try to explain the TN_i variable and its components (TC_i, TP_i) as computed in the model above (see equations [1], [2], and [3]). The regression model specified for this purpose has the following elements:

$$TC_i^g = f(TXP_i, LAN_i, EMPL1 \ldots 4_i, AGEHEAD_i,$$
$$CHL_i, NUM_i, EARNPERS_i, WORCOP_i,$$
$$TCARD_i, UPPER_i, VILSIZE_i, DIS_i,$$
$$CITYGRT_i, CITYSMAL_i, URBAN_i), \quad (7)$$

where

i	= the number of households observed in rural and urban samples; i runs from 1 to 2,367;
g	= components and aggregates of income transfers by commodities and commodity groups; g runs from 1 to 13;
TC_i^g	= annual income transfers to or from households through the commodity group or ration (g) in Egyptian pounds per capita;
TXP	= total household expenditure per capita per year in Egyptian pounds;
LAN	= farm size, if the household cultivates land; if not, it equals 0;
EMPL	= dummy variables for employment groups, classified by the

[26] On diversity in rural employment, see Samir Radwan and Eddy Lee, *The Anatomy of Rural Poverty: Egypt 1977* (Geneva: International Labour Office, 1980).

main occupation of the head of the household:

EMPL 1: if self employed = 1, else = 0;

EMPL 2: if farm worker = 1, else = 0;

EMPL 3: if nonagricultural worker = 1, else = 0;

EMPL 4: if unemployed or outside workforce = 1, else = 0;

AGEHEAD = the age of the head of the household;

CHL = the proportion of children in a household; the number of children 5 years or younger divided by the number of family members;

EARNPERS = the number of people earning income divided by the total number of people in the household;

WORCOP = the number of workplace cooperatives in which the household is a member;

TCARD = the number of ration cards held by a household;

VILSIZE = the size of a household's village (the number of observations in the village is used as a proxy, as the number of cases randomly drawn in each of the sample villages is a constant fraction of village size);

DIS = the distance to the capital of the governorate, in kilometers (this is 0 for the urban sample);

CITYGRT = a dummy variable that equals 1 if a household is in Cairo, Giza, and Alexandria and 0 otherwise;

CITYSMAL = a dummy variable that equals 1 if a household is in a city with fewer than 100,000 inhabitants and 0 otherwise; and

URBAN = a dummy variable for the total urban sample that equals 1 if the household is in an urban area and 0 otherwise.

Each of the components of the net income transfer and the net transfer itself is explained by the same set of exogenous variables. The analysis allows for two kinds of explanation.

The first is an assessment of the effect a particular determinant has on components of income transfers. This means reading the results of the analysis compiled in Table 23 by lines. For example, the degree and direction of the regional orientation of the various price and marketing policies can be identified on this basis.

The second is an explanation of what causes the variance in the per capita income transfers from each of the branches of the subsidy and rationing system. This means reading the parameter estimates in Table 23 by columns. In this way it may become clear, for example, what determines the fluctuations in income transfers from the bread and flour distribution system for households.

Some Major Findings

The net effects of the food price and subsidy policy show a rural bias, whereas subsidies transferred by government-controlled food marketing show a moderate urban bias. This finding shows up in the parameter estimates for the variable URBAN in the models for net transfers and for government distribution. While the increase in real income that an urban inhabitant received from explicit subsidies was LE 9.2 greater than the increase a rural inhabitant received, all else being equal, the urban inhabitant faced a LE 17.9 loss if open-market price distortions are taken into account. The urban bias of the government-controlled system was established mainly by the larger transfers from the bakery system, the ration system, and the cooperative system. However, this was more than offset by the smaller transfers to urban households from cereals sold on open markets and negative transfers from the meat market.

The inhabitants of the big cities (greater Cairo, Alexandria) are not more subsidized by the system than people in small cities, and living in a small or a large village made little difference in the amount of subsidies received. This finding looks somewhat different if the components of the subsidy system are looked at individually. Big-city dwellers receive a significantly larger transfer with the basic ration and frozen meat from cooperatives but this is offset by other components, particularly flour. People in small cities (fewer than

48

Table 23—Determinants of the income distribution effects of food subsidies and price distortions on food markets

								Dependent Variables						
	Government Channels						Open Market					Total Income Transfer in Consumption	Net Income Transfer in Consumption and Production	Mean of Independent Variable
Independent Variable	Basic Ration	Additional Ration	Purchase from Cooperatives	Frozen Meat	Flour and Bread	Total	Cereals	Sugar, Oil, and Tea	Meat and Fish	Beans and Lentils	Total			
Intercept	3.691	1.226	0.033	1.431	8.488	14.869	21.902	−0.325	0.988	−0.542	22.024	36.89	38.500	…
TXP	−0.00112‡	−0.0000832	0.00114‡	−0.000310	0.00244‡	0.00207‡	0.00307‡	−0.000027	−0.0245‡	−0.00026‡	−0.022‡	−0.0197‡	−0.0130‡	368.58
LAND	−0.0306*	−0.0078	−0.0114	−0.0119	−0.308‡	−0.369†	−0.215†	−0.00708	−0.386‡	−0.00311	−0.611‡	−0.9802‡	−7.205‡	0.899
EMPL1	0.920‡	−0.1189	−0.349*	−0.419	1.331	1.365	−1.293	−0.125*	0.0147	0.0757	−1.328	0.0377	−4.333	…[a]
EMPL2	0.744†	−0.229	−0.439*	−0.623	2.011	1.465	1.013	−0.201†	0.339	0.0828	1.234	2.699	−0.698	…[a]
EMPL3	1.122‡	−0.028	−0.0137	0.137	3.055†	4.272‡	−1.101	−0.076	−0.0055	0.0671	−1.115	3.157	−1.372	…[a]
EMPL4	0.746‡	0.094	0.00387	−0.214	2.464*	3.094*	0.796	−0.074	0.246	0.0674	1.036	4.129*	−0.398	…[a]
AGEHEAD	0.027†	0.00581‡	0.00561*	−0.00202	0.0615‡	0.098‡	0.047†	0.00402‡	−0.045*	0.00251†	−0.086†	0.012	0.0643	47.79
CHL	−2.947‡	−0.432†	0.733†	0.0140	−7.094‡	−9.726‡	−5.498‡	0.1599*	0.3978	0.128	−4.812*	−14.537‡	−15.05†	0.150
NUM	−0.364‡	−0.158‡	−0.0527‡	−0.1089‡	−0.639‡	−1.323‡	−0.396‡	0.0176‡	0.394‡	−0.00467	0.012	−1.311‡	−0.0411	6.11
EARNPERS	−0.274	−0.479‡	0.552†	0.524*	−2.564*	−2.240*	−0.907	0.0968	−1.168	0.118*	−1.861	−4.101*	−8.465*	0.329
WORCOP	0.177†	−0.0611*	0.0158	0.197*	0.368	0.698*	0.144	0.041†	0.149	−0.064‡	0.27	0.968	−0.359	0.397
TCARD	2.403‡	0.725‡	0.065	0.446‡	1.296†	4.935‡	−0.017	0.0336	0.204	0.099‡	0.319	5.254‡	6.493‡	1.126
UPPER	−0.441‡	0.141†	0.1919*	0.00231	7.983‡	7.877‡	−5.949‡	−0.556‡	−3.636‡	0.275‡	−9.867‡	−1.990*	−7.159‡	…[a]
VILSIZE	0.00194	−0.0013	−0.00106	−0.0218‡	−0.012	−0.0343	−0.037	0.000681	−0.0138	−0.00121	−0.052	−0.0860*	−0.0995	13.86
DIS	0.0078†	0.0005	−0.00118	−0.00291	0.011	0.0153	−0.012	−0.0033‡	−0.050†	0.0053‡	−0.0704‡	−0.055†	−0.126†	20.67
CITYGRT	0.408†	−0.1656*	0.0283	1.291‡	−1.413	0.149	−1.573*	−0.0544	−0.355	0.046	−1.936	−1.787	−0.9019	…[a]
CITYSMAL	−1.097‡	−0.760‡	−0.0738	−0.655†	0.154	−2.432*	0.666	−0.0711	1.268	−0.115*	1.748	−0.684	2.565	…[a]
URBAN	1.855‡	0.711‡	1.042‡	0.250	5.305‡	9.163‡	−13.868‡	0.084	−6.151‡	0.229‡	−19.706‡	−10.543‡	−17.912‡	…[a]
T-ratio	67.2	29.2	22.8	11.6	19.3	34.3	27.6	24.7	58.6	15.3	49.5	22.6	25.0	
R^2	0.34	0.18	0.15	0.08	0.13	0.21	0.17	0.16	0.31	0.11	0.27	0.15	0.16	
Mean	6.30	1.23	1.04	1.04	14.18	23.79	7.96	−0.23	−12.87	−0.29	−5.44	18.35	16.51	

Source: Data from the household survey made by the International Food Policy Research Institute and the Institute of National Planning, Cairo, 1981/82.

Notes: In all the regressions listed, the degrees of freedom were 2,348. The independent variables are defined in Appendix 2.

Basic rations include sugar, oil, tea, and rice. Additional rations include those commodities, at higher prices, plus beans and lentils. Purchases from cooperatives include the same commodities included in additional rations. The category "flour and bread" includes only the flour and bread distributed through government channels. Flour sold on the open market is included in cereals.

[a] This is a dummy variable.

* The estimated parameter is significant at the 85 percent level according to t-statistics.

† The estimated parameter is significant at the 95 percent level according to t-statistics.

‡ The estimated parameter is significant at the 99 percent level according to t-statistics.

100,000 inhabitants) get less from rations and from meat. No important deviations in distribution are indicated by the variable VILSIZE in the components of the transfer system.

The net transfers received by people living in remote areas of the country are somewhat smaller than those received by people in more accessible areas. This is largely an effect of the prices on the open market, although the government system balances a good deal of this comparative disadvantage. This effect of the system is represented by the variables UPPER and DIS. Egyptians in Upper Egypt get significantly less from basic rations but more from additional rations, cooperatives, and especially from the flour and bread network. The latter finding is consistent with an earlier assessment by governorates of the government cereal distribution system, which showed strong support of Upper Egypt.[27] On the other hand, inhabitants of Upper Egypt do have smaller transfers from cereals on open markets because of higher prices, and lose significantly from purchases of sugar, oil, and tea on open markets. This is caused by the extremely high preference for sugar consumption in the region. In combination with losses on open meat markets, this reduces the total transfer on the consumption side. Moreover, taxes on farm production in Upper Egypt were implicitly higher because of sugarcane and cotton pricing, which contributes to the significant net loss.[28]

People living in remote villages further away from the capital of their governorate receive larger transfers with the basic ration and are not neglected by the government distribution system. But prices on open markets are higher at these locations. These prices impose losses from open market transactions and finally cause the value of the net transfer to be negative. The effect is relatively small, though statistically significant.

Food price policy in total has a progressive effect on income distribution but food distribution directly controlled by the government has a regressive effect. Transfers from rations declined as income grew but transfers from purchases at cooperatives (sugar, oil, tea, rice) and subsidized bakeries and flour shops increased. This means that richer households gain, in the aggregate, more

from this branch of the system than the poor: a 10 percent increase in income yields a 0.42 percent increase in the income transfer incorporated in the directly managed distribution system. Increased meat consumption in high-income groups basically establishes the progressiveness of price policy for income distribution: the net sum of consumer gains decreases by 3.95 percent if income increases by 10 percent.

It is already evident from the tabulations of income transfer effects by farm-size classes that net transfers shrink as farm size increases (see Table 21). This is stressed by the estimation results for the LAN variable in the regressions. All income transfer components are reduced as farm size increases, many quite substantially (see Table 23).

The income transfer accrued by nonagricultural wage earning households was significantly higher than the transfer accrued by those that do not earn wages. Households headed by a wage laborer outside agriculture receive more subsidies from the government system because their transfers with the basic ration are larger and they use the bread and flour system more. In the ration system, all the four groups of households distinguished by employment categories have positive marginal transfers. This implies that the group not included (which basically represents households living on capital income and remittances) gains less from this system.

Another indication of the more favorable position of wage earners in the system is the increase in the transfer from basic rations and frozen meat gained from being a member of a workplace cooperative. This type of cooperative is open only to wage earners and government employees.

Having a ration card not only allows for significant income transfers from the ration system but from other government-controlled food channels, too. The income transfer from the basic and additional ration is—as one would suppose—very much a function of whether the household has a card. It may be surprising that the estimated parameter for the related variable (TCARD) is not closer to the mean of per capita transfers incorporated in the basic and additional ration. However, part of it is captured by the intercept. The variance of the dependent variable is also

---

[27] Ibid., pp. 44-46.

[28] Cotton varieties of lower quality grown in Upper Egypt are procured at lower prices.

fairly large. This is partly explained by the demographic and locational variables (that is, CHL, UPPER, CITYSMAL, URBAN).

The ration card is frequently used for ad hoc rationing of commodities not included in the basic ration. This explains why transfers from frozen meat and flour from flour shops are higher for cardholders.

The difference between the parameter estimated for TCARD in the total consumption transfer and net transfers may not be immediately obvious. It implies that farm households without a card have an additional loss. It should be recalled that although the regulation is not totally enforced, farms bigger than 10 feddan are not eligible for the basic ration. This nonlinear relationship between farm size and income transfer from subsidies is captured by the TCARD variable.

Large households and households with a large proportion of small children are less supported by the system. Some components of the rationing system are designed on a per household and not on a per capita basis. In larger households this reduces transfers per capita from the ration, the cooperative, and the flour system. The variable NUM yields negative parameters for transfers from all government-controlled food channels (Table 23). This effect is eliminated in the net transfer, which includes the effects on farm production because farm households with an abundant labor supply tend to shift toward more labor-intensive livestock production, which is protected. Of course, households having higher proportions of children do not experience this effect. Delayed registration of newly born children on the ration card may be a reason for the significant decrease of per capita income transfers from rations. Second, children's consumption of subsidized cereals such as flour and bread is below the average, which partly explains the lower transfers in the related parts of the system.

Two other demographic factors of distribution effects are depicted by the analysis: households with an older head manage to accrue larger income transfers within the government system and if the share of earners in the household increases, the transfers received tend to decrease. The latter happens although transfers from purchases at cooperatives increased.

7

SUBSIDIZED STAPLE FOODS IN FARM HOUSEHOLDS AND THE HOUSEHOLDS' RESPONSE IN PRODUCTION, CONSUMPTION, AND MARKETING

The following analysis deals mainly with the subsidized cereal commodities in farm households. Farm households, being both food producers and consumers, are affected by food subsidy policies in a particular fashion. As producers they are burdened by the depressing effect import subsidies have on prices of wheat and maize and by export restrictions on rice. An integral component of this price policy is the compulsory delivery of paddy at prices below market prices. On the other hand, some livestock producers gain from subsidized feed supplies (yellow maize) distributed in a quota system.

As consumers, farm households gain from having low-price cereals available. In general, farm households that are net purchasers of grain for human consumption and animal feed are better off in the system, while households that might produce a surplus are worse off.

The actual effects that changes in grain prices and price ratios have on resource allocations depends on the prices of competing commodities and, possibly, on either the stability of subsidized food supplies in rural areas or farmers' perception of the riskiness of these supplies. As labor affects food production and processing as well as acquisition, the composition of a household may influence the net effects of the system. Finally, farm households may perceive a difference in quality between subsidized cereal products, such as bread, and products they produce themselves and may attach an intrinsic value to consumption of the latter. Such factors determine the actual ability and desire of farm households to substitute subsidized cereals for cereals they produce themselves. In the short run, in households that have increased access to subsidized cereals, an increased marketing of their own produce may occur. In the long run, farm production patterns and households' food processing activities would change. These processes are largely determined by farmers' resource endowments, such as the amount of land and the availability of family labor. Therefore, the resources, production, and marketing activities of farm households were assessed in the survey. The results are discussed in this chapter.

The rural survey of 1,389 households included in the analysis shows that 790 households cultivated land. The total land area captured was 1,799 feddan. A comparison of the farm size structure reported in the survey with information from more broadly based surveys reveals that the survey was reasonably representative (see Table 24). If compared to available data from 1975, notable differences appear only in the shares bigger farms had in area. However, a shift of land from large farms to medium-size farms since 1975 does not seem unlikely as population growth and inheritance rules continue to reduce farm size.

The seasonal cropping pattern reported in the survey for 1980/81 is very close to the one reported in official statistics for the winter crops. Among summer crops some overreporting of cotton and rice and underreporting of maize occurs (Appendix 3, Table 43). As farm production was not a criterion for stratification in the survey, a bias toward the rice growing areas in the northern Delta may have occurred.

Implications of Farm Production Structures for Equity-Oriented Production Policies

Some interesting features of production patterns show up in a breakdown by farm size of the land sown with major cereals. The shares of wheat and maize in total area were much larger on small farms than on big ones. The share of area sown with maize fell espe-

Table 24—Patterns of cereal cropping, livestock production, and farm size

| | | Farm Size | | | | |
Share Category/Commodity	Landless	0 – 1 Feddan	1 – 3 Feddan	3 – 5 Feddan	More than 5 Feddan	Total
			(percent)			
Share of all farms						
1975 data	...	39.4	40.6	12.4	7.6	100.0
Survey	...	40.3	37.6	15.3	6.8	100.0
Share of total area						
1975 data	...	12.4	33.8	19.8	34.0	100.0
Survey	...	10.2	33.2	28.5	28.1	100.0
Share of total area of farms of given size[a]						
Wheat	...	31.4	30.1	22.2	27.1	27.2
Maize, sorghum	...	60.6	35.5	22.0	21.4	30.3
Rice	...	9.7	24.7	36.4	27.7	27.4
Share of total area sown with crop						
Wheat	...	11.8	37.0	22.7	28.5	100.0
Maize, sorghum	...	20.4	39.3	20.2	20.1	100.0
Rice	...	3.6	30.3	37.1	29.0	100.0
Share of total livestock						
Buffalo	7.8	28.8	39.1	17.1	7.1	100.0
Cattle	7.0	22.6	40.3	20.1	10.0	100.0
Animal units, including poultry[b]	8.0	20.0	38.6	20.0	13.4	100.0
Sheep, goats, and camels per feddan[c]	...	1.60	0.95	0.57	0.39	0.81

Sources: Data from the household survey made by the International Food Policy Research Institute and the Institute of National Planning, Cairo, 1981/82; and data from the Egyptian Ministry of Agriculture.

[a] It should be noted that total area, not cropped area, is used.

[b] Animal units are aggregated on a feed requirement basis. Buffalo, cattle, sheep, goats, camels, and poultry are included.

[c] Soliman, Fitch, and Aziz reported the following figures for animal units per feddan: for farms with less than 1 feddan, –1.52; for those with 1-3 feddan, 0.72; for those with 3-5 feddan, 0.64; for those with more than 5 feddan, 0.21; for all farms, 0.63. These figures include donkeys, but exclude poultry, which makes them only roughly comparable with the figures above (Ibrahim Soliman, James B. Fitch, and N.A. Aziz, "The Role of Livestock Production on the Egyptian Farm," Economics Working Paper 85, Agricultural Developments Systems Project, Ministry of Agriculture, Cairo, and the University of California—Berkeley, Cairo, July 1982, p. 7).

cially rapidly as farm size increased. Rice showed an opposite change: its share tended to increase with farm size (see Table 24).

These patterns are mainly to be explained by the interplay between grain and livestock production on the farm level, which is a consequence of the output price ratios and differences in factor scarcities by farm size. The desire of farm households to be self-sufficient may also have played a role. Wheat and maize are the major subsistence crops of the farm population. In most areas bread is baked from a mix of wheat and maize flour. But subsistence food requirements alone do not determine this cropping pattern. Probably even more important is the comparative advantage in livestock production that small farms with large supplies of labor have. This advantage in labor supply, together with the high effective protection of meat and milk and the implicit taxation of other major products, leads to the extreme livestock intensity of Egypt's small farms. About four times as many animals—as measured by starch requirements—are kept per unit of land on small farms as on big farms (see Table 24). The difference in intensity is even greater for buffalo and cattle because bigger farms have larger shares of poultry production. About 37 percent of the buffalo are kept by landless households and farm households with less than 1 feddan. This pattern of livestock intensity tends to enforce the observed feed orientation in the cropping pattern of small farms.

Consumption of cereals that a household has produced itself is still important on Egyptian farms. On small farms about 80 percent of the wheat produced, 70 percent of the maize, but only 30 percent of the rice is actually consumed by the farm household (see Table 25).

Table 25—Shares of cereals used for human consumption and animal feed from a farm household's own production, by farm size

Commodity/Use	Farm Size				
	0 – 1 Feddan	1 – 3 Feddan	3 – 5 Feddan	More than 5 Feddan	Total
	(percent)				
Wheat					
Human consumption	79.5	65.4	62.3	39.6	59.7
Animal feed	0.9	1.6	3.2	3.1	2.3
Maize					
Human consumption	68.5	62.9	63.9	49.1	62.4
Animal feed	19.7	21.1	15.4	12.6	18.5
Sorghum					
Human consumption	38.3	41.7	33.4	49.6	41.1
Animal feed	49.1	47.6	36.1	13.4	39.7
Rice					
Human consumption	29.2	21.9	26.2	22.8	24.1

Source: Data from the household survey made by the International Food Policy Research Institute and the Institute of National Planning, Cairo, 1981/82.
Note: The shares not consumed by people or fed to animals were sold.

The production patterns have important implications for the design of agricultural development strategies that would combine growth with equity in agriculture. An obvious solution, for instance, to the problem of inefficiency in allocation of resources inherent in the protectionist meat price policy might be an adjustment of output prices. This would require increased imports of animal products, at least in the short run. However, in addition to the negative implications such an adjustment would have for foreign exchange, the detrimental impact on equity in agriculture would have to be considered, as livestock is concentrated on the small farms. Introducing measures to increase productivity in the small farmers' livestock sector might be an alternative. Shifting supply curves by improving animal husbandry and using feed more efficiently would certainly be more equitable.

Another policy implication is given by the cereal cropping pattern. The increase in wheat and rice yields from new technologies such as improved varieties, fertilizer, and pest control would have no effect on equity for farms growing wheat, but a negative effect for farms growing rice. Increases in maize yields would combine the growth effects and equity effects. This is evident from differences in the patterns of cereals production on small farms from those on medium and bigger farms (Table 25).

Cereal Balances of Farm Households and the Role of Subsidized Cereals

The supply and disappearance of cereals in farm households is assessed here in a balanced accounting system. Basically the balances have the following components for each household production unit (i) in a given year:

$$PRD_i + PUO_i + PUS_i - STR_i$$
$$= HUM_i + ANI_i + SAL_i + SED_i, \quad (8)$$

where

PRD = the production of cereals in kilograms per year (all cereals and cereal products are given in wheat grain equivalents),

PUO = purchase from the open market (including wage payments received),

PUS = purchases from subsidized government outlets,

STR = changes in stocks during the period of observation,

HUM = human consumption,

ANI = livestock feed,

SAL = the total sales on the open market,

54

including wage payments in kind, and

SED = seed and losses.

Simplifying assumptions were necessary for changes in storage, as it was not possible to do a complete accounting of opening and ending stocks of all cereals in the survey, which covered one year with its two cropping seasons. Harvests in 1981/82 were not extreme in either direction. It was basically assumed that ending stocks equaled opening stocks; special emphasis in the analysis is put on subsidized cereals (PUS_i), their importance on the supply side of the balance, and farm households' responses to fluctuations in the supply of subsidized cereals.

Table 26 gives an overview for the aggregate balance of all cereals. Several conclusions can be drawn from it. Cereal consumption per capita hardly increases with farm size. It is, overall, fairly high in per capita terms;[29] the composition of this consumption, however, does vary by farm size. Subsidized cereals, according to the table, made up one third of cereal consumption in rural households (farm and nonfarm). Rural households received about twice as much subsidized cereal from the government in Upper Egypt as in Lower Egypt. Landless households acquired about the same amount as households with less than 1 feddan, but as farm size increased households' use of subsidized cereal decreased. Even medium and big farms purchased considerable amounts of cereal. At the same time, they sold some of their own produce. Farm households in Egypt are generally well integrated into the market.

While Table 26 includes grain for animals, it does not focus on grains purchased primarily as feed. These grains, including yellow maize and commercially prepared feed mixes, are a significant input into production, and the subsidies on them were included in the transfers discussed in the previous chapter. Although there were rations of subsidized feed at the agricultural cooperatives, most purchases were from the open market (Table 27). Apparently the upper income groups obtained a higher percentage of their purchased feed from the cooperatives. The price of yellow maize at cooperatives averaged 6.5 piasters a kilogram but nearly 11 piasters on the open market. The price of feed varied greatly as prepared mixes for different animals were priced differently.

An Analytical Assessment of the Acquisition of Subsidized Cereals by Farm Households

An attempt is made here to use cross-sectional survey information to assess the determinants of the acquisition of subsidized cereals and cereal products by farm households. A reduced-form estimate of an econ-

Table 26—Aggregate cereal balances for rural households, by region and farm size

	Supply			Disappearance		
		Purchased		Sales and	Human	Animal
Region/Farm Size	Production	Open Market	Subsidized	Seed	Consumption	Feed
	(kilograms/capita/year of wheat equivalent)					
Upper Egypt	137	143	147	53	326	49
Lower Egypt	191	166	79	96	314	27
Landless	0	197	129	0	304	23
Farms						
0 – 1 feddan	98	160	131	22	329	38
1 – 3 feddan	268	141	78	112	328	49
3 – 5 feddan	361	108	59	186	314	30
More than 5 feddan	607	95	55	378	332	43
All farms	171	158	104	80	319	35

Source: Data from the household survey made by the International Food Policy Research Institute and the Institute of National Planning, Cairo, 1981/82.
Note: Wheat, flour, bread, maize, rice, sorghum, and barley are included.

---

[29] It should be noted that these quantities are not intakes because losses within the household are not accounted for.

Table 27—Annual purchases of yellow maize by rural households for animal feed and feed mix, by expenditure quartile

| | Expenditure Quartile | | | |
Commodity/Source	1st	2nd	3rd	4th
	(kilograms/household)			
Yellow maize				
Cooperatives	9.9	11.5	25.0	33.3
Open market	28.6	40.8	31.5	31.8
Feed mix				
Cooperatives	2.1	0.4	19.8	12.1
Open market	65.7	69.8	89.4	180.9

Source: Data from the household survey made by the International Food Policy Research Institute and the Institute of National Planning, Cairo, 1981/82.

Note: Female heads of household occasionally reported additional purchases of yellow maize for poultry in the preceding month that were not reported by male heads of household.

Expenditure quartiles were determined by ranking rural households according to total reported expenditures per capita. The 1st quartile had the smallest expenditures; the 4th, the largest.

ometric model is applied, with aggregate subsidized cereal acquisition per capita (SUBN) as an endogenous variable.

If a household prefers cereals it produces itself to subsidized purchased ones, or if the sales price of a household's own produce plus the shadow costs of processing (milling and baking) is lower than the purchase costs of subsidized cereal products, then the increased availability of the cereals a household produces (OWN) should reduce the acquisition of subsidized cereals. Ranking the means of the open market wheat prices for the 77 villages surveyed shows that the average for the lowest quartile is 6.3 piasters per kilogram (Table 28). The official subsidized price for *balady* flour is 6.5 piasters. The search and transportation costs to be added to the subsidized flour price may often exceed the processing costs of wheat produced by the household, thus making the latter competitive. As milling by-products, used mainly for livestock feed, sell for roughly the same price as the wheat grain,

the extraction rate of the subsidized flour does not matter for this comparison. Nor does this comparison answer the question of whether there is a comparative advantage in producing wheat rather than other crops, in view of the subsidized supply of cereals. It addresses only the short-run competitiveness between purchases of subsidized wheat and the wheat households produced themselves, which may affect the marketing and storage decisions of farm households.

The distribution system across the country, especially the system for flour, includes a variety of regular or occasional rationing mechanisms and differing degrees of access to the commodities by location. Therefore acquisition of subsidized cereals is partly a result of availability in the villages, accounted for by several variables (BAK, FLSHOP, DELTA, DIS), and partly a result of households' choice and purchasing power. Thus, the income of households may affect the amount of subsidized cereals acquired. A positive income elasticity may be expected, especially at the margin in those locations where the supply of subsidized cereals is unconstrained at the fixed price, although the high per capita grain consumption of Egypt might lead to the suspicion that cereal products are clearly viewed as inferior. This empirical question is assessed through inclusion in the model of the per capita expenditure variable (TXN), which is assumed to represent income reasonably well. Farm households' choice to acquire subsidized cereals or to use grain they produce themselves or that they purchase on the open market is hypothesized to depend on the ratio of the prices of subsidized cereals to the open market price of cereals. As the price of subsidized cereals is more or less uniform throughout the country, only the open market price (PCE) needs to be incorporated in the model.[30] It is hypothesized that an increase in the ratio of the open market price to the subsidized price would lead farm households to increase their effort to acquire more cereals from the outlets that sell the subsidized commodities. Such efforts include, for instance, waiting and traveling to the outlets, which yield higher payoffs the bigger the wedge between the open market and subsidized prices. Thus, it can be ex-

---

[30] It is somewhat simplifying to speak of the price as uniform. Some minor differences in the local prices of subsidized grains are in fact observed, and the average price of subsidized cereals may in fact differ by location, depending on what subsidized commodities are available (that is, bread or flour).

Table 28—Cereals prices in villages and subsidized cereals distributed

Open Market Prices Ranked by Village Means	Wheat		Maize	
	Price	Distribution	Price	Distribution
	(LE/ardeb)	(kilograms/capita/year)	(LE/ardeb)	(kilograms/capita/year)
1st quartile	9.4	106	11.0	116
2nd quartile	10.2	118	13.2	118
3rd quartile	11.4	115	14.6	120
4th quartile	14.2	136	17.4	129

Source: Data from the household survey made by the International Food Policy Research Institute and the Institute of National Planning, Cairo, 1981/82.

Notes: The lowest mean prices are in the 1st quartile; the highest, in the 4th.

One *ardeb* of wheat approximately equals 150 kilograms, one *ardeb* of maize approximately equals 140 kilograms.

pected that the acquisition of subsidized cereals will respond positively to changes in the open market prices of cereals.

To sum up, the actual acquisition of subsidized cereals by farm households is determined by access to outlets such as bakeries and flour shops, the location of villages, the open market prices of cereals, the income and grain production in the households (farms), and the demographic characteristics of the household. A regression model including these determinants yields the following results for the acquisition per capita of subsidized cereals:

$$SUBN = 10.057 + 0.00942 \, TXN$$
$$(3.92)$$

$$+ \quad 111.527 \, PCE - 0.00654 \, OWN_{cer}$$
$$(2.99) \qquad (-3.99)$$

$$+ \quad 10.280 \, BAK + 56.641 \, FLSHOP$$
$$(0.98) \qquad (3.52)$$

$$- \quad 74.624 \, DELTA + 0.0859 \, DIS$$
$$(-7.62) \qquad (0.41)$$

$$- \quad 4.879 \, NUM - 28.335 \, CHL; \qquad (9)$$
$$(-3.52) \qquad (-0.88)$$

$\bar{R}^2 = 0.168$; degrees of freedom = 780;

where

SUBN = per capita acquisition of subsidized cereals per year in kilograms of wheat grain equivalents;

TXN = total expenditures per capita per month in piasters;

PCE = the open market price of cereals (an index weighted by the production shares of the cereals);

OWN_{cer} = total grain produced by the household in kilograms per year;

BAK = a dummy variable that equals 1 if there is a bakery in the village and 0 if there is not;

FLSHOP = a dummy variable that equals 1 if there is a flour shop in the village and 0 if there is not; and

DELTA = a dummy variable that equals 1 if the household is north of Cairo and 0 if it is not.

A significant positive response of subsidized cereals to income (TXN) is estimated. The respective income elasticity computed at mean values is 0.21. The availability of government-licensed bakeries and flour shops in the village increased consumption of subsidized cereals, as expected. The dummy variable for the Delta region shows the effect of regional orientation in the distribution of subsidized grains toward Upper Egypt. Positive effects of household size are depicted by the variable NUM: the bigger the household, the lower the per capita cereal consumption, other things remaining equal.

The parameter estimates for the production variable (OWN) need some cautious interpretation. The significant negative parameter for the production variable means that the acquisition of subsidized cereals decreased as the household's production of grain increased, as hypothesized. As dynamic adjustments in consumption and production should not be analyzed on the basis of the cross-sectional data, it is difficult to discriminate strictly between the two possible causal relationships: whether subsidized cereal acquisition is high on farms that produce little grain because production is low or whether production is low because the availability of subsidized cereals is high. Both relationships have meaning. A model estimation of the effects of subsidized cereals on production by farm households demonstrates that subsidized cereals reduced production even if farm size and government-ordered cash crop orientation (cotton, sugarcane) are taken into account. (This model is discussed later in this chapter.) The production variable in the model of subsidized grain acquisition above accounts mainly for the substitution between household-produced grain and purchased, subsidized grain that occurs as the production of grain increases.

The parameter estimate for PCE can be interpreted as indicating that—as hypothesized—the higher the local open market price of cereals, the more subsidized grain households attempted to and actually did acquire. However, the relationship between local prices on open markets and the government's regional cereal distribution also requires attention. To the extent that the government channels subsidized cereals into regions with short supplies from domestic production, cereal prices in the open markets of those regions may be high despite the government's large supplies of subsidized cereals. The relationship between subsidized cereals and local prices is discussed further below.

Substitution by Farm Households Between Subsidized Cereals, Purchases from the Open Market, and Cereals the Households Produce

The fairly equal per capita consumption of cereals observed among farm-size classes is the final outcome of complex processes of substitution between the various cereal commodities at several stages of processing, acquired by households at different marketing outlets and at different rates of subsidization. Wheat consumption actually decreased as farm size increased while rice consumption did the opposite (see Table 29). Bigger farms obtained a much smaller amount of subsidized cereals because they purchased less of practically all subsidized cereal products with the exception of *shami* bread and yellow maize. The latter is mainly used for animal feed. However, the most important

subsidized wheat commodities in this bundle showed different rates of decrease: the subsidized *balady* flour purchased by big farm households corresponds to 37 percent of the quantity purchased by small farm households. The reduction in the quantity of *balady* bread purchased was even greater, as big farm households purchased only 20 percent of the quantity small farmers did (see Table 29). In this breakdown by farm-size classes, bread turns out to have been more targeted toward the poor than flour was in rural areas, but the poor's share in wheat consumption was lower (see Figure 3).

As farm size goes up, households tend to consume cereals they produce themselves instead of cereals they purchase. In the process, subsidized cereals are substituted for much more rapidly than cereals purchased on the open market: while big farmers purchased 59.5 percent as much cereal from open markets as small farmers, they purchased 42.0 percent as much subsidized cereal (figures computed from per capita data, Table 29).

Government Procurement and Subsidized Cereals on Farms

Significant quantities of the cereals produced are procured by the government. For rice, this procurement is based upon a compulsory delivery system of fixed quantities per unit of land allocated for rice production under the government area allotment plan. Wheat is—with a few local exceptions—procured voluntarily. Compulsory procurement affects the availability of cereals for consumption by farm households that produce them. Rice in particular is procured at a high implicit tax rate. This is for the benefit of the consumers receiving the rice through the ration and cooperative marketing system. To the extent that farm households lose a share of their grain to the procurement system and are forced to buy on the open markets, they have to sell cheap and buy back dear. On the other hand, as was pointed out above, farm households' participation in the subsidized cereals distribution scheme was significant.

This leads to the question of whether the distribution and procurement of subsidized cereals are balanced. Table 30 was compiled to provide an answer. It shows that at the

Table 29—Cereal balances of farm households by farm size

Components	Farm Size			
	0 – 1 Feddan	1 – 3 Feddan	3 – 5 Feddan	More than 5 Feddan
	(kilograms/capita/year/of wheat grain equivalent)			
Cereal production	97.7	268.1	360.9	606.5
Wheat	30.1	87.5	96.4	210.6
Rice (milled)	10.9	70.9	144.0	214.0
Maize	41.2	78.1	63.4	84.4
Sorghum	13.1	13.6	20.8	25.6
Barley	0.0	1.6	3.2	21.7
Subsidized cereals	131.1	78.4	59.2	55.0
Balady flour[a]	80.2	44.5	34.4	29.7
Fino flour[a]	20.0	10.8	12.1	5.7
Balady bread[a]	17.3	10.0	4.4	3.5
Afrangi bread[a]	2.0	1.1	0.3	0.4
Shami bread[a]	0.6	0.6	0.1	1.2
Rice (milled)				
Rationed	6.5	5.8	4.8	4.3
From cooperatives	0.7	0.8	0.2	0.8
Maize (yellow)	2.5	3.3	1.8	8.2
Sales of cereals	15.0	84.0	149.6	293.1
Wheat	3.7	18.9	21.7	86.5
Rice (milled)	6.5	48.3	93.8	136.5
Maize	3.0	3.8	6.0	18.2
Sorghum	0.4	1.0	5.1	6.8
Human consumption[b]	329.2	327.6	314.5	332.3
Wheat and wheat products[b]	232.3	203.0	184.4	183.0
Rice (milled)	24.9	37.4	52.3	63.7
Maize and maize flour	53.1	71.5	57.2	55.4
Sorghum	13.3	7.1	8.0	14.2

Source: Data from the household survey made by the International Food Policy Research Institute and the Institute of National Planning, Cairo, 1981/82.

[a] The conversion to wheat grain equivalents was based on the extraction rates of the flour. The conversion of bread took moisture into account.

[b] This includes barley.

mean and measured in physical quantities, farm households with less than 3 feddan took more out of the subsidized cereal distribution system than they delivered to the procurement system. Farmers with 1-3 feddan, for instance, acquired subsidized cereals (bread, flour, maize, and rice) equal to 29.2 percent of their total cereal production, but they delivered rice and wheat equal to only 19.6 percent. The situation was different for the bigger farmers, who delivered more than they took from the subsidized cereal system. The low share of procurement in the total production of small farms was not due as much to a lower procurement quota as to a much higher share of maize production, which is not a procurement crop.

Total cereal production (wheat, rice, maize, sorghum, and barley) is the denominator for the figures computed in Table 30,

which also show the self-sufficiency ratios of the farm-size classes. The farms with less than 3 feddan were less than completely self-sufficient. It should be noted, however, that this is a result not only of the demand for food in these households but is also a result of animal feed requirements in livestock-intensive, small-farm enterprises.

The analysis shows some interesting regional differences between Lower and Upper Egypt. Procurement was higher in Lower Egypt because rice production is concentrated there. In addition, the amounts of subsidized cereals received were smaller—not only in relation to local production but in absolute terms too (Tables 27 and 30). The higher procurement of wheat in Upper Egypt only slightly offsets this major difference. Rural self-sufficiency is higher in Lower Egypt than in Upper Egypt.

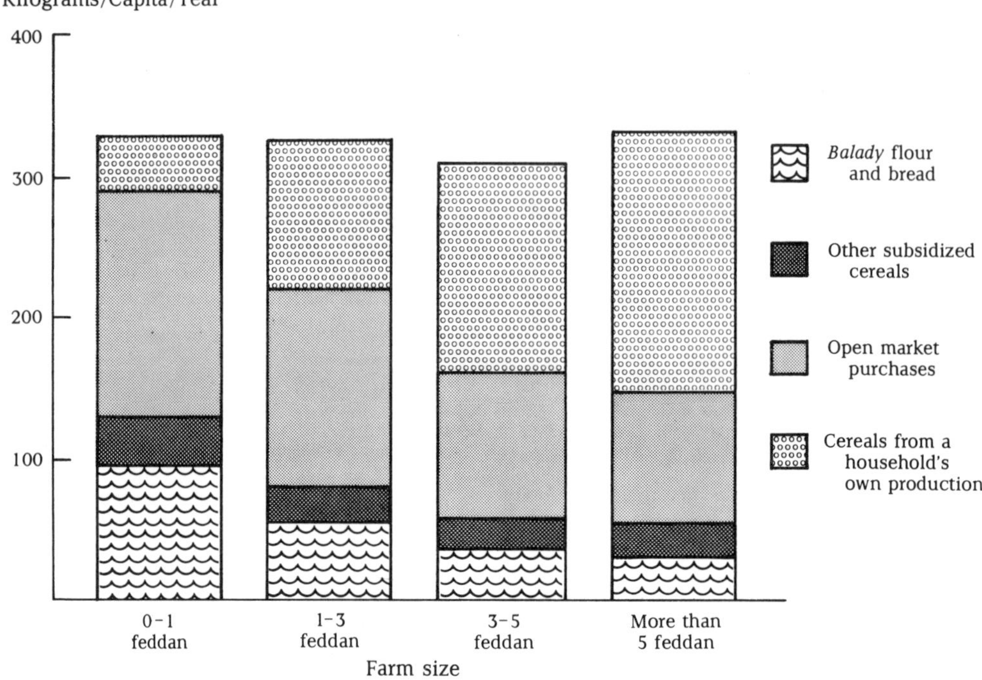

Source: Data from the household survey made by the International Food Policy Research Institute and the Institute of National Planning, Cairo, 1981/82.

Subsidized Cereals and Local Prices and Price Stability

Wheat and wheat flour that is imported for distribution with subsidies and sold principally without restrictions is the major reason why domestic cereal prices are depressed below international prices. While this general picture appears to be quite clear, the relationship between food subsidies and local prices is not. The rural survey showed that there were large differences between local prices. Prices between villages or even settlements belonging to a village frequently differ in the same season by a margin that seems to exceed transportation costs. Market imperfections in the broadest sense can have a large effect on local prices and price stability. A longer-term observation of cereal markets in some Delta villages stresses this finding.[31] Prices of the two major cereals—wheat and maize—show roughly the same degree of variance in our rural survey: the coefficients of variance were 17.8 for wheat and 17.5 for maize.[32]

An obvious hypothesis would be that local prices and the distribution of subsidized cereals have a negative relationship; that is, the more subsidized cereals are available the more depressed local prices are. However, the empirical results show just the opposite: a ranking of the 77 villages by the mean prices of wheat and maize in the villages shows that subsidized cereal consumption per capita was highest in those villages where open market prices were highest (see Table 28). This is explained by the fact that

---

[31] de Treville, "Food Processing and Distribution Systems," pp. 26-45.

[32] The coefficient of variance expresses the standard deviation as a percent of the mean value, so 17.8 means that on the average the price of wheat deviates 17.8 percent from the mean value.

Table 30—Cereal procurement, subsidized cereals consumed, and self-sufficiency, by farm size and by region

Commodity	Farm Size				All Rural Households		
	0 – 1 Feddan	1 – 3 Feddan	3 – 5 Feddan	More than 5 Feddan	Upper Egypt	Lower Egypt	Total
	(percent of total cereal production)						
Paddy sold to the government	5.2	14.2	19.6	17.9	6.1	19.2	15.4
Wheat sold to the government	2.0	3.4	3.2	10.3	10.9	2.3	3.9
Subsidized cereals consumed	134.5	29.2	16.4	9.1	107.8	41.3	60.4
Cereals purchased on the open market	163.5	52.7	30.0	15.7	104.4	86.9	92.0
Self-sufficiency[a]	29.7	81.8	114.8	182.5	41.9	60.8	53.8

Source: Data from the household survey made by the International Food Policy Research Institute and the Institute of National Planning, Cairo, 1981/82.

Note: All rural households include farm and nonfarm households.

[a] The self-sufficiency figures are production as a percentage of human cereal consumption.

subsidized cereals are supplied to districts or governorates by quota (as flour is), if their distribution to consumers is not rationed (as rice and flour, to some extent, are). This implies that the observed pattern that subsidized cereal consumption showed when mapped against prices may reflect a government supply function, which directs subsidized cereals to those regions of the country where basic food is scarce.[33] Despite this redistribution of cereals, high price regions—in general—do not necessarily become low price regions. The large supplies of subsidized cereals that go to Upper Egypt, especially to the sugarcane belt, are a case in point.

A second hypothesis shall be tested with surveyed price data: does the marketing of subsidized cereals decrease or increase local price instability? The effects the subsidized distribution system have on local price stability are worth consideration as increased instability may induce misallocation in production and consumption and thus add to the social costs of the system. As was pointed out above, supplies at government-controlled outlets for subsidized flour and bread are not always stable. This does not, however, necessarily mean that the amounts the government supplies are deliberately varied to balance seasonal fluctuations from local supplies, although the distribution of beans and lentils does include such a counter-cyclical strategy. But the instability of flour and bread supplies may, of course, increase the instability of local prices, depending on the correlation between the fluctuations of government supplies and supplies from local production.

To get an indication of local price instability, each farm household (i) was asked to report the highest and lowest prices (PH_i^j; PL_i^j) observed for basic cereals (j) during the preceding year. From this information a price instability coefficient (PI_i) is computed:

$$PI_i^j = (PH_i^j - PL_i^j)/PL_i^j. \qquad (10)$$

Village means of the coefficient were then correlated with the availability of subsidized cereals in the households, and with a dummy variable testing for the effect of a bakery on local (village) price stability. The results indicate that local price instability was reduced significantly where bakeries were operating. But the total supplies of subsidized cereals (bread and flour) show an insignificant relationship with the coefficient. These results coincide with findings that the supply of subsidized bread available at bakeries was fairly regular, but that flour supplies were less regular. The pattern observed here again indicates that key variables were affected differently by different branches of the food subsidy system.

---

[33] This finding is consistent with an analysis of governments' cereals distribution by governorates. Alderman, von Braun, and Sakr, *Egypt's Food Subsidy and Rationing System*, pp. 42-49.

The Response of Farm Households to Subsidized Cereals in Production, Marketing, and Consumption

Farm households with different capacities of resources, such as land, take different advantages from the subsidies on cereals (Table 29). Numerous factors in addition to resource capacities, household size, and demographic composition determine the decisions of farm households on the quantities and mix of the production, marketed surplus, and consumption of cereals. These include the costs of providing food from what the household produces, purchasing prices and food acquisition costs from outside the farm, the cost of preparing edible cereal products (including opportunity costs), storage costs, the farm-gate sales prices of the household's produce, the comparative advantage of other crops and livestock, behavioral traditions, and factors such as the risk that food will not be available in the market, price risk, the risk that crops of individual cereals will fail, and the price and yield risks of cash crops with their compound effect on income.

Response in Production

The distribution scheme for subsidized food is expected to influence resource allocation because of its effects on prices, price ratios, income, and the price risk factors faced by farm households. And it affects food production and consumption on the farm through resource allocation. The effects of the depression of cereal prices on farm incomes were described in the previous chapter. The effects of the depression on production were estimated in a sector-level study.[34] A major finding of that study is that wheat production would certainly increase substantially if farmers received wheat prices that were not depressed, that is, prices that corresponded to international prices, with all others remaining constant. These results were obtained using a partial analysis under the assumption that all other prices are con-

stant. Such an analysis is not realistic. An alternative policy scenario with no distorted agricultural prices, that is, with all prices at their international equivalents, reveals that wheat would lose even its current comparative advantage because of a drop in the value of straw used for livestock feed. Thus, under free trade, Egypt might grow less wheat than it does now!

The production response to agricultural policy is analyzed here for households to provide some insight into farmers' behavior under an extended food subsidy scheme operating in rural areas. The production effects of food subsidy schemes may differ even if basic cereals in alternative schemes to be compared are subsidized equally but the schemes are designed differently. The bread and flour system may be seen as an example, as was shown by the behavior of households of different farm sizes in substituting *balady* bread and *balady* flour for grain they produced themselves (Figure 3).

An increase in the availability of subsidized food has three effects on the interplay between the production, consumption, and marketing of a farm household. First, such an increase is expected to increase consumption of the subsidized commodities, decrease consumption of what the household produces and purchases on the open market, and thus increase net sales of the subsidized commodities at the market price, which is above the subsidized price at government-controlled outlets. These short-run effects—without resource reallocation—increase the incomes of farm households as long as a possible negative price effect on the local open market does not offset the gains mentioned. Second, if the reliability of subsidized food supplies is increased, the risk of occasional shortages is reduced, and so is the demand for on-farm storage; combined with this, the comparative advantage in growing subsistence crops is reduced, which induces a shift to production for the market of more profitable but possibly more risky crops. Third, a reduction in the time spent storing and preparing food (for example, in baking bread) makes more time available that may be spent on farm production or for leisure. As long as this time is not spent acquiring food instead (waiting in line, traveling to the bakery, and so forth), a

---

[34] See von Braun and de Haen, *Effects of Food Price and Subsidy Policies.*

welfare benefit results. The third effect will be addressed in a later chapter; the following analysis focuses on the first and second.

All cereals and cereal products are included in the analysis. These are wheat, wheat products, rice, maize, sorghum, and barley. Production, marketing, and consumption functions for the aggregate of cereal products are estimated independently. Separate estimates were also made for the three major cereals (wheat, rice, and maize) to test for behavior that is peculiar to a commodity, but these results are not reported in detail. As the models are based on cross-sectional data, dynamic adjustments are not included. This is, of course, a shortcoming in analyses of price response in production. But it is not viewed as a key issue in this farm-level analysis. It has already been dealt with in a model analysis of agriculture as a whole.[35] The models are not designed explicitly as an interdependent system, which necessarily would have to be built on dynamic interrelations; rather they are designed to show major relationships in the production-consumption unit of farm households within the constraints of the cross-sectional information available.

Production of cereals (PRD) depends upon the land and labor resources of the farm (LAN, LAB), and is influenced by a set of variables accounting for local and regional production conditions. These variables include a dummy for the Delta region (DEL), dummies for cotton and sugarcane growers (COT, SUC), the instability of yields at the location (YSB), and the instability of prices at the location (PSB). The resources of the farm, together with the relevant output prices and price ratios (PCM, PWS), and a proxy for feed demand (LIV), determine the comparative advantages of grain production on the farm. The variable representing household size (NUM) accounts for the demand specific to the household size for the cereals produced by the household. The availability of subsidized cereals to the farm households, accounted for by variables in the model (SUB, BAK), is included in the specification to test for direct substitution in cereal production induced by the supply of subsidized cereals to farm households. Thus, the

production component of the cereal balance (equation [1]) is explained by:

$$PRD_i = f(LAN_i, LAB_i, DEL_i, COT_i, SUC_i,$$
$$YSB_i, PSB_i, PCM_i, PWS_i,$$
$$LIV_i, NUM_i, SUBN_i, BAK_i), \qquad (11)$$

where

LAB = the amount of male labor available in a farm household (given in number of male adult equivalents; child labor is valued at 0.3 male adult equivalents);

COT = a dummy variable that is 1 for cotton growers and 0 for other producers;

SUC = a dummy variable that is 1 for sugarcane growers and 0 for other producers;

YSB = the instability of cereal yields (j) as reported by farmer (i):

$$YSB_i = \sum_j a_{ij} [(YH_{ij} - YL_{ij})/YL_{ij}],$$

where

a_{ij} = the production share of crop j in total cereal production of farm (i) with j running from 1 to 3 (wheat, rice, and maize);

YH = the highest yield during the preceding 5 years;

YL = the lowest yield during the preceding 5 years;

PSB = the instability of cereal prices; sum of PI_i^j weighted by shares of the crops in production;

PCM = the ratio of the cereal price to the milk price;

PWS = the price of wheat straw (village mean per bundle); and

LIV = livestock on the farm in animal units (aggregated on the basis of starch requirements).

The results of the regression analysis are given in Table 31. They will be discussed with the estimation results on marketing

---

[35] Ibid.

Table 31—Results of regressions on the effect of subsidized cereal distribution on cereal production, marketing, and consumption of farm households

Dependent Variable		Independent Variables and Coefficients	$\overline{R}^2$	Degrees of Freedom
Production				
PRD	=	$3{,}161.7 + 868.0$ LAN $+ 103.5$ LAB $+ 357.3$ DEL $- 376.3$ COT $\quad(40.2)\qquad(1.61)\qquad(2.72)\qquad(-3.01)$		
	$-$	$1{,}165.4$ SUC $- 1{,}457.2$ YSB $- 10{,}108.4$ PSB $+ 140.4$ PCM $\quad(-3.68)\qquad(-2.00)\qquad(-3.29)\qquad(0.36)$		
	$+$	37.61 PWS $- 40.42$ LIV $- 13.72$ NUM $- 0.1498$ SUB $- 265.1$ BAK $\quad(3.08)\qquad(-1.39)\qquad(-0.63)\qquad(-2.82)\qquad(-1.83)$	0.73	776
Marketing				
SAL	=	$-43.518 - 25.66$ NUM $+ 208.3$ CHL $+ 3.789$ DIS $+ 0.1950$ PRD $\quad(-4.80)\qquad(1.64)\qquad(4.20)\qquad(13.2)$		
	$+$	127.7 PCE $+ 77.82$ DEL $+ 379.3$ LIQ $- 22.54$ LAN $- 992.1$ PSB $\quad(0.89)\qquad(1.85)\qquad(3.00)\qquad(-1.87)\qquad(-1.06)$		
	$-$	0.4187 PRQ $- 0.0049$ SUB $\quad(-12.63)\qquad(-0.22)$	0.30	690
Consumption				
HUM	=	$416.11 + 0.0211$ TXN $- 57.05$ PCE $- 16.42$ NUM $- 162.78$ CHL $\quad(5.35)\qquad(-1.00)\qquad(-7.14)\qquad(-3.08)$		
	$+$	0.01907 PRD $- 135.1$ SUC $+ 0.7628$ SUBN $\quad(7.02)\qquad(-3.48)\qquad(13.47)$	0.38	781

Source: Data from the household survey made by the International Food Policy Research Institute and the Institute of National Planning, Cairo, 1981/82.

Notes: The figures in parentheses are t-statistics. The variables are defined in Appendix 2.

and consumption after the specification of those models has been described.

Response in Marketing

The determinants of the marketable surplus of a farm household, apart from size and demographic characteristics (NUM, CHL) and the taste of the household, are the production capacity of the farm and the comparative advantages between crops on the supply side and income and prices on the demand side. In Egypt, forced procurement (PRQ) reduces the supplies available for sale on open markets. Occasional cash requirements (LIQ) may increase sales above normal at any given time. Such disturbances and the location of the farm (DIS) are taken into account in the following analysis of cereal sales on the open market (SAL). When modeling the marketed surplus with a reduced form approach for a given time period (year), demand and supply determinants must be condensed.[36] This has some implications for the specification of the variables for income and resource capacity, which are closely related. To bypass this problem, just the production variable (PRD) and the land variable (LAN) were included in the model. An increase of the land variable would include part of the increase in demand expected from rising income. As supply is accounted for by another variable (PRD), such an increase would thus reduce the

---

[36] For a complete marketed surplus model with forced deliveries, see Alain de Janvry, Gamal Siam, and Osman Gad, "The Impact of Forced Deliveries on Egyptian Agriculture," *American Journal of Agricultural Economics* 65 (August 1983): 493-501.

marketable surplus. In order to assess how the prevailing open market price affects a household's substitution of subsidized grain for grain it produces, the open market price of cereals (PCE) is included in the model with the variable representing households' access to subsidized grain (SUB). Including variables on household demographics (NUM, CHL), as well as information on local price instability (PSB) to account for the market situation in a particular location (price risk), leads to the following model for the sales component of the cereals balance (equation [8]):

$$SAL_i = f(NUM_i, CHL_i, DIS_i, PRD_i, PCE_i,$$

$$DEL_i, LIQ_i, LAN_i, PSB_i, PRQ_i, SUB_i), \quad (12)$$

where

LIQ = the special liquidity requirements of the household during the observation periods (the shares of expenditures for weddings, funerals, and medical treatment, and of debt repayments in total expenditures), and

PRQ = the quantity of rice sold to the government (compulsory deliveries).

It should be noted that only private sales are included (in SAL) as government procurement is mainly exogenously determined. Results of the regression analysis for equation (12) are listed in Table 31.

Response in Consumption

The consumption of cereals in farm households may be affected by changes in other components of the cereal balance (equation [8]). A rewriting of the cereal balance makes it clear that farm households have many instruments at hand with which to balance the food needs of the household in the short run if, for instance, a shortage in the household's production (PRD) occurred:

$$HUM_i = PRD_i + PUO_i + PUS_i + STR_i$$

$$- ANI_i - SAL_i - SED_i. \quad (13)$$

But the feasibility of a food security strategy for the household depends very much on the proper functioning of rural markets (PUO, SAL), and on the household's purchasing power. The availability of subsidized food (PUS) may be important for such adjustments as the amount stored (STR) on small farms is small. Some potential for adjustment by small farms is provided by livestock, which may either be reduced to free grain for human consumption or it may be used as an asset serving as collateral for borrowing to cover a period of income or production loss. The latter possibility is included only indirectly in the modeling of cereal consumption because total expenditure is used as a proxy for income.

Per capita cereal consumption by farm households is modeled as a function of income (TXN), cereal price (PCE), and the size and demographic structure of the household. Moreover, supplies from what the household produces and the availability of subsidized supplies (PRD, SUBN) are included to account and test for particular effects in the consumption of supplies by source. Because of the special demand situation in farms growing sugarcane, a dummy variable is included to distinguish this particular group (SUC). Thus, the consumption function for total cereals used as food (HUM) reads:

$$HUM_i = f(TXN_i, PCE_i, NUM_i, CHL_i,$$

$$PRD_i, SUC_i, SUBN_i), \quad (14)$$

where

HUM = human consumption of cereals, in kilograms per capita per year (using wheat grain equivalents); and

TXN = expenditures per capita per month in piasters.

The estimation results are included in Table 31.

Major Findings

Some major findings of this analysis and their implications for evaluating the food subsidy scheme are summarized in the following.

The availability of subsidized cereals in farm households decreases grain production, but farm households that produce more grain make

less use of subsidized cereals. A bakery in the village induced a reduction of grain production at the location by 13.4 percent, other things remaining the same, and if the amount of subsidized cereals acquired by the household increased by 10 percent, grain production dropped by 0.5 percent (computed from the equation for PRD in Table 31).[37] These effects of the distribution of subsidized cereals on production turn out to be significant after differences in farm size and the government area allotment for cash crops (cotton and sugarcane) are accounted for in the model (see variables LAN, COT, and SUC in the equation for PRD in Table 31).

With increasing grain production on the farm, farm households tended to acquire less subsidized grain. Thus farm households that produced more grain received smaller amounts of the subsidies incorporated in government-controlled cereal distribution. A 10 percent increase in production of cereal by a household led—at the mean—to a 1.2 percent reduction in the amount of subsidized cereals acquired (calculated from the model on subsidized grain; see SUBN and PRD).

Responsiveness to differences in the prices of food and feedgrains and the strong response of grain production to the prices of inputs for livestock production (straw) emphasizes the effect of livestock protection on grain production. The demand for livestock feed and its effects on the prices of cereal by-products affected crops differently: maize production was higher—as additional analysis showed— while overall grain production was lower the more livestock a farm had. In addition, wheat production was affected in a particular way because of the importance of wheat straw for fodder. An increased straw price (PWS) significantly increased the incentive to grow wheat. This increased total grain output as well (see PWS in the equation for PRD in Table 31).

Price instability has a strong disincentive effect on grain production. To the extent that the distribution of subsidized cereals stabilizes local grain prices, it has an incentive effect on cereal production. The strong effect of price stability on overall grain production and on production of wheat and rice —but not for produc-tion of maize, the main subsistence crop—is an interesting phenomenon (see PSB in Table 31). A 1 percent increase in the instability index reduced grain production by 1.1 percent. This implies that a policy for managing the system for distributing subsidized grain that takes the stabilization issue into account may carry large rewards for farm production. The effect of bakeries on price stability assessed in the previous section somewhat compensated for the negative effect bakeries had on local production.

The variable representing yield instability (YSB) also had an important effect on grain production. It accounts for the effects the local technical environment—such factors as soils, water supply, pest infestation, and insecure input supplies—had on grain production.[38] Farmers tend to reduce grain production if crop failures are more likely. The extension of the government food distribution system to rural areas certainly facilitates this. An increase of 1 percent in the yield instability index reduced grain production by 0.5 percent (Table 31).

The amount of labor available in the farm household is positively related to grain production. To the extent that subsidized food is labor-saving a positive effect on production is possible. Wheat production was especially affected by the (male) labor supply in the household. The wheat harvest is the major peak season of labor demand in agriculture. The provision of subsidized grain may have had labor-saving effects in the households (saving mainly female labor in baking bread), which may then have affected allocation of both male and female labor on the farm and, thus, grain production. One additional laborer (male) available for farm production increased total household grain production by 5.2 percent (Table 31).

Total sales of cereals are higher in the Delta. Furthermore, in remote areas farm households market larger quantities. While the first part of this finding is a more or less straightforward observation captured by the regression analysis, the second part needs some explanation. Farmers in remote areas, measured by the distance to a governorate capital (DIS), have fewer incentives to grow fruits and vegetables, which have fairly high trans-

---

[37] All elasticities mentioned in this discussion are computed using the mean values of the variables used in the regression models.

[38] The variable was constructed to incorporate these production determinants implicitly because this type of farm management information could not be collected in the survey.

port costs. The variables for cereal production may not completely account for such specialization. If farmers in remote areas were generally poorer, this would also have shifted their demand and thus have left a greater surplus to be marketed. Intercorrelation between the land and the income variable (LAN, TXN) made it impossible to refine the approach (see Table 31).

Higher price instability tends to reduce sales. Total cereal marketing is not responsive to cereal prices (see PCE in the equation for SAL in Table 31). Though the reduction was not very significant, marketing was reduced if prices tended to be more unstable. Farmers kept more grain as carryover stocks. This result does not stem from lower production at locations with unstable prices; the production variable accounts for that in this specification.

About 20 percent of farm production is privately marketed. As expected, marketing increases as production does but, at the margin, less is marketed when holdings are larger. The private marketing of grain ranged between 16 percent (for rice) and 24 percent (for maize) of production. Through the separate specification of grain production and farm size (PRD, LAN), the effects of production volume and farm size were separated in the explanation of sales. As expected, for most farms, sales increased as production did. But somewhat surprisingly, at first glance, they decreased significantly for the bigger farmers (assuming nothing else changed; see LAN, in Table 31).

Two effects account for most of the reductions of marketed surplus on bigger farms. First, because bigger farms had higher incomes, they consumed more and had less available for sales, other conditions being equal. The LAN variable functions partly as a proxy for income in this sense. Because of the correlation between the land and income variables (expenditures), no particular income variable was included. Second, yields decreased significantly as farm size increased. In particular the group of farms with more than 5 feddan reported much lower yields than smaller farms. This is consistent with expectations, as the intensity of production on small farms is usually higher. The decreased sales from bigger farms (after correction for production volume) also resulted from demographic differences between small and big farms, but this is accounted for separately and does not affect estimates for the LAN variable. The bigger farms had more people in their households (for example, farms with less than 1 feddan had 6.2 persons on the average; and farms with more than 5 feddan had 11.4 persons per household on the average). Demographic factors such as household size and the share of children in the household were taken into account and showed significant and plausible results. Sales decreased as household size rose and, with size held constant, increased as the proportion of children in a household rose.

Sales of grain are significantly influenced by the short-term cash requirements of farm households. This finding is supported by the estimates for the variable LIQ, representing liquidity requirements for certain unavoidable expenditures that exceeded normal household expenditures. Outlays for weddings, funerals, medical treatment, and debt repayment are included. At the mean, 12.6 percent of the total expenditures of farm households was used for such spending. An increase of this share by 1 percentage point (for example, from the mean value of 12.6 to 13.6 percent) increased grain sales by 2.7 percent (see Table 31). This stresses that grain stocks and their drawdown were still important in balancing the cash needs of Egyptian farm households. As grains provide a savings tool it is not unlikely that this affects the amount produced as well. Grain is certainly a supplement to livestock used as savings, though this is not specifically tested here.

Availability of subsidized cereals does not significantly affect the grain sales of farm households, but it does increase total per capita consumption. Contrary to expectations, the increased use of subsidized cereals did not significantly increase the marketed surplus of grain produced on farms (SUB in Table 31). One might have expected that the households would have tended to use subsidized cereals as a substitute for consumption of cereals they produced themselves and thus would have implicitly resold subsidized bread, flour, or maize. But this was not suggested by the empirical analysis.

The main adjustment to the availability of subsidized cereals occurred in consumption, not in the production and sales of farm households. An additional kilogram of subsidized cereals per capita raised consumption by 763 grams per capita (Table 31). The related negative effect on consumption of household-produced grain, an effect that works through the relationship between grain production and distribution of subsidized cereals, offsets only a marginal share of this additional consumption (see PRD in the equations in Table 31).

Even after correcting for income, prices, demographics, production, and so forth, sugar producing households consume significantly less grain. The effect of cash cropping on consumption requires more attention in research. Here the significant negative effect that growing sugarcane has on consumption is just noted (SUC in the equation for HUM in Table 31).

8

CONSUMER RESPONSE TO PRICE AND INCOME CHANGES

Among the basic tools for ascertaining change in consumption patterns following a policy change are marginal propensities to consume (MPC) and income and price elasticities derived from demand equations. When policies are targeted to benefit specific subgroups of a population, it is necessary to estimate those parameters in a manner that is flexible enough to measure the different responses of the subgroups. Furthermore, when different policy instruments are applied to different commodities, it is important to be able to make such estimates on a disaggregated level. Obtaining such estimates is seldom straightforward. Obtaining them for Egypt is no exception. As many commodities have prices fixed by government policy, the price variation necessary to estimate price parameters, which is already limited by the nature of a cross-sectional survey, is reduced further. In addition, because the distribution system is complex, consumers generally purchase the same commodity at several prices. Estimates using average prices would be misleading. Accordingly, the estimates used in the report are based on marginal prices and consumption observed in the open market. The next section discusses the methodology used in making these estimates.

Methodology for Estimating Demand Parameters

Demand estimation in the Egyptian context must account for the complex structure of the marketing system in order to avoid biasing the estimates and to make it possible to understand the unique implications of the system. Particular characteristics include fixed rations; goods available at fixed prices but in limited supply—this leads to queuing and appreciable search costs; an open market in which prices exceed those of the cooperatives but at which queuing is not reported; and variations in the prices observed in open markets in different regions.

The first characteristic is dealt with by estimating the consumer response from excess demand curves.[39] Although most consumers can obtain rations at price P_r, the amount received is limited to Q_r. They may obtain more at the higher price P_o, the open market (or cooperative) price, although for many consumers the quantity demanded at P_o, $Q(P_o)$, is less than Q_r and, therefore, no further purchases are made. The excess demand is defined as $Q(P_o) - Q_r$ and is, in effect, a rescaling of the demand curve so that the origin is at Q_r. As a consumer has only one margin, marginal responses of the excess demand curve are the same as those of the total demand curve, although the relevant elasticities should be obtained using total demand.

Estimations are based on the following model:

$$Q_{Tj} = Q_{oj} + Q_{cj} + Q_{rj}$$
$$= f[P_o, y + \Sigma (P_{oj} - P_{rj})Q_{rj}], \quad (15)$$

where

P_{oj} = the open market price of good j,

P_{rj} = the ration price of good j,

Q_{Tj} = total demand for good j,

Q_{cj} = the per capita quantity of good j purchased from cooperatives, in grams,

Q_{oj} = the per capita quantity of good j purchased from the open market,

---

[39] While a few economists have investigated the implications of rationing on consumer demand, such studies are applicable only to systems in which rations are binding. Most Egyptians consume more than what they get from rations (see Chapter 3). For further discussion of rationing and demand, see Angus Deaton, "Theoretical and Empirical Approaches to Consumer Demand Under Rationing," in *Essays in the Theories and Measurement of Consumer Behavior in Honor of Sir Richard Stone,* ed. Angus Deaton (Cambridge: Cambridge University Press, 1981), pp. 55-72.

Q_{rj} = the per capita quantity of rations of good j, and

Y = income.

Demand is a function of all income, including the implicit income transfer of the potentially resalable ration. Rearranging,

$$Q_{oj} = f[P_o, Y + \Sigma (P_{oj} - P_{rj}) Q_{rj}] - Q_{cj} - Q_{rj}. \quad (16)$$

An advantage to the formulation in equation (16) is that it allows a test for whether $\partial Q_{oj}/\partial Q_{rj} = -1$ and therefore aids in assessing whether income transfers linked with food programs are perceived differently than their cash equivalents are.[40]

As indicated in Chapter 4, not every family consumes quantities above the ration allotment and, when they do, the purchase may be from either the open market or the cooperative or, infrequently, both. This presents two problems for the estimation. The first problem is that, as open market prices exceed cooperative prices, it is important to model the decision of where to shop as a rational choice reflecting the environment and the characteristics of the family. This is done by including the time spent searching for a commodity and the waiting time as independent variables in the regressions. The theoretical justifications and implications of such a model are discussed in greater detail in the following chapter. At this point, concentrating on income and price parameters, it is sufficient to note that for each commodity, equations were estimated to measure determinants of excess demand from the cooperative, Q_{cj}, and from the open market, Q_{oj}. That is, $Q_{Tj} = Q_{cj} + Q_{oj} + Q_{rj}$.

Since, for all practical purposes, $Q_{cj} = 0$ when $Q_{oj} > 0$ and vice versa, the two components were estimated independently according to the relationship in equation (16).

The second problem is econometric. If the proportion of families that do not purchase either at the cooperative or on the

open market is appreciable, estimates from the entire sample may be biased. This general problem was first pointed out by Tobin.[41] Consider the general relationship:

$$Q_j = X\beta + u_j, \quad (17)$$

and the expected value of the error, $E(u) = 0$. If sample selection is such that one observes Q_j when $X\beta + u > 0$ and 0 if $X\beta + u < 0$, then the assumption of normality of the error term used in least squares regression does not hold. Similarly, if the sample is truncated to exclude those cases for which the observed $Q = 0$, then $E(u) \neq 0$. Tobin shows that for equation (17),

$$E(Q) = X\beta F(Z) + \sigma f(Z), \quad (18)$$

where σ is the standard deviation of the error term, $Z = X\beta/\sigma$, $f(Z)$ is the unit normal density, and $F(Z)$ is the cumulative normal density.

Furthermore, the expected value of the observed consumption that is not equal to 0, Q^*, is

$$E(Q^*) = X\beta + \sigma[f(Z)/F(Z)]. \quad (19)$$

If Q is estimated as a function of X alone, the estimate is biased if and only if both Q^* and X are correlated with $\sigma f(Z)/F(Z)$. The problem, then, in effect, is a missing variable problem.

Tobin proposes that the parameters be estimated using a maximum likelihood method. Pitt has recently used such a method to estimate demand parameters for Bangladesh.[42] Tobin's model is based on a probit estimation of likelihood, and so is called Tobit.

Heckman points out, however, that the Tobit model includes some restrictions that are frequently overlooked. In particular, the model constrains the determinants of entry in a market to be the same as the determinants of quantity of purchases once the market is

---

[40] See the discussion in Eileen T. Kennedy and Per Pinstrup-Andersen, *Nutrition Related Policies and Programs: Past Performances and Research Needs* (Washington, D.C.: International Food Policy Research Institute, 1983).

[41] James Tobin, "Estimation of Relationships for Limited Dependent Variables," *Econometrica* 26 (January 1958): 24-36; Zvi Griliches, B. Hall, and J. Hausman, "Missing Data and Self-Selection in Large Panels," *Annales de l'INSEE* 30-31 (1978): 137-176; and James J. Heckman, "Sample Selection Bias as a Specification Error," *Econometrica* 47 (January 1979): 153-162.

[42] Mark M. Pitt, "Food Preferences and Nutrition in Rural Bangladesh," *Review of Economics and Statistics* 65 (February 1983): 105-114.

entered. There is no a priori reason why this should be. For example, search costs may be "per purchase" and not "per unit."

For a similar issue with labor markets, Heckman proposes that an estimate be made of the right-hand term of equation (19) and that it be included in a regression of nonzero observations on X. In particular, a probit equation is established with the dependent variable defined as 1 if $Q > 0$ and as 0 otherwise. This equation predicts the probability of entry and can be used to estimate the right-hand term of equation (19), which is referred to in statistical literature as the inverse of the Mills ratio. In general, one is not particularly interested in the coefficient of the Mills ratio—indeed, frequently it is statistically not significant due to collinearity—but its inclusion will eliminate the bias from the missing variable.

Following McDonald and Moffit, the components of the population parameters needed are from each of the two regressions:[43]

$$\partial Q/\partial X = F(Z)(\partial Q^*/\partial X)$$
$$+ E(Q^*)[\partial F(Z)/\partial X]. \quad (20)$$

The total change in Q is composed of the change in Q of those households whose consumption is above the limit, weighted by the probability of being above the limit plus the change in that probability weighted by the expected value of Q if that change is greater than zero.

When dealing with marginal changes in consumption, when either the cooperative or the open market may be the margin, equation (20) is (omitting commodity subscripts):

$$\partial Q_T/\partial X = F(Z_c)(\partial Q_c^*/\partial X)$$
$$+ E(Q_c)[\partial F(Z_c)/\partial X]$$
$$+ F(Z_o)(\partial Q_o^*/\partial X)$$
$$+ E(Q_o)[\partial F(Z_o)/\partial X]. \quad (21)$$

As there is no price variation in the cooperative, it is necessary to assume that $\partial Q_o^*/\partial X = \partial Q_c^*/\partial X$. This modification of equation (20) was used to calculate the marginal propensities discussed below.

In general, the two-step approach should be interpreted as a logical rather than a temporal order of decisionmaking. That is, when interpreting results it must be recognized that the decision whether to purchase is made simultaneously with the decision of how much to purchase. In the Egyptian context, however, there is a further complication that lends greater justification to the two-step method. Purchase behavior in the multi-tiered market has a probabilistic element introduced by the uncertainty of finding a desired good in the cooperative market. As discussed below, this uncertainty has the nature of a local disequilibrium and spills over into other markets.

The first step of the measurement then is to estimate the probability of market participation with the dependent variable being 1 if the family consumes the good in the particular market and 0 otherwise.

$$Pr_{ci} = a + \beta_1 TXN + \beta_2 NUM + \beta_3 Pr_{oi}$$
$$+ \beta_4 WAIT + \beta_5 SEARCH$$
$$+ \beta_6 RATION + \beta_{zi} Z_i, \quad (22)$$

where

Pr_{ci} = a dummy variable that is 1 if household i buys at a cooperative and 0 otherwise;

Pr_{oi} = a dummy variable that is 1 if household i buys on the open market and 0 otherwise;

WAIT = the time spent waiting for the good at the cooperative, in minutes;

SEARCH = the time spent searching for a good at the cooperative, in minutes. This is defined as the reported time needed to reach the cooperative divided by the estimated probability that the good was available in the store (for a discussion see the following chapter);

RATION = a dummy variable defined as 1 if the household received the commodity as a ration in the preceding month and 0 if it did not; and

---

[43] John F. McDonald and Robert A. Moffitt, "The Uses of Tobit Analysis," *Review of Economics and Statistics* 62 (May 1980): 318-321.

Z   = a group of regional and demographic variables, including the number of family members, the proportion of children in the family, and the degree of urbanization.

Using the estimated value $\hat{Pr}_{ci}$, the Mills ratio can be calculated. The conditional demand equations then are:

$$Q^\star_{oj} = a + \beta_1 LTX + \beta_2 LTX2 + \beta_3 BTX$$
$$+ \beta_4 CTX + \beta_{5i} LPRICE_i + \beta_6 Q_{ri}$$
$$+ \beta_{zi} Z + \beta_m \text{Mills Inverse}, \qquad (23)$$

where

LTX   = the logarithm of TXN;

NTX   = the number of people in the household times LTX;

CTX   = the percentage of children younger than 5 in the household times LTX;

LPRICE = the logarithm of the ith price; and

Mills Inverse = 1/Mills ratio from equation (22).

And,

$$Q^\star_{cj} = a + \beta_1 LTX + \beta_2 LTX2 + \beta_3 NTX$$
$$+ \beta_4 CTX + \beta_{5i} LWAIT_i + \beta_6 Q_{ri}$$
$$+ \beta_{zi} Z + \beta_m \text{Mills Inverse}, \qquad (24)$$

where LWAIT is the logarithm of the ith waiting time at the cooperative.

The difference in equations (23) and (24) reflects the asymmetry in the decisionmaking process. Once the decision to purchase at a cooperative is made, the open market price is not relevant. Furthermore, as the cooperative price does not vary, cooperative purchases alone can be used to study the effects of income, demography, and time.

Similarly, once the decision to purchase on the open market is made, the time of waiting at the cooperative is not relevant, although price variations can be useful in investigating responses to price.

The marginal propensity to consume and the expenditure elasticities from equations (23) and (24) will vary with a household's expenditures and family composition. There is no single best way to model family characteristics, as they affect both the purchases of the individual commodities and the real value of household income.[44] The approach here is pragmatic and is used to avoid any potential bias from missing variables in the association of family size and per capita expenditures.

For four classes of commodities—cooked beans, *tamiya* (a processed food), fruit, and vegetables—data were collected only on weekly expenditures. Therefore, instead of a quantity on the left-hand side of equation (23), budget shares, W_i, were used. No prices were included as independent variables. As there are only open market sales for these goods and since the number of nonconsumers was relatively small, the estimates for these goods were made with ordinary least squares on the entire sample.

For both theoretical and practical reasons, the error terms for one commodity are likely to be correlated with the error terms for others. The standard approach that includes such information is Zellner's seemingly unrelated regressions (SUR). The particular nature of the two-step estimations makes the application of Telser's modification of the techniques to the second step the most practical approach.[45] These second-step equations were also weighted for heteroskedasticity, with the assumption, proposed by Prais and Houthakker, that the variance of Q is proportional to the square of its expectation.[46] In general, the two procedures resulted in smaller income parameters than the OLS estimates, and gave somewhat higher t-statistics for most variables.

---

[44] For discussions, see Angus Deaton, *Three Essays on a Sri Lankan Household Survey*, Living Standard Measurement Study, Working Paper 11 (Washington, D.C.: World Bank, 1981); and Robert A. Pollack and Terence J. Wales, "Demographic Variables in Demand Analysis," *Econometrica* 49 (November 1981): 1533-1551.

[45] Lester G. Telser, "Iterative Estimation of a Set of Linear Regression Estimates," *Journal of the American Statistical Association* 59 (1964): 845-862.

[46] S.J. Prais and H.S. Houthakker, *The Analysis of Family Budgets* (Cambridge: Cambridge University Press, 1955); and Henri Theil, *Principles of Econometrics* (New York: Wiley, 1971).

Income Parameters

The estimated income elasticities shown in Tables 32 and 33 give total response for the different population groups, estimated at the appropriate mean values. The total elasticity is comprised of weighted entry and response parameters in keeping with equations (20) and (21). The components reported are the weighted responses. It is important to note that the component of the total elasticity due to entry is calculated from the derivative of the probability of consuming in excess of rations. The appropriate divisor when converting these marginal responses to demand elasticities is total consumption from all sources, includ-ing rations and home production. The estimations from which these parameters are derived are presented in Appendix 3, Tables 44-60.

The estimated income elasticities are quite plausible. In urban areas, fresh meat, chicken, fish, milk, eggs, and fruit had the highest elasticities. Rationed commodities in general had modest elasticities, while *balady* bread, frozen meat, fish, cooked beans, and *tamiya* had negative elasticities for at least a portion of the sample. A few comparisons are possible with elasticities computed from urban areas for the 1974/75 Household Budget Survey.[47] The elasticities for 1981/82 reported here were lower than many calculated from the earlier period, which is in keeping with the higher average

Table 32—Commodity expenditure elasticities for urban areas

	1st Expenditure Quartile			Other Expenditure Quartiles		
Commodity	Weighted Entry Elasticity	Weighted Response Elasticity	Total	Weighted Entry Elasticity	Weighted Response Elasticity	Total
Sugar	0.006	0.130	0.136	0.018	0.187	0.205
Oil	0.011	0.065	0.076	0.027	0.070	0.097
Tea	0.001	0.105	0.105	0.001	0.126	0.126
Rice	0.000	0.364	0.364	0.000	0.132	0.132
Beans	0.040	0.049	0.089	0.084	0.056	0.140
Lentils	0.002	0.328	0.330	0.001	0.183	0.184
Fresh meat	0.120	1.461	1.581	0.123	0.542	0.665
Fresh chicken	0.000	0.680	0.680	0.000	0.313	0.313
Fresh fish	0.060	0.831	0.891	0.063	0.295	0.358
Frozen meat	−0.127	0.199	0.072	−0.452	0.302	−0.150
Frozen chicken	0.000	0.552	0.552	0.000	0.407	0.407
Frozen fish	−0.080	0.287	0.206	−0.228	0.036	−0.192
Balady bread	−0.018	−0.002	−0.020	−0.054	0.008	−0.047
Shami bread	0.052	0.194	0.246	0.084	0.121	0.205
Balady flour	−0.040	0.127	0.087	−0.020	−0.045	−0.065
Fino flour	0.032	0.556	0.588	0.061	0.156	0.217
Pasta	0.000	0.511	0.511	0.000	0.242	0.242
Eggs	0.136	1.232	1.368	0.150	0.387	0.537
Milk	0.061	1.513	1.574	0.097	0.572	0.670
White cheese	0.132	0.073	0.205	0.131	−0.172	−0.042
Cooked beans[a]	...	...	0.23	...	...	−0.39
Tamiya[a]	...	...	0.49	...	...	0.30
Fruit[a]	...	...	1.71	...	...	1.11
Vegetables[a]	...	...	0.80	...	...	0.51

Source: Data from the household survey made by the International Food Policy Research Institute and the Institute of National Planning, Cairo, 1981/82.

Notes: Expenditure quartiles were determined by ranking urban households according to total reported expenditures per capita. The 1st quartile had the smallest expenditures; the 4th, the largest.

Mean expenditures for the 1st quartile were LE 14.5, and the family size was 6.44; the mean expenditures of the other quartiles were 43.6, and their family size was 5.16.

[a] These figures were obtained from estimates of budget shares.

---

[47] See Karima Korayem, *The Impact of the Elimination of Food Subsidies on the Cost of Living of the Urban Population in Egypt* (Geneva: International Labour Organisation, 1980).

Table 33—Commodity expenditure elasticities for rural areas

	1st Expenditure Quartile			Other Expenditure Quartiles		
Commodity	Weighted Entry Elasticity	Weighted Response Elasticity	Total	Weighted Entry Elasticity	Weighted Response Elasticity	Total
Sugar	0.000	0.144	0.144	0.000	0.121	0.121
Oil	0.000	0.136	0.136	0.000	0.109	0.109
Tea	0.008	0.239	0.247	0.016	0.215	0.231
Rice	0.000	0.564	0.564	0.000	0.264	0.264
Beans	0.035	0.153	0.188	0.065	0.138	0.205
Lentils	0.022	0.227	0.249	0.035	0.165	0.200
Fresh meat	0.033	1.094	1.127	0.024	0.358	0.372
Fresh chicken	0.000	0.726	0.726	0.000	0.231	0.231
Fresh fish	0.172	0.770	0.942	0.157	0.275	0.432
Frozen fish	0.000	1.824	1.824	0.000	0.631	0.631
Balady bread	−0.027	0.071	0.044	−0.072	0.078	0.006
Shami bread	0.178	0.000	0.178	0.159	0.000	0.159
Balady flour	0.000	0.241	0.241	0.000	0.319	0.319
Fino flour	0.149	0.770	0.919	0.174	0.412	0.596
Open market flour	0.000	0.358	0.358	0.000	0.210	0.210
Balady and open market flour	0.000	0.323	0.323	0.000	0.320	0.320
Pasta	0.039	1.011	1.050	0.033	0.445	0.478
Eggs	0.101	1.460	1.561	0.078	0.504	0.582
Milk	0.021	0.140	0.161	0.027	0.089	0.116
White cheese	0.064	0.570	0.634	0.077	0.290	0.367
Grain wheat	0.000	1.321	1.321	0.000	0.589	0.589
Grain maize	0.000	0.802	0.802	0.000	0.558	0.558
Cooked beans[a]	...	...	0.68	...	...	0.48
Tamiya[a]	...	...	1.40	...	...	0.78
Fruit[a]	...	...	1.17	...	...	0.85
Vegetables[a]	...	...	0.85	...	...	0.58

Source: Data from the household survey made by the International Food Policy Research Institute and the Institute of National Planning, Cairo, 1981/82.

Notes: Expenditure quartiles were determined by ranking rural households according to total reported expenditures per capita. The 1st quartile had the smallest expenditures; the 4th, the largest.

Mean expenditures for the 1st quartile were LE 10; the mean expenditures of the other quartiles were LE 25.2 per month and their family size was 6.4.

[a] These figures were obtained from estimates of budget shares.

consumption in the later period. One exception is the elasticity for refined *(fino)* flour, which was reported to be an inferior good for most of the population in the middle of the 1970s, but which had an elasticity of 0.59 for the urban poor and 0.22 for others in 1981/82.

Expenditure elasticities in rural areas in 1981/82 differed significantly from those in urban areas. Rural expenditure elasticities for *fino* and *balady* flour, cooked beans, and *tamiya* were higher than those in the cities. On the other hand elasticities for milk and fruit were lower. The difference between rural and urban milk demand is particularly striking and reflects, in part, the higher consumption of cheese in rural areas. These elasticities undoubtedly also reflect marketing channels, or their absence. Urban consumers frequently purchase sterilized milk, which keeps without refrigeration, while few villagers have a way to preserve fluid milk other than to make cheese. Marketing probably also influenced the difference in elasticities for tea. There are fewer tea or soda stalls in rural areas and, therefore, tea is not an inferior good there, while it is in the cities.

Balady bread was an inferior commodity in the cities while the income elasticity was positive in the villages, but the elasticity in both regions was small enough to be considered negligible. The elasticities for *shami* bread (aggregated with *fino*, or *afrangi*, loaves in these estimates) were moderate. The elasticities estimated for flours in the rural area exceeded those in the urban, as did the elasticities for pasta (macaroni and noodles combined).

Overall, the income elasticities declined with income. Such a pattern is common. Indeed, it is built into a basic semilog equation for normal goods. The form used in this study, however, is more flexible as it includes the square of LTX (LTX2). If the coefficient of LTX is positive and that of LTX2 is negative and significant then the elasticities decline more rapidly than predicted by a semilogarithmic form, in which the elasticities vary inversely with quantity. The coefficient of LTX2 was generally negative and significant in the urban estimates. Elasticities declined less rapidly with income in rural areas, as indicated by the coefficient of LTX2, which was frequently not significant in preliminary estimates and was, therefore, excluded in subsequent work. This also reflects lower variance of total expenditures in rural areas.

As family size varied with income, additional flexibility in the average expenditure elasticities is provided by the NTX term. As poorer families were larger, on the average, and as the coefficient of NTX was generally negative, this term moderates the decline of expenditure elasticities over total expenditure.

With a few exceptions, the entry components of the total income elasticities were small, and frequently not significant. For a few commodities—frozen meat and fish as well as *balady* bread and flour in urban areas and *balady* bread in rural areas—the probability of entry declined with income, although the size of purchases depended on entry increases. This result, which is not possible with a decomposition of a Tobit estimation, is quite plausible. So are the zero entry elasticities for *balady* and open market flours, grain wheat, and maize in rural areas and for rice in both rural and urban areas. They are plausible because these goods are major consumption items and over a range of income changes households will change the amounts they purchase but will not eliminate the goods from the diet. This does not mean that every household consumed these goods—random timings and institutional factors affect the probability that they would purchase a good during the survey—but it does imply that income was not a determinant. It is, however, somewhat surprising that given the large total elasticity for fresh chicken, the entry component of the elasticity was zero in both rural and urban areas. While the rich consumed far more chicken and meat than the poor, the latter were no less likely to consume chicken at least once during the month and only slightly less likely to consume meat during the survey period.

Price Parameters

The price responses in Tables 34 and 35 reveal that there are a number of difficulties in attempting estimations when price variance is limited. In general, the price elasticities estimated for commodities that were rationed and also available at the cooperative were not significant (these are reported as 0 in the tables regardless of the sign) or were even significantly positive. The estimates of price elasticity for meat, chicken, fish, and other open market goods like pasta or cheese were larger in absolute value and, in general, significantly negative. Some of the differences in these estimates, then, reflect the nature of the data and the relatively standardized prices for staple commodities.[48] For some goods, such as breads and frozen products, the price variation was too small to even attempt to estimate a response. Such cases do not imply that the most probable response is zero, but only that it is not possible to ascertain statistically what the response would be.

In both urban and rural areas, the price elasticities for meat and chicken were large, with a significant portion coming from the entry equations. The price responsiveness for fish was apparently less than for other animal products. The elasticities for eggs and cheese were large in both rural and urban areas. The elasticity for milk was larger in urban areas than in rural, which may reflect the larger portion of dairy products that comes from fluid milk in the cities.

The price elasticities for bread deserve some discussion. The degree of substitution in urban areas may be high because flour (as opposed to bread) is not the foundation of the urban diet. Breads and, to a lesser degree, rice and *fino* flour are substitutes. The computed urban price elasticities came mainly from the entry equations. While the probability that an urban consumer purchased

---

[48] Many results that seemed significant in single equation estimations did not prove to be so in the seemingly unrelated approach.

Table 34—Own-price elasticities of commodities for urban areas

Commodity	1st Expenditure Quartile			Other Expenditure Quartiles		
	Weighted Entry Elasticity	Weighted Response Elasticity	Total	Weighted Entry Elasticity	Weighted Response Elasticity	Total
Sugar	0	0	0	0	0	0
Oil	0.071	−0.071	0	0.071	−0.071	0
Tea	0	−0.173	−0.173	0	−0.135	−0.135
Rice	0.011	−0.155	−0.144	0.016	−0.144	−0.128
Beans	0	0	0	0	0	0
Lentils	0	0	0	0	0	0
Fresh meat	−1.672	−1.207	−2.879	−0.435	−0.385	−0.820
Fresh chicken	−0.621	−0.962	−1.583	−0.161	−0.306	−0.467
Fresh fish	−0.219	−0.625	−0.845	0.000	−0.211	−0.211
Balady flour	−3.791	1.195	−2.593	−3.791	1.195	−2.593
Fino flour	0	0	0	0	0	0
Pasta	−0.116	−0.496	−0.612	0	−0.297	−0.297
Eggs	−0.407	−0.621	−1.028	0	−0.206	−0.206
Milk	−0.349	−0.528	−0.877	−0.171	−0.260	−0.431
White cheese	−0.842	0	−0.842	0	0	0

Source: Data from the household survey made by the International Food Policy Research Institute and the Institute of National Planning, Cairo, 1981/82.

Notes: The elasticities reported as 0 were not significant.

Expenditure quartiles were determined by ranking urban households according to total reported expenditures per capita. The 1st quartile had the smallest expenditures; the 4th, the largest.

Table 35—Own-price elasticities of commodities for rural areas

Commodity	1st Expenditure Quartile			Other Expenditure Quartiles		
	Weighted Entry Elasticity	Weighted Response Elasticity	Total	Weighted Entry Elasticity	Weighted Response Elasticity	Total
Sugar	0	0	0	0.093	0	0.093
Oil	0	0	0	0.268	0	0.268
Tea	−1.190	−0.147	−1.337	0	−0.135	−0.135
Rice	0	0	0	0.362	0	0.362
Beans	0	−0.327	−0.327	0.369	−0.210	0.149
Lentils	−0.275	0	−0.275	0	0	0
Fresh meat	−0.262	−1.898	−2.158	0	−0.609	−0.609
Fresh chicken	−0.322	−0.834	−1.156	0	−0.269	−0.269
Fresh fish	−0.473	0	−0.473	0	0	0
Balady flour	0.169	0	0.169	0	0	0
Fino flour	0	0	0	0	0	0
Open market flour	0	−1.900	−1.900	0	−1.113	−1.113
Balady and open market flour	−0.243[a]	−0.498	−0.498	0.219[a]	−0.449	−0.449
Pasta	0.768	−0.638	−1.406	0	−0.220	−0.220
Eggs	−0.983	−1.737	−2.720	0	−0.528	−0.528
Milk	−0.258	−0.240	−0.498	−0.078	−0.123	−0.201
White cheese	−0.414	−0.508	−0.922	−0.031	−0.243	−0.274
Grain wheat	0	0	0	0	0	0
Grain maize	0	0	0	0	0	0

Source: Data from the household survey made by the International Food Policy Research Institute and the Institute of National Planning, Cairo, 1981/82.

Note: The elasticities reported as 0 were not significant.

Expenditure quartiles were determined by ranking rural households according to total reported expenditures per capita. The 1st quartile had the smallest expenditures; the 4th, the largest.

[a] This is significant at the 0.10 level.

balady flour declines as the price of *balady* flour increases, the probability that the consumer bought bread and also *fino* flour increases. This pattern, then, is quite plausible, but it does hinge on an understanding of the source of the price differences in *balady* flour, much of which came from packaging. In many urban areas flour was available only in small bags selling for 8 piasters, while bulk purchases sold for 6.5 piasters. Few open market sales were observed in the cities. If the price reflected unmeasured limits on quantity, part, but probably not all, of the observed response would reflect that.

Lower income consumers in rural areas had an elasticity for open market flour that was close to that of lower income consumers in urban areas. The rural price, however, reflects the open market price and can be assumed to be free of quantity restrictions. The choice of substitutes was wider as trade in grains in rural areas was more widespread. Consumers might have chosen to mill their own flour at a local mill. Some but not all consumers had a choice of purchasing bread, while others may have been able to obtain flour from government stores.

It should be noted that the aggregation of grain wheat consumption, both from the market and from home production, accounts for the majority of the total production of that grain. If the remainder were sold after being milled as flour, it would be consistent with the likelihood that between one-half and two-thirds of the flour sold on the open market was from imported grain. This flour was frequently purchased in bulk from government shops and transported to other markets or sold in smaller amounts. Open market flour, then, is not necessarily a different commodity from flour in government stores, although there were quality differences sometimes.

On the other hand, there was virtually no significant price response for rural *balady* flour, and what has been measured reflects a positive entry elasticity for the rural poor. Considering this and the nature of the open market sales, which can be presumed to be the marginal sales for many households, regressions were run pooling open market and *balady* flours in rural areas. The income and price parameters from this aggregation are in keeping with aggregate time series estimations and are the most plausible candidates for projections to use for setting policy.

The second round of the rural sample offers another way to determine price parameters. Using a first-difference form of equation (23), it was possible to regress the changes in the quantities consumed by each household on the change of the prices the households faced and on the changes in total expenditures and rations. Regional differences and other taste factors are thereby controlled. The limited price variances still present difficulties; open market prices changed only moderately in the few months between the surveys. Nevertheless, the elasticities yielded are plausible, even if some allowances need be made for statistical significance (see Table 36).

Table 36—Income and price parameters from first difference equations for the rural sample

	Income Elasticities			Price Elasticities		
Commodity	1st Expenditure Quartile	Other Expenditure Quartiles	t-Statistic	1st Expenditure Quartile	Other Expenditure Quartiles	t-Statistic
Sugar	0.20	0.15	3.36	−0.16	−0.12	1.18
Oil	0	0	0.08	0	0	0.04
Tea	0.19	0.15	2.28	−0.35	−0.28	2.24
Rice	0.96	0.40	1.68	−0.28	−0.12	0.16
Beans	0	0	0.02	−0.77	−0.71	1.10
Lentils	0.91	0.59	1.56	−0.83	−0.54	1.14
Aggregate flour and bread	0.58	0.46	5.96	−0.68	−0.53	0.96

Source: Data from the household survey made by the International Food Policy Research Institute and the Institute of National Planning, Cario, 1981/82.

Note: Expenditure quartiles were determined by ranking rural households according to total reported expenditures per capita. The 1st quartile had the smallest expenditures; the 4th, the largest.

The price response measured for the Delta rice growing region from the rice regression was positive, probably because in the post-harvest period, the time of the first survey round, private sales were officially prohibited and private mills were closed. Although a fair amount of sales were recorded, it is not unlikely that there were some restrictions that were not present in the second round.

In general, Tables 34 and 35, and Tables 37 and 38 as well, indicate that the absolute values of price and cross-price elasticities were lower if expenditures were higher. This is, in effect, a hypothesis maintained when working with normal goods and a semilog functional form, as the elasticities are inversely related to total consumption. Variables that allowed the price parameters to vary by expenditure class were included in preliminary regressions but most proved not to be significant. As these parameters were frequently correlated with other price and expenditure terms, such results were generally not included in subsequent work. The data, then, do not allow us to disregard the pattern of declining absolute values of price elasticities. Indeed, when the interaction term for price and expenditure class did prove

significant it usually indicated that the differences in the price responses were more pronounced than the semilog relationship alone implied.

For example, the interaction variable was significant at the 10 percent level in eight urban estimations. Seven of these interaction terms indicated that the price responsiveness of the lower quartile was greater, all of the terms being for commodities not available in the ration system. It should be noted that with meat, chicken, and fish, the poor are more likely to stop consuming the product with a rising price and, furthermore, if they buy, they will reduce the quantity of fish and chicken more sharply when the price rises. For rice in urban areas, however, the interaction term indicates that the absolute value of the net price coefficient was smaller.

The situation in the rural market was more complex. The price parameters for entry estimated for the poor proved to be significantly different from those for the general population for all of the commodities that were also available in ration shops. As the apparent relationship for the general population is positive, however, this usually

Table 37—Cross-price elasticities of commodities for urban areas

Commodity	Expenditure Quartiles	
	1st	Others
Balady bread with *balady* flour	0.73	0.68
Balady flour		
With *fino* flour	2.07	3.04
With maize	0.84	1.23
Fino flour with *balady* flour	1.40	0.85
Eggs with rice	−0.09	−0.09
Meat with fish	1.05	0.30
Fish		
With meat	1.85	0.67
With *balady* flour	−2.07	−0.75
Chicken with rice	0.35	0.12
Rice with noodles	0.24	0.15
Sugar with *balady* flour	0.22	0.20
Beans with lentils	−1.32	−0.60
Lentils with rice	−2.32	−1.53

Source: Data from the household survey made by the International Food Policy Research Institute and the Institute of National Planning, Cairo, 1981/82.

Note: Expenditure quartiles were determined by ranking urban households according to total reported expenditures per capita. The 1st quartile had the smallest expenditures; the 4th, the largest.

Table 38—Cross-price elasticities of commodities for rural areas

Commodity	Expenditure Quartiles		Commodity	Expenditure Quartiles	
	1st	Others		1st	Others
Rice			*Balady* flour (continued)		
With noodles	0.34	0.15	With wheat	0.29	0.38
With *balady* flour	0.90	0.32	With rice	−1.06	−1.37
With meat	3.01	1.27	With open market flour	−1.06	−1.37
With maize	−1.03	−0.37	*Fino* flour		
Beans with *balady* flour	1.28	0.89	With maize	2.43	1.11
Lentils			With wheat	−1.68	−0.77
With rice	−0.32	−0.21	Open market flour		
With *balady* flour	1.51	0.98	With rice	0.38	0.22
Meat			With *balady* flour	−0.38	...
With wheat	−1.37	−0.67	With maize	0.43	0.25
With fish	0.14	0.05	Pasta with rice	0.11	0.04
Chicken			Eggs with maize	−0.08	−0.03
With rice	1.45	0.59	Milk		
With beans	−0.51	−0.22	With maize	−0.38	−0.21
With meat	−2.20	−0.95	With meat	0.72	0.40
Fish			With beans	−0.14	−0.08
With meat	3.07	0.95	With flour	0.17	0.09
With beans	0.61	0.19	With cheese	0.27	0.15
With *balady* flour	1.03	0.27	Cheese		
With chicken	−0.95	−0.29	With meat	0.49	0.29
Frozen fish			With flour	0.25	0.15
With beans	3.77	1.27	With milk	−0.07	−0.04
With chicken	−8.36	−2.81	Wheat		
Balady bread			With open market flour	1.61	1.27
With maize	1.60	1.30	With rice	0.65	0.51
With flour	−0.42	−0.42	With meat	7.04	5.50
With meat	1.39	1.36	With maize	−0.96	−0.76
With wheat	−0.72	−0.72	Maize		
Shami bread with *fino* flour	2.01	0.75	With rice	1.03	0.68
Balady flour			With meat	−3.16	−2.09
With maize	1.20	1.55			

Source: Data from the household survey made by the International Food Policy Research Institute and the Institute of National Planning, Cairo, 1981/82.

Note: Expenditure quartiles were determined by ranking rural households according to total reported expenditures per capita. The 1st quartile had the smallest expenditures; the 4th, the largest.

implies only that the net effect for the poor was not appreciably different from zero.[49] Positive associations between the probability of entry and prices were also observed for *balady* flour, although in this case the association was for the poor only. The poor were less likely to purchase meat, fish, chicken, pasta, eggs, milk, and cheese the higher their prices. Furthermore, those poor who did purchase meat reduced the quantity consumed more sharply as price increased than did the rest of the population that consumed the same amount.

An increase in the probability of purchase with higher prices runs counter to intuition, yet since it occurred for most of the main staple commodities in the rural sample, it is unlikely to have been merely a statistical oddity. One possible explanation may be the cash constraints that made some individuals unable to take full advantage of either the possibility of storage if prices fluctuated or of economies of scale in purchases. This may be particularly true for flour if it were cheaper in 100 kilogram sacks than in small purchases. (Purchases of flour in quantities

[49] In the initial estimates, the price ratio of cooperative and open market prices was used as a regressor. This gave a different pattern, but as the cooperative plays a minor role in the rural area, cooperative prices may be proxy for institutions in the analysis.

of less than 5 kilograms per visit cost, on the average, 10 percent more than larger purchases.) The cost of a given quantity of a commodity then would be higher for the poor. This would generate a positive statistical relationship between the probability of purchasing and price but would not affect the relationship observed between the quantity purchased and price.

However, flour is the only commodity that the poor are more likely to begin purchasing with higher prices. The phenomenon is observed in the general population for other commodities.

One must also consider the difficulty of measuring the supply response. Neither the source of the open market commodities nor the behavior of the suppliers is well documented. If high demand areas also increased supplies of open market commodities, the association of prices and number of purchasers in a single equation estimate could be positive. It is noteworthy in this respect that the association in the equations with commodities that were less regulated and more widely used was not positive.

Cross-price effects can provide a broader picture of the total price effect. The urban sample yielded few of these, most likely because the prices were uncorrelated. Positive cross-price elasticities, which indicate that commodities are substituted, were observed with the prices of *balady* flour, *fino* flour, and *balady* bread. Conversely, the *fino* flour price is positively correlated with the purchase of *balady* flour. Similarly, as the price of meat rose, more fish was purchased and vice versa. Noodles appear to have been a substitute for rice, and maize appears to have been a substitute for *balady* flour. Lentils and beans appear to have been highly complementary to rice, indicating that as the price of rice increased fewer lentils and beans were purchased. This could have been expected with lentils, which are used with rice in *koshari,* but it is somewhat surprising for beans, which are generally eaten with bread.

A greater number of cross-price elasticities were significant in the rural estimates, although the problem of supply simultaneity must be considered. Rice consumption increased as noodle prices did and vice versa. It also increased with the price of *balady* flour and meat, although the response was

larger than expected. Lentils were, again, complements of rice, while both lentils and beans were substitutes for flour. In general one would expect cross-price elasticities between animal products, indicating substitution to have been positive. The relationship of meat and fish prices was, but chicken appears to have been a complement of fish, frozen fish, and meat, although the responses observed were not symmetrical. There was no regional pattern of correlation for these prices that could explain such an occurrence. Furthermore, frozen fish and fresh fish purchases were slightly negatively correlated, yet the cross-price elasticities of both commodities with the price of chicken were negative.

The response of consumers to increases in flour prices is noteworthy. When the price of flour, defined as the price of government flour if it was reported to be available and open market flour otherwise, increased, consumers not only decreased their purchases of flour but also increased their purchases of wheat, maize, rice, beans, meat, fish, milk, and cheese. Purchases of *shami* bread responded to *fino* flour prices. Even more surprising was that the cross-price elasticity of *balady* flour with the open market price of flour was apparently negative, as was the reverse elasticity. What may have happened was a reverse causality; the more likely consumers were to obtain *balady* flour, the lower the price of open market flour, because the relationship between the prices of open market and government flour appears to have been complex and the elasticities reported must be used with caution. The price elasticities arrived at here may be roughly compared with estimates derived from a complete expenditure system for food and nonfood demand in Egypt, which are based on more aggregated price and quantity information by expenditure class for 1958/59, 1964/65, and 1974/75.[50] Those results are comparable to the elasticities derived from the direct estimates reported here. For example, von Braun's estimates of own price elasticities for urban low income households are, for bread and cereals, −0.28; for pulses, −0.60; for meat, fats, and milk, −1.21; and the estimates reported here are, for rice, −0.14; for pasta, −0.61; for meat, −2.9; for chicken, −1.6; and for milk, −0.88.

---

[50] Joachim von Braun, *Ernaehrungssicherungspolitik in Entwicklungslaendern—Oekonomische Analyse am Beispiel Aegyptens* (Kiel: Kieler Wissenschaftsverlag Vauk, 1984).

Other Demographic Effects and Effects by Area

The two-step method of estimations allows one to investigate both the probability that a producer will enter a given market and his response after he does enter. The variable for home production, which is defined as one if a family produces a given good or a close substitute, and zero otherwise, makes this test possible. Producers of sugar, *ghee*, beans, milk, cheese, and eggs were statistically less likely to purchase the good on the open market. This was true of producers of eggs in urban areas as well. In some cases this was dramatic; for example, while 23 percent of the villagers produced cheese, only 3 percent of those who purchased it were producers. The figures are 40 percent and 20 percent for rural producers of eggs and 19 percent and 12 percent for rice producers. It is, of course, not surprising that many producers did not need to obtain what they consumed from the open market, nor is it strange that some producers found that their production was insufficient. It is, however, important to note that the marginal response of producers, conditional upon entry, was not statistically different from other consumers, as the lack of statistical significance of most production variables in the response equations indicates. This held true for bread, flour, and grains as well. In addition, the observation is the same whether land per capita or a dummy variable is used for producers, although the statistical fit varies. One can then use aggregate land ownership statistics to predict market entry and to use the overall marginal propensities to predict purchases by both farm and non-farm families.

The coefficient of the variable NUM was usually positive in the entry equations, which indicates that larger families had to purchase more frequently. This may reflect an inability to obtain enough for storage. It also indicates that family marketing costs were greater, although not necessarily the costs per person.

The variable NTX, which indicates the effect of family size on income elasticities, was generally negative. This implies that, at the same per capita income, a larger family had a lower propensity to spend on food. Although this is frequently interpreted as meaning that larger families have economies of scale, these economies may be for nonfood as well as food items.

Thus if two families had equal per capita incomes, the larger family had a higher real income. As income elasticities for food generally declined with income, this higher real income was reflected in the food purchases of the family. From a policy standpoint, this is consistent with a view that while welfare and food policies should take family size into account if transfers are intended, the transfers do not need to be increased proportionally with family size to achieve equal welfare effects.

The interaction term CTX was also generally negative, although it was frequently not significant. This indicates that a family with small children spent less on food than a family of the same size and income without them. This term proved to be significant and positive for milk in urban areas. Furthermore, although the variable for the share of children in a family seldom proved to be significant (probably because of collinearity problems) the term was highly significant in both urban and rural areas in determining the probability that a family would purchase milk.

The variables for residence in Cairo and Alexandria and for rural residence in Upper Egypt frequently proved to be significant. In urban areas they generally indicated that large city dwellers were less likely to make open market purchases. In rural areas, the variable for residence in Upper Egypt proved to be consistent with the higher average sugar purchases and the lower purchases of rice, oil, and fresh fish in that region. An additional variable for a female head of household was included in preliminary runs although it rarely proved to be significant. It was significant and negative with tea, which reflected the social role of that commodity. Note, also, that in regressions for total food expenditures the variable for a female head of household was not significant, but it was significant for similar regressions for total calories. This indicates that households with a female head purchased a different bundle; one that contained slightly cheaper sources of calories.

The parameters in the tables can be used for projections of changes in demand under various policy options. Furthermore, one can use the income parameters as an indicator of the degree that subsidies on a good are targeted to low-income consumers. Subsidies on commodities with low elasticities such as *balady* flour in the cities and *balady* bread in both urban and rural areas are neutral or slightly targeted. Conversely, subsidies on commodities with high income elasticities such as pasta and *fino* flour are skewed to benefit the upper income groups. In this regard, it would appear that using subsidies to promote the consumption of milk would also be skewed to benefit the urban rich.

Similarly, the price elasticities in Tables 34 to 36 indicate that consumers of rice and sugar are not particularly responsive to price. Hence, reductions of the subsidies on these items will decrease both government outlay and consumers' real income, but will have only a small effect on total demand. On the other hand, the larger price elasticities for *balady* flour indicate that consumers readily substitute that commodity for others when the price of *balady* flour drops, and that they reduce their consumption when it rises. There is similar evidence of substitution with other goods, such as meat products, eggs, and pasta.

9

CONSUMERS' TIME ALLOCATION

Prices for a group of commodities in Egypt are set by the government and not allowed to fluctuate according to variations in demand and supply. Unless the government's supply response is infinitely elastic—that is, its supply curve is horizontal—there will be times when local supply and demand are not in balance. If as a result of this disequilibrium the quantity demanded at the current price exceeds the quantity supplied, then nonprice mechanisms will be needed to allocate supply. Most simply, the government can allocate using fixed quotas. It does this at the prices of the basic and additional rations. At the cooperative, however, there are no official quotas. At times, these goods are allocated by an ad hoc per customer or per visit limit imposed by the shopkeepers. Furthermore, it is only natural to expect that at times certain customers, including friends and relatives, will receive preferential treatment, but one can consider these to be irregularities in a pattern by which goods are allocated according to the willingness of consumers to devote time to their acquisition.

This chapter will discuss the implications that nonprice mechanisms for clearing markets have for household decisionmaking and consumer welfare.[51] Further analysis of the results of demand estimations is presented in the subsequent chapter.

Household Decisionmaking with Uncertain Supplies

In recent years, several economists have explored the implications of disequilibrium.[52] The essential feature of such a model is that demand does not equal supply. Consumers may demand more of a commodity at price P_t than suppliers bring forth, or suppliers, including laborers, may offer more than buyers demand. This occurs because, for a variety of reasons, P_t is sticky. This is surely true for a number of markets in the Egyptian economy, in which supply is frequently determined by a complex system of bureaucratic allocative decisions.

Given knowledge of its budget and prices, a household may determine that its optimal consumption is D_{ht}. If D_{ht} is unobtainable in the market, the household may choose to look somewhere else or at another time. Alternatively, it can reallocate its budget according to the quantity constraint it faces.

It can be demonstrated easily that a constraint on the quantity of a single good can "spill over" into markets for other goods, with demand for substitutes usually increasing. Furthermore, once the household's budget has been revised to take into account the constraint on the supply of the *ith* good, the household must verify that the new demand will not be curtailed by constraints on the *jth* good. Were the constraints on quantity in each market fixed, then quantity rationing theory could be applied to the analysis of demand. However, in some markets in Egypt the quantity constraints are stochastic. The effective demand of a household can be formulated as the demand that maximizes expected utility given the probability that quantity will be constrained. However, effective demand must be continually revised, for while expected utility can be determined by the subjective probability that quantities will be constrained $[\hat{P}_r(R_i)]$, where R_i is a restriction on the purchase of good i, the only possible status for a market at a given time is either $P_r(R_i) = 0$ or $P_r(R_i) = 1$. When it has this information, a household can reevaluate its vector of effective demand for all goods.

---

[51] For relevant theory on this see Yoram Barzel, "A Theory of Rationing by Waiting," *Journal of Law and Economics* 17 (April 1974): 73-95; Janos Kornai, *The Economics of Shortage,* 2 vols. (Amsterdam: North-Holland, 1980); and Donald A. Nichols, E. Smolensky, and T. N. Tideman, "Discrimination by Wasting Time in Merit Goods," *American Economic Review* 61 (June 1971): 312-323. A detailed discussion of these issues is given in Harold Alderman, "Allocation of Goods Through Non-price Mechanism: Implications of Rationing and Waiting Times in Egypt" (Ph.D. dissertation, Harvard University, 1984).

[52] For a review, see Richard E. Quandt, "Economic Disequilibrium Models," *Econometric Review* 1 (No. 1, 1982): 1-65.

Suppose that a household originally estimated the probability that the quantity of goods j and k would be constrained as 0.5 for each and, subject to these expectations, desires m units of the first good and n of the second. Suppose, however, that m units are not available. If j and k are substitutes, then under most conditions the constraint on j will lead to a revision of demand for k to p units (p > n). It should also be apparent that if the quantity of the *jth* good available is greater than m units, then actual trade may exceed m as m was the optimal amount when $\hat{P}_r(R_j) = 0.5$. Similarly, if more than m units of j are available, the revised demand for good k should be lower than the original n units. No revision would be necessary when $P_r(R_i) = \hat{P}_r(R_j) = 1$ or 0.

The example above illustrates two points. First, when temporary restrictions on quantity exist, they introduce a specific form of uncertainty in the analysis of consumer spending patterns. The distinction between the unconstrained demand of a household and actual purchases offers an additional justification for the two-step measurement used in this study. More important, the example points to the need to consider search and waiting costs. Without the costs of searching, there would be no reason to accept a restricted demand when there is a nonzero probability of finding a market in which supply is greater than or equal to demand or a probability of finding such a condition in the future. This is because the utility of a restricted demand can, at the most, be equal to the utility of demand with no quotas and is generally less.

If the benefits of searches over time or place are to be considered, a concept of the opportunity costs of time is needed.[53] Demand, then, can be expressed as

$$D_{ht} = f(P_t, T_{ht}, Y_{ht}, Z_{ht}), \qquad (25)$$

where T_{ht} is a vector of the time required by the household to make a purchase including search costs, Y_{ht} is the income of the household, and Z_{ht} is an exogenous variable. The household maximizes its utility according to a time budget as well as a cash budget. Essentially, this removes the problem of disequilibrium, which comes from rigid cash prices. Even when those prices are sticky, time prices are not, and they rise toward infinity as shortages occur.

Equation (25) also allows one to look at another component of the marketing process. The household may find that local supply exceeds demand but view the waiting time as "prohibitive." It again faces the choice of searching or reallocating. Each component of the vector of time prices in equation (25) can be viewed as consisting of these two elements, searching and waiting. Furthermore, it should be recognized that both components of time prices contain probabilistic elements:

$$\hat{T} = T_s/P_r + E(\text{wait}) \mid S_{ht} > Q_{ht}, \qquad (26)$$

where $\hat{T}$ is average expected marketing time, T_s is the average time it takes to obtain information on the availability of the good, P_r is the probability of the good being available, $E(\text{wait})$ is the expected length of the queue when the good is in stock, S_{ht} is supply, and Q_{ht} is actual household consumption. If the lines are shorter than expected and $S_{ht} > Q_{ht}$, the household may be expected to revise its budget based on the new information and to build up stocks of the commodity. Even if lines are of an average length, if $S_{ht} > Q_{ht}$, the probability of finding the good is 1. This reduces $\hat{T}$ and results in current purchases exceeding expected purchases.

The reason for using time in the analysis of demand is not merely to improve the fit of the price and income parameters and avoid potential biases in them. The effect of institutional arrangements on food demand should be known if the distribution of basic food commodities is to be understood and if the effects of changes in the institutional environment on total and group-specific demand are to be considered. Furthermore, time, being both a consumption good and a factor of production, has a value in and of itself. An analysis of the effect of a commodity marketing system on welfare, then, should include its effect on this scarce factor. One notes, furthermore, that the willingness to wait is frequently a means by which goods are distributed. It is sometimes proposed

---

[53] There is a large literature on leisure and time in household decisionmaking. See, for example, Gary Stanley Becker, "A Theory of the Allocation of Time," *Economic Journal* 75 (September 1965): 493-517; and Reuben Gronau, "Leisure, Home Production and Work—The Theory of the Allocation of Time Revisited," *Journal of Political Economy* 85 (December 1977): 1099-1123.

that waiting time be used to target subsidized goods on specific groups.

The tie with more conventional rationing is most apparent when the origin of the queue is considered. The concern is less with the time taken to distribute a scarce commodity, but the process of gaining priority rights (first come, first served) to it. As an illustration, consider a case in which goods are distributed instantaneously, one to a consumer, to the first N consumers who enter an outlet when it opens. The $N+1th$ individual to arrive receives nothing. Since each customer seeks to be N or earlier, yet desires to minimize waiting time, each will attempt to arrive only a moment before the $N+1th$ consumer. If all consumers are perfectly informed, the line will form instantaneously with exactly N individuals at time $t = t(N)$ before opening. Each individual in line will consider the benefits greater than or equal to the costs of waiting. Each potential customer not in line will consider the time excessive for the benefit obtained. If the store increases the total number of goods available, hence the number of beneficiaries, the line will form, instantaneously, somewhat later; that implies a shorter wait, since $t(N+1) < t(N)$. If scarcity of a substitute for the commodity or rising income leads to increased demand for the good at the outlet with N staying fixed, the line will form earlier. (The same holds true if the store offers two units to each of the first N customers.) Note that the waiting time varies although distribution is assumed to be immediate.

Now suppose that the store requires M minutes to dispense a good to a customer. The first individual will arrive $t(N) - M$ minutes before the outlets open, the second $t(N) - 2M$, and so forth, so that each still waits only $t(N)$ total minutes.[54]

The problem is different if there is no limit to the quantity purchased per visit. From the perspective of a two-part tariff, the consumer enters the queue if the consumer surplus of the entire purchase exceeds the costs of queuing. The consumer then makes a purchase according to the marginal costs. Otherwise, he or she stays out of the queue. This assumes that no resale is permitted or the individual transaction costs make such sales unprofitable.

On the other hand, if resale carries no transaction costs, then the first consumer in the queue would purchase all the quantity and sell it at the market clearing price P_o'. This is because the average cost would decline monotonically with quantity, creating a situation analogous to a natural monopoly. Ironically, if all consumers are perfectly informed there will be no queue at all; one consumer will arrive $t'+1$ minutes before the time of sale, where t' is the time that the consumer whose time has the next lowest opportunity costs considers equivalent to the profits from resale. Models with some mixture of limits on per visit purchases (quantity rations of a sort) and transaction costs for resale, then, seem most plausible.

The prices of time, then, may serve the same function as cash prices in clearing a market. The costs to consumers, however, are not captured by any producers, hence there is a deadweight loss relative to a conventional price equilibrium. This is illustrated in Figure 4. If supply is completely inelastic, then the net loss in consumer surplus relative to a market clearing price is zero—in either case a consumer surplus of $Q_r(P_o + wt_o)$ is sacrificed from the rationed position with nominal price P_o. When the price of time clears the market, suppliers receive only $Q_r \times P_o$, so there is a deadweight loss of $Q_r \times wt_o$. If supply is elastic, then queuing with prices at P_o entails a loss in consumer surplus of $\frac{1}{2}(P_o + wt_o - P')(Q')$ relative to the open market position. The producer surplus in the market cleared by time is less than that of a market cleared by price by $\frac{1}{2}(P'-P_o)(Q_r+Q')$.

The use of queues to clear markets may also have consequences for distribution. Nichols, Smolensky, and Tideman reasoned that the deadweight loss and congestion of public facilities are motivated by considerations of equity and that these considerations may be effectively served by waiting time costs.[55] The asset of time is distributed more equally than financial assets are. Furthermore, they argued, opportunity costs are likely to be positively correlated with wages and income. If there is a marginal external benefit to the consumption of a particular good—merit goods in their study—then it may be efficient to subsidize the costs of

---

[54] This example follows Barzel, "A Theory of Rationing."

[55] Nichols, Smolensky, and Tideman, "Discrimination by Wasting Time."

Figure 4—Loss to consumers when time clears markets

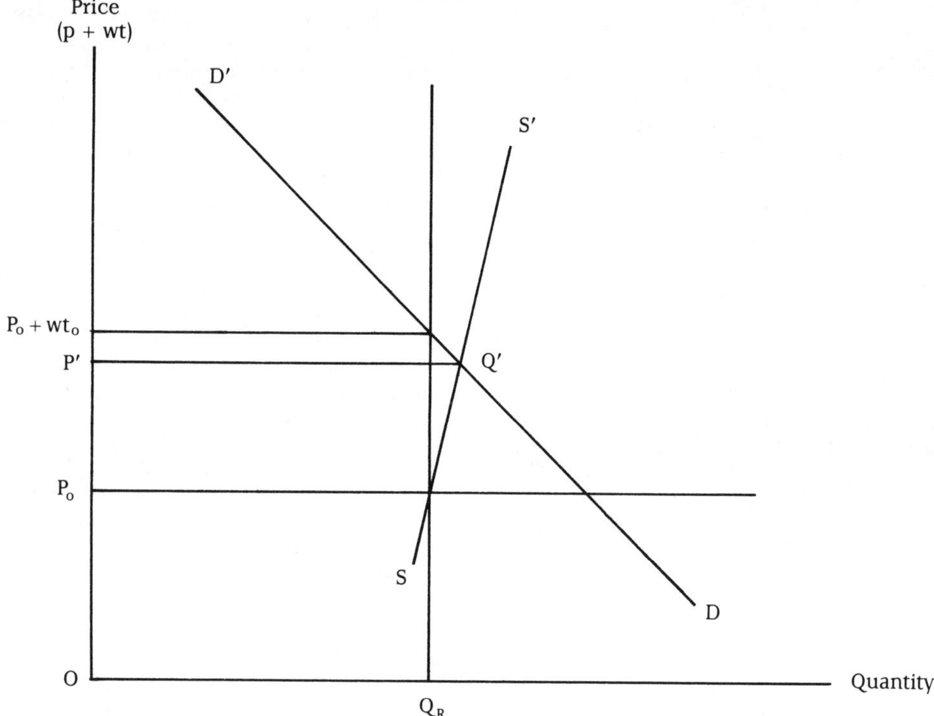

that good in cash and to use waiting time to target the limited supply of the subsidized good.

There are several reasons why the conclusion of Nichols, Smolensky, and Tideman may not hold. If there is no alternative market for the good (at a higher cash price) then the increase in the demand for a good that occurs when incomes rise can offset the decrease in demand caused by the price effect and the higher opportunity cost of time that it can be assumed higher income groups have. Moreover, this assumption about opportunity costs may be false. Finally, if the time price serves as the first of a two-part tariff under various assumptions of market structures, the upper income group with its larger total purchases will have a higher total surplus from standing in a queue and, therefore, will be more willing to pay the costs.

Basic Data on Marketing Times

While the analysis attempts to test the assertion that waiting times influence consumer behavior much as cash prices do, the former cannot be observed directly in a visit to a market. As indicated in equation (26), the expected time costs are a function of the time necessary to travel to the outlet to gather information on the availability of goods, the probability that the goods will be available, and the expected or average waiting time.

Table 39 indicates that there was little difference between income classes in the average waiting time or traveling time to ration shops. As expected, rural consumers had further to travel, but reported shorter waits upon arriving. This is in keeping with the greater number of persons per shop in urban areas indicated from aggregate data.[56]

---

[56] See Alderman, von Braun, and Sakr, *Egypt's Food Subsidy and Rationing System.*

Table 39—Average time taken to acquire food, by expenditure quartile

Location/ Expenditure Quartile	Time to Ration Store	Average Wait for Rations	Average Time Spent Shopping at the Cooperative[a]	Average Wait for Bread	Travel Time to Flour Shop	Time Spent Baking Bread[b]
	(minutes/month)		(hours/month)	(minutes/month)		(hours/month)
Urban areas						
1st	19.1	47.1	2.48	30.0	. . .	32.7
2nd	16.3	45.6	2.68	30.8	. . .	31.5
3rd	16.6	48.8	2.39	37.4	. . .	38.4
4th	14.0	53.0	1.76	29.3	. . .	38.1
Rural areas						
1st	27.2	28.1	1.20	. . .	20.8	51.5
2nd	34.0	31.8	1.27	. . .	30.5	48.8
3rd	25.0	33.9	1.43	. . .	22.9	41.9
4th	25.6	31.8	1.49	. . .	24.9	38.3

Source: Data from the household survey made by the International Food Policy Research Institute and the Institute of National Planning, Cairo, 1981/82.

Note: Expenditure quartiles were determined by ranking urban and rural households according to total reported expenditures per capita. The 1st quartile had the smallest expenditures; the 4th, the largest.

[a] For urban areas this is calculated as the number of visits to the cooperative times travel time plus the number of purchases of sugar, oil, or rice times average waiting time. It was assumed that if more than one of these three commodities were purchased, they were all purchased at the same time. The data do not allow a similar method of calculating the shopping time for rural areas. For them, the average shopping time is the sum of the average wait and travel time for consumers alone.

[b] These figures are for only the households that baked.

The longer time spent shopping at the cooperatives is an artifact of differences in the data and methodology of the samples. In urban areas, the number of visits and the number of purchases were recorded. This makes it possible to calculate shopping times as products of travel times and waiting times with a conservative assumption (conservative in the sense that purchasing times are this large or greater) that all other commodities are purchased at the same time as is the item requiring the largest time investment. In rural areas the shopping time is the sum of travel time and average waiting time for those individuals who used the cooperative in the previous month.

Although the average times for shopping at the cooperative did not appear to be large, they represent the time spent purchasing a few commodities only. Table 40 shows the average waiting times for selected commodities. For all commodities, the waiting times were appreciable and longer in the general cooperatives than in those restricted to employees of large factories or government offices. Somewhat surprisingly, the waiting times for purchasing bread were also long. Either there are a number of neighborhoods in which the capacity of bakeries or outlets is insufficient for peak demand or consumers value freshness and loaf quality enough to want to be at the shop when the bread arrives.

Obtaining the ration quota takes approximately one hour. This commitment of time, however, results in purchases that have a higher value on the open market so that the average family obtains an implicit transfer of nearly LE 4 embodied in the monthly ration. As LE 4 per hour is an astronomical wage rate in Egypt, it is unlikely that many families did without their rations because waiting times were long.

Waiting at the cooperative is a different issue. First, in urban areas (where more information was available) waiting times at cooperatives were somewhat higher on the average than at ration shops. Moreover, the waiting did not guarantee a fixed bundle and may have had to be done several times each month. Finally, given the higher, although subsidized, prices in cooperatives, the cash value earned per unit of time may have been small. For an average waiting time of over 2.5 hours, consumers obtained an implicit transfer of less than LE 1. This gave an implicit wage of LE 0.4 an hour. The average wage for the individuals who reported that they did the shopping was LE 0.51, ranging from LE 0.36 for the poorest quartile to LE 0.71 for the highest expenditure quartile. This wage was calculated by dividing the

Table 40—Average waiting time for selected commodities at urban cooperatives

Commodity	Public Cooperative	Workplace Cooperative
	(minutes)	
Sugar	54	37
Oil	50	31
Rice	93	55
Frozen beef	105	48
Frozen chicken	46	23
Frozen fish	56	29

Source: Data from the household survey made by the International Food Policy Research Institute and the Institute of National Planning, Cairo, 1981/82.

weekly reported income for an individual's secondary occupation by the hours worked each week, unless less than 5 hours were worked in that endeavor each week, in which case the basic occupation was used. This defines the secondary employment as the marginal use of time, although, as reported in the survey, the secondary job frequently had a higher implicit wage. Egyptians are notorious moonlighters, frequently working in a secure and moderately prestigious government or public sector post in the morning and working at a higher paying private job in the evening. A government clerk who also drives a taxi will give the civil service post as the primary employment, although the wage rate is probably higher behind the wheel.

In apparently two-thirds of the households in rural areas and 58 percent in urban, the person who obtains the ration or the commodities from the cooperative decides the food budget.[57] Nearly 40 percent of the urban shoppers also had jobs (14 percent of them were self-employed) and another 12 percent were full-time students. In the rural areas more than 34 percent were self-employed and 8 percent were students. The difference between urban and rural shoppers

reflects the number of self-employed farmers who also take responsibility for shopping. More than half of the shoppers in both urban and rural areas were male.

This probability variable used in applying equation (26) to the demand analysis was constructed by summing the total number of purchases of a specific commodity in a census tract and dividing that by the sum of visits to the cooperative for that commodity reported by respondents. The values of the variable, then, are for a census tract rather than for an individual. There is, however, a conceptual difficulty with the probability variable that the waiting time variable does not have. Suppose the residents of a district believe that the probability of finding rice at the cooperative is low. They would make few visits, if any. Accordingly, if fewer than three visits were reported for the entire tract, regardless of the outcome, the probability for the tract was set to 0.2. This, then, assumes that if only one or two visits were made in a census tract and one or both were successful, the successes would reflect special circumstances. The probability 0.2 is an arbitrary floor, but it is unlikely that the results would be sensitive to small changes.

Table 41 presents information on the average size of purchases from the cooperative and the number of purchases in a month for those consumers who obtained a given commodity. Repeated visits indicate that limits were set on the size of each purchase, although cash constraints could have produced a similar pattern. For example, the number of families who frequently purchased chicken and the numbers who made large purchases suggests that monthly quotas for these commodities were not enforced uniformly. Indeed, the pattern for chicken was very similar to that for fish, although the latter was available without quotas. Although the percentage of large purchases of frozen beef were smaller than for chicken, a large share of the consumers made more than one visit. This may indicate that the size of purchases was limited but the number of them was not. Of the staple commodities, only sugar was purchased frequently. Again this

---

[57] The second round of the survey allowed a cross-check of the responses to the question, "Who does the food budget?" In only 272 of the 453 cases was the response by the female head of household the same as that of the male. In another 64 cases, the woman responded that the decision was joint, while the man named an individual, and in 29 cases the woman named an individual while the man responded that the budget was jointly determined. In 88 cases the responses came from different individuals.

Table 41—Frequency and size of purchase from urban cooperatives

Consumer Groups	Sugar	Oil	Rice	Beans	Lentils	Frozen Meat	Frozen Chicken	Frozen Fish
					(percent)			
Share of consumers making 1 purchase in a month	46	65	70	75	79	58	48	63
Share of consumers making 2 purchases in a month	35	38	22	17	17	23	29	27
Share of consumers making more than 2 purchases in a month	19	7	8	8	4	20	23	10
Share of consumers obtaining more than 2 kilograms per purchase	44	12	13[a]	18	18	29	58	60
Share of consumers obtaining more than 3 kilograms per purchase	18	5	12[a]	7	5	7	30	30

Source: Data from the household survey made by the International Food Policy Research Institute and the Institute of National Planning, Cairo, 1981/82.

[a] The figures for rice are for purchases greater than 5.0 and 7.5 kilograms per purchase.

could indicate that the average size of a purchase was limited, although a moderate number of consumers made purchases greater than the 2 kilogram limit suggested by the cooperative management.[58] While purchases of oil, beans, and lentils could be expected to be small and infrequent given the modest demand for them, it is somewhat surprising that few families made large or frequent purchases of rice. Whereas there are more shortages of rice in the regions of the Delta where large amounts of it are consumed, the limited supply of rice may have limited the number of purchases and the average size of a purchase. This would have raised the time spent purchasing a unit of rice and, in accord with the model, would have increased the number of open market purchases. The results of the test of that model are given in the next chapter.

[58] Alderman, von Braun, and Sakr, *Egypt's Food Subsidy and Rationing System*.

10

EFFECTS OF MARKETING OBSTACLES ON CONSUMER BEHAVIOR

Consumers have a choice of standing in queues to buy rationed goods or paying higher prices on the open market. They can be expected to adjust their consumption patterns to maximize total household welfare by trading off cash for convenience. This should affect both demand at cooperatives and distribution.

A family must allocate its time over an array of production and consumption activities in a manner analogous to the process of allocating cash. If consumers have the choice of obtaining a commodity at a low cash price but with high time costs, stemming from both long lines and high search costs, or of paying a higher cash price with greater convenience, consumer behavior should reveal the relative values of time and goods to the families in the sample.

In keeping with the analogy between allocations of time and cash, a series of demand equations was estimated using measures of time costs as independent variables along with monetary prices, income, and household characteristics. The method used parallels that used to measure income and price response, and is discussed in more detail in Chapter 8.

Although a similar methodology was used throughout the sample, the role of time allocation is examined in greater detail for urban areas. This is because the choice between open market purchases and cooperative purchases is more apparent in the cities. The probability that six staple commodities—sugar, oil, tea, rice, beans, and lentils—and frozen meat, chicken, and fish as well, would be available was estimated by adding up the number of purchases in a census tract and dividing that total by the number of recorded attempts to make a purchase. In addition, the expected waiting times were recorded for six of these commodities; tea, beans, and lentils were excluded. The waiting time for bread was also recorded. When waiting time was recorded, the total time of purchasing was estimated with waiting time as one regressor and the time spent going to the cooperative divided by the probability of finding the goods as another. Only the searching time was used for other commodities. These equations are reported in the tables of Appendix 3. The waiting time elasticities from the estimates are presented in Table 42.

First and foremost among the general conclusions that can be drawn from the estimates is that time matters. There are eight possible coefficients for waiting time in the estimates for entry equations. Seven of these are significant and negative and the other (*fino* bread) is negative for the lowest income group. Similarly, there are eight estimates for search time. These include beans and lentils, for which there is no information on waiting time, and exclude breads. Of these eight, seven are negative and significant while the estimate for oil is negative but not significant. In addition, four of the eight cross-time parameters for entry into the open market are significant and positive; a fifth is positive and significant at about the 0.15 level (two-tailed test).

Of course, it is not really surprising that time matters. The more interesting questions are how does it matter and how much. The results reported in Appendix 3 indicate that, for all six cooperative commodities for which there are observations of both search and waiting times, the coefficient of search time is less than that of waiting. This is logical. The price of waiting in line is, at the margin, a real individual cost, either of the individual's own time or of the compensation paid to another. Search time, however, is calculated from the families' average travel time to the cooperative and the probability of the good being available at any given visit in the district. It is quite likely, however, that the consumer obtains information about the availability of a good at a lower cost than the calculated term measures. For example, suppose that the individual has to go only halfway to the cooperative to obtain information from a neighbor. The variable search cost would then equal twice the real search cost and the estimated derivative would be

Table 42—Time elasticities for commodities sold at cooperatives and on the open market in urban areas

| | 1st Expenditure Quartile | | | | Other Expenditure Quartiles | | | |
| | Weighted Entry Elasticity | | Weighted Response Elasticity | | Weighted Entry Elasticity | | Weighted Response Elasticity | |
Commodity	Cooperatives	Open Market	Cooperatives	Total	Cooperatives	Open Market	Cooperatives	Total
Sugar	−0.106	0.081	0.000	−0.025	−0.090	0.076	0.000	−0.014
Oil	−0.127	0.000	0.000	−0.127	−0.105	0.043	0.000	−0.062
Rice	−0.185	0.124	0.021	−0.040	−0.094	0.087	0.015	0.008
Frozen meat	−0.332	...	0.000	−0.332	−0.579	...	0.000	−0.579
Frozen chicken	−1.235	...	0.000	−1.235	−0.752	...	0.000	−0.752
Frozen fish	−1.068	...	0.000	−1.068	−0.624	...	0.000	−0.624
Balady bread	...	−0.047	0.065	0.018	...	−0.047	0.065	0.018
Fino bread	...	−0.358	0.212	−0.146	...	0.053	0.111	0.164
Cross-time elasticities								
Fresh meat with frozen meat	...	0.000	...	0.000	...	0.000	...	0.000
Fresh chicken with frozen chicken	...	0.637	...	0.637	...	0.214	0.000	0.214
Fresh fish with frozen fish	...	0.063	...	0.063	...	0.000	...	0.000
Balady flour with bread	...	0.220	...	0.220	...	0.000	...	0.000
Fino flour with bread	...	−0.290	...	−0.290	...	0.000	...	0.000

Source: Data from the household survey made by the International Food Policy Research Institute and the Institute of National Planning, Cairo, 1981/82.

Note: Expenditure quartiles were determined by ranking urban households according to total reported expenditures per capita. The 1st quartile had the smallest expenditures; the 4th, the largest.

half the real derivative, although the sign and significance would be unaffected.

The estimated coefficients of the regressions are not actually the coefficients of time costs, but of time. They are, then, the product of the coefficient of time and the cost of time per visit, for one estimates $Q = (\beta \times w)(\text{TIME}) = C(\text{TIME})$ where w is the opportunity cost of time and β is the elasticity of waiting time. Ideally, the model would be used to calculate w. The parameter w is, however, not identified directly. Under the original assumption of the direct analogy of time and cash prices, $\partial Q/\partial P = \partial Q/(w \times \text{TIME})$ and, in principle, one could use the ratio of the derivatives to estimate w. Unfortunately, the price parameters proved difficult to obtain by income group. Nevertheless, the estimates will be used below to investigate the size of w, but before risking that it is worthwhile to look at other features. Note that although w is not identified, the elasticities in Table 42 are unaffected, as w cancels out in the calculation. The elasticities of net waiting time are plausible. They are small but negative for sugar, oil, and rice, and are much larger for chicken, fish, and meat. Their sizes are close to the expected sizes of the price elasticities for the frozen commodities and oil but they may be a trifle low for rice and sugar. The search elasticity for beans is −0.14 and for lentils, −0.10.

Closer inspection reveals another important pattern. There was little response to time observed in the conditional demand equations (equation [24]). Most of the effect of time was from entry into either a cooperative or the open market. The effect of time that depended upon entry can be used to help determine whether the cost of time was per visit or per unit and also to give some information on hoarding. Looking first at bread, for which there were no limits on quantities purchased, the longer waiting times were associated with larger purchases once a consumer entered the queue (see the coefficient of $\text{LWAIT}_{\text{bread}}$, Appendix 3, Table 45). The net effect for *balady* bread was virtually negligible, as the entry and conditional response effects cancelled each other. The net effect for *fino* bread was negative for the poor, but positive for the rest of the population, implying, on face value, that consumers were overcompensated or hoarding. As *fino* bread stores better than *balady* bread, this may be an indication that purchases of this bread replaced purchases of *balady* bread. If so, it would be a type of cross-time effect that is somewhat masked because the variable for bread waiting time is not distinguished by type of bread.

As indicated in Table 41, more than half the consumers of sugar at the cooperative made repeated purchases. One would expect, then, that the waiting costs for sugar consumers were marginal. The conditional response equation produced negative coefficients for both search and waiting time but these are statistically insignificant and remain so if either are introduced singly. The coefficient of time for rice in the conditional equation is positive; consumers apparently compensate for waiting time but the poor could not do this completely. The other coefficients for search time or waiting time in the cooperative response equations are negative, but insignificant. The time variable in the conditional response equation has less variance than it does in the corresponding full-sample entry equation. It is possible that the limited variance of this term renders the estimates insignificant when in fact there was a response to time conditional upon entry. The alternative hypothesis is that waiting was an entry cost but not a variable cost.

The model included covariance terms in order to test whether the poor were more likely to stand in line to obtain the limited supply of subsidized staples and frozen produce. The coefficients of the product of the terms for waiting time and class test whether the poor respond more readily to time than the others. If so, the interaction term would have a sign opposite to that of the general population, but it would probably be smaller. The estimates provide no statistical evidence that the poor were ardent queuers. There is some evidence that they were actually less likely to queue. They were statistically more responsive to waiting time for rice, fish, and lentils although the evidence for lentils comes from search costs and not waiting time. Furthermore, the poor were discouraged from buying *fino* bread when waiting time was longer while the general population was indifferent. Similarly, the cross-time response of the poor for *balady* flour was positive, as expected, while the general population was unresponsive.

It is unlikely that there would not be a difference between the responsiveness of consumers for other commodities because the variance in the parameters was insufficient. The overall time response parameters are generally estimated with precision ($p < 0.001$). It is difficult to imagine that there was a real difference in the responsiveness of the poor that eluded estimation.

A principal finding here, then, is really negative. It can be said with some confidence that waiting times did not target scarce subsidized goods on the poor. The implications for policy hold, even if it is difficult to measure opportunity costs or expected wages directly.

If time costs are analogous to market prices then the parallel between $Q = a + \beta_1 P$ and $Q = a + \beta_2 wT = a + cT$ can be used. Under this relationship β_1 should equal β_2 and

$$C_{poor}/C_{other} = (w_{poor}/w_{other})$$
$$\times (\beta_{1poor}/\beta_{1other}). \quad (27)$$

The ratio of the average wages of poor shoppers to the average for the rest of the shoppers was 0.64. When the time response of the poor was not different from that of the general population, the assumption that wage rates indicated the opportunity cost of time would imply that the ratio of the price response was 1.56. If the poor proved more responsive to time, the implied ratio of time parameter would be larger. For example, the estimated time response for rice and frozen fish implies ratios of price response parameters of 2 and 2.4 respectively.

The price elasticities reported for a number of commodities in this study—for example, meat, chicken, and fish—tend to be larger for the poor. This was noted in a number of other studies. But the relationship in equation (27) does not deal with elasticities but derivatives. For normal goods, the ratio of the poor's marginal response to price to the marginal response of the general population would be smaller than the elasticities. For example, while the ratios of price elasticities for meat and chicken in urban areas were 3.5 and 3.4, the ratios of marginal responses were only 1.16 and 1.55. For rice, the latter ratio was less than 1. For other commodities, the absence of data on the responses to price do not allow one to establish the price response ratio or to fix the opportunity cost values. Given the information on responses to time, however, it is likely that the ratio of opportunity costs of the poor to the opportunity costs of the general population was somewhat higher than the ratio of wages. That is, the ratio of time costs are likely to be somewhat higher than 0.64, though not necessarily as high as 1.

Since, however, the parameters of time response above come from entry equations, it is worthwhile to reformulate the inquiry in terms of a two-part tariff. As noted in Chapter 9, waiting times can be considered as a payment to enter the market, but the marginal costs of entry are purely in terms of cash. It was also noted that, to allow application of a two-part price, the model must include a mechanism so that it is not possible for a single individual to procure the entire stock for resale. This can be done by simply assuming either that the transaction costs of reselling the stock are prohibitive (or become so as volume increases) or that purchases are limited, but only to amounts less than what most households would demand.

In such a model, a consumer participates if and only if the desired purchase times the difference in the cash price of the two markets exceeds the waiting cost:

$$Q_i^* (P_{oi} - P_{ci}) > w \times TIME, \qquad (28)$$

where TIME is the time spent waiting to purchase a commodity. Furthermore, for the marginal entrant, equation (28) is an equality.[59] Note that the gain here comes from the difference in the two prices and not consumer surplus as it is generally defined.

From the conditional response equations it is possible to calculate how much a consumer can be expected to purchase if he or she enters the market. Therefore, $\hat{Q}$, expected family purchases, can be estimated.

Suppose that equation (28) can be represented as an equality. The consumer either gains from being in a queue or finds that the loss is slight. Implicitly, then, each cooperative or queue indicates the break-even point for the consumer, with each showing up at exactly the time before opening that allows the market to clear (see Chapter 9). Markets are sufficiently separated that the travel time to alternative markets exceeds the gain and, therefore, waiting times do not equilibrate between markets. In this situation,

$$w = \hat{Q}(P_{oi} - P_{ci})/TIME. \qquad (29)$$

One more simplifying assumption was risked, that the poor shop in different markets or wait in different queues than the rest of the population (this could come about if the poor live in different areas). The estimated $\hat{Q}(P_o - P_c)$ for sugar was then regressed against waiting times multiplied by a dummy for either the poor or the nonpoor population. The regression was then

$$
\begin{aligned}
Surplus = \;& 29.4 WAIT \times CLASS\ 1 \\
& (12.39) \\
& + 38.3 WAIT \times NONPOOR; \\
& (25.83) \qquad\qquad\qquad (30)
\end{aligned}
$$

$R^2 = 0.46.$

A similar estimate with rice gave

$$
\begin{aligned}
Surplus = \;& 18.7\ WAIT \times CLASS\ 1 \\
& (10.14) \\
& + 25.5\ WAIT \times NONPOOR; \\
& (23.68) \qquad\qquad\qquad (31)
\end{aligned}
$$

$R^2 = 0.40;$

where CLASS 1 has a value of 1 when the household is in the poorest quartile and 0 otherwise, and NONPOOR has a value of 1 when the household is in the other 3 quartiles and 0 otherwise. Prices and wages were in piasters.

The experiment is subject to a number of caveats, readily apparent from the assumptions listed above. It fails to account for joint purchases, which would increase the gain from waiting, and it assumes away the possibility that the household bundle could be obtained in more than one visit. Nor does it account for the fact that the estimated gain is endogenous and, within limits, could be increased by a consumer merely by purchasing for storage. The model also does not correct for the utility or disutility of the actual act of shopping.[60] Despite all those caveats, the wait predicted for market clearance is close to the time costs estimated from observed wages. Furthermore, the ratio of the time costs of the poor and the overall

---

[59] For a review, see Harold Alderman, "Impact of Income and Food Price Changes on Food Acquisition by Low-Income Households: A Review of the Evidence," report prepared for U.S. Agency for International Development, Office of Nutrition, Washington, D.C., July 1984.

[60] James Tobin uses a variant of equation (29) to define the costs of a ration currency. $r_j = (P_b - P_o)/P_A$ where P_b is the black market price, P_o is the official price, and P_A is the price in ration points ("A Survey of the Theory of Rationing," *Econometrica* 20 [October 1952]: 521-553).

population was 0.77 in one estimate and 0.73 in the other, which is more or less what was expected.[61] These results seem all the more plausible as the omission of joint purchases depresses the gain and, therefore, the implied clearing wage. The correlation of purchases is not known, although evidence indicates that it is far from perfect. For example, the majority of purchasers of open market rice had patronized the cooperative for one of the six staples in the preceding month. That is, rice was not purchased at the same time that other goods from the cooperative were.

These results of equations (30) and (31) are close to the wage rates, which lends support both to the view that wage rates were close to opportunity costs and to the view that queuing times served to bring supply and demand into balance, a function normally attributed to prices. As the measurement of the wage rates and the response to time were performed simultaneously, the model is underidentified and, hence, the data can support both views, but cannot prove either. In addition, this evidence, and the absence of regularly observed time responses in the conditioned response equations, supports the view that time costs are the first of a two-part tariff, which is modified in some unspecified manner by upper limits on purchases or by prohibitive transaction costs for resale.

One more issue about waiting time needs to be addressed. A variable for servants was included in the entry equations in an interaction term with waiting time. This term is not confined to servants but took a value of 1 if the family sent an individual other than a household member to do the shopping. Frequently, the individuals were not paid directly for this service, although it is likely that some reciprocal obligation was incurred when the family asked a neighbor to assist. If the payment was a flat fee, because the servant was paid per day or per trip, the length of the wait would be irrelevant and the interaction term in the cooperative entry equations would be positive. Such was the case only for rice. Many of the people using servants were elderly or invalids (13 percent were from the poorest quartile and 23 from the next quartile), which suggests that the family or individual sometimes exhibits a reluctance to ask services from a neighbor having a similar reluctance to queue.

Time Allocation in Bread Baking

As indicated in Chapter 3, virtually all rural households and a quarter of urban households baked bread. Table 39 indicates that there were substantial differences in the time allocated to baking. Rural families, particularly the poor, spent more hours baking than families in the cities did. There was little difference in the number of individuals involved each time bread is baked (means of 2.3 for rural families and 2.4 for urban families), and urban families actually spent more time per session (5.6 to 4.8 hours). Rural families, however, baked more frequently. More than half (54.6 percent) of the rural families reported baking at least once a week, while only 30.6 percent of the urban families who baked did it that often.

Baking bread, then, took up large amounts of the families' time and it was relatively expensive as it uses an appreciable amount of fuel. If bread was baked from cereals (or flour) purchased on the open market, the cost of flour was usually close to or exceeded the flour equivalent price in the subsidized bread. If subsidized flour were used as an input, bread might be produced at a somewhat lower cost.[62]

The extra costs of home baking were probably incurred for two reasons. First, as anthropological studies and interviews indicate, families prefer homemade bread.[63] Homemade bread keeps longer because its moisture content is lower and it is considered cleaner. Second, bread was not available in all villages and some urban neighborhoods. More home baking was done in areas where respondents said local availability is insufficient. In urban areas, 35 percent of the families baked in neighborhoods where not enough bread was available, compared to 22 percent elsewhere in the cities. The cor-

---

[61] For a discussion, see Robert A. Pollack and Michael L. Wachter, "The Relevance of the Household Production Function and Its Implications for the Allocation of Time," *Journal of Political Economy* 83 (April 1975): 255-277.

[62] The *balady* loaf of 169 grams and 39 percent moisture contains a flour equivalent of 103.1 grams sold at 1 piaster. This is equal to a flour equivalent price of 9.7 piasters per kilogram. The mean value of flour prices is 9.4 piasters per kilogram on the open market. *Balady* flour at the flour shop is sold at 6.5 piasters per kilogram.

[63] See de Treville, "Food Processing and Distribution Systems."

responding figures for rural areas were 99 percent and 92 percent.

As bread is almost universally baked by women, the time spent baking should also be determined by the number of women in a household and their opportunity cost. Baking should be positively related to the availability of labor and flour and to income, and negatively related to the price of cereal or flour and to the availability of commercial bread. Regressions were run to test some of these assumptions. These regressions are, to a degree, counterparts to the demand regressions on the choice of flour and bread.

The dependent variable of the model is the time households spend baking bread. As long as the technology and working intensity of this process are fairly uniform, this variable may also be used as a proxy for the quantity produced. The total time in a month spent baking by a household (BT) is defined as the product of the number of persons baking (P), time per session (hours, T), and the usual frequency of baking (every . . . day, F), thus $BT = P \times T \times (30/F)$.

Since virtually all of the rural population bakes, it was possible to run the regressions using ordinary least squares. For the urban sample, a two-step probit-OLS method, similar to the demand estimates, was used.

The results are shown in Appendix 3, Table 53. They support the hypothesis that the availability of female labor was a major determinant of baking at home. An additional female laborer increased bread baking 15 percent in rural households and 23 percent in urban ones. The variable for children indicated that families with a higher proportion of children spent less time baking, particularly in the rural areas. This probably reflects the time required for child care and the smaller demand for bread. Also, as assumed, the presence of a bakery reduced home baking appreciably while temporary shortages increased baking. In rural areas the existence of a bakery in the village reduced baking 52.3 percent, while shortages of bread increased baking 20.7 percent.

The view that home baked bread was considered to be a superior food commodity in rural areas is confirmed by the positive income elasticity of the time spent baking. In the urban areas, however, baking time was negatively correlated with income. The availability of subsidized flour increased home baking significantly in both urban and rural areas. The importance of the availability of female labor to a household and the influence of the availability of subsidized bread and flour makes it clear that the decision to bake is influenced by economic concerns.

Evidence of the Effect of Institutions on Consumer Behavior

The demand equations were estimated from excess demand over ration quantities (basic and extra). It could be expected that the probability of entry would decrease with the availability of rations and the amount purchased in either the open market or the cooperative would decrease one unit for every unit of ration. The entry equations were consistent with such expectations; 7 of the 12 coefficients for RATION in the urban sample were negative and significant at the 5 percent level while none were positive. In the rural sample, the coefficient for ration was negative and significant in five of the six open market entry equations.

A test was made for the hypothesis that the coefficient of the rationed quantity was not different from -1; that is, that consumers' behavior was consistent with the hypothesis that rations were perfect substitutes for nonrationed commodities. The hypothesis had to be rejected. In the response equations, the coefficient for four of the six commodities in urban open markets was different from -1, while the hypothesis was rejected for all of the commodities in cooperatives. Similarly, the hypothesis was accepted only for rice in the rural sample. The coefficient of ration quantity was different from -1 for each of the other commodities. Indeed, for beans and lentils it was apparently significantly greater than 0. Note that this test was performed only for those consumers who purchased in either the open market or the cooperative and excluded those consumers for whom the rations may have been marginal.

Consumers generally perceived meat as a different commodity when it was fresh than when it was frozen. Consequently, there is less reason to expect that a similar test of the substitution of frozen and fresh commodities will give a coefficient of -1. Nevertheless, as the absence of variance in the price of frozen meat precluded a more conventional test for substitution elasticities within a Slutsky matrix, the quantity of frozen meat purchases was included as a regressor in the equations for fresh meat. In the three urban cases the coefficient was significantly less than zero but also different from -1, implying that substitution was moderate but not perfect.

Another way to look at the effect of ration transfers is to look at the differences in marginal propensities by including an interaction term, LTX $\times$ TRANSFER (transfer income). In this case, LTX used all expenditures, including transfer income at its nominal value. It tested whether individuals with transfer incomes increased their food expenditures in a functional relationship with the transfer income (H_o:∂ food expenditure^2/∂NTX∂ TRANSFER $= 0$). The coefficient of LTX $\times$ TRANSFER was positive but insignificant ($\beta = 1.27 \times 10 - 5$, $t = 1.27$). Finally, the model was run with a dummy variable term for individuals without ration cards $\times$ LTX. This model is below.

$$LFX = -7.44 + 2.86 - 0.12LTX2 - 0.02NTX$$
$$\quad\quad\;\; (11.32)\;\;(8.55)\quad\quad\;\;(3.09)$$

$$+\;\; 0.13NUM + 0.02CITYGRT$$
$$(2.66)\quad\quad\;(0.96)$$

$$-\;\; 0.008NORAT \times LTX;$$
$$(1.79) \quad\quad\quad\quad\quad\quad\quad\quad (32)$$

$$R^2 = 0.74;$$

where LFX is the log of the food expenditures of a household.

This model was run with expenditures in piasters; the average expenditure elasticity for an urban family with 5.4 members and spending LE 30 per capita was 0.82. While the expenditure elasticities of individuals with no ration card was different, this difference was small and only marginally significant. With expenditures of LE 30, the difference was only 0.06. It is difficult to say whether the difference was endogenous (having a ration card changed spending behavior) or exogenous (the spending behavior of families without cards was never the same as their neighbors'). In any case, the difference was too small to imply much for policy.

In addition to the primary conclusion that families responded to waiting time as they would have to a two-part tariff, the study points to a secondary conclusion, that consumers treated rationed goods somewhat differently than perfect substitutes and implicit income transfers would imply.

Were consumers able to purchase according to their preferences and time and budget constraints, demand could probably be explained as a function of household characteristics, income, price, and waiting time. If, however, institutional arrangements prevent a consumer from obtaining his or her family's choice of commodities, then the characteristics of the outlets should be significant in explaining what the family purchases. The analysis presents evidence that the characteristics of the outlets are significant. For example, a member in a workplace cooperative in the cities was more likely to purchase sugar, rice, and lentils from a cooperative than other consumers and less likely to purchase sugar, oil, and rice in the open market. The corresponding coefficient for membership in a workplace cooperative was less than zero at the 10 percent level for the open market purchase of lentils. The size of the coefficients was particularly high. For example, the estimated probability that a member of a workplace cooperative would purchase sugar at the cooperative was 0.37 higher than that he or she would purchase it outside. The probability was 0.6 for rice and 0.3 for meat. The pattern was also seen in the equations for the purchase of chicken and fish. This may mean either that there was a greater probability of finding the goods in the workplace cooperative or that the inclinations to spend time in lines while at the workplace differed in ways that were not captured in the other coefficients of the estimates.

It is worth noting that the positive and significant income elasticities for frozen meat and chicken in the response equations indicate that the stated means of distribution by quotas was not binding. Were frozen meat distributed per family per month, the coefficient for income would be 0. There is, however, no evidence that purchases of these commodities, conditional on market entry, followed a pattern different from unconstrained free market behavior.

Bread purchases were influenced by the availability of outlets. For example, in urban areas, the probability of purchasing *balady* bread was positively associated with the availability of *balady* bread, while the families who purchased the bread, even though it was available locally (31 percent of the total purchases), did not have a different purchase pattern from the rest of the sample. When bread was not sold in the neighborhood the probability of purchasing flour was also statistically higher. The opposite pattern was observed with flour availability. For example, 35 percent of the consumers of flour did not find it available in the neighborhood, yet the purchasing pattern of this group, conditional upon entry, was not statistically different.

Such patterns are more pronounced for rural areas. The coefficient of bread availability was highly significant and positive with bread purchases and, as expected, strongly negative with flour purchases. Also, as in the urban sample, the availability of bread had no influence on bread purchases conditional on entry. The availability of flour in a village was negatively associated with the purchase of open market flour, but positively associated with the probability of purchasing *balady* flour. An additional variable, for limits on the size or availability of purchases at the public outlet, had the expected negative sign for the probability of purchasing *balady* and *fino* flours and positive for the profitability of purchasing open market flour. The institutional variables also affected the conditional purchases in rural areas. When there was a flour shop in the village the monthly purchases of *balady* were smaller. The net coefficient of the two equations, however, remains positive. This implies that when there is no flour shop locally, consumers purchase *balady* flour

less often but in larger quantities per visit, and their total purchases are less than if there is a shop. The corresponding coefficients for open market flour were of the opposite sign. Looking at the coefficients for the two flours combined, overall purchases were more frequent if a local shop were available, but, conditional upon entry, the average size of purchase was not affected. Somewhat offsetting this were local limits or shortages that did reduce purchases of *balady* flour, conditional upon entry, and total flour purchases as well. This was observed even after the differences in the prices of flour from the two sources were controlled. From a policy standpoint, this implies that a measurable amount of the growth in flour consumption in recent years can be attributed to the increased availability of government outlets, which reduces the effective prices of flour faced by consumers.

This process is likely approaching saturation and, therefore, the rate of growth in flour consumption will probably slow, although given the parameters from equations (14) and (16), continued income growth, falling real prices, and no other restrictions, this growth will still be positive.

11

RESEARCH CONCLUSIONS AND POLICY IMPLICATIONS

IFPRI took a broad approach to its study of the Egyptian food subsidy system. The need to evaluate the implications of the system for foreign trade and the economy as a whole, the effects of subsidies for agriculture, and the effects of the system on income distribution and nutrition in order to cover the costs and benefits of the policy comprehensively were evident at the outset of the research.[64] Although a rigorous cost-benefit analysis was not attempted, the research focused on the fiscal and economic costs and the distributional and nutritional benefits of the subsidies. The basic conclusions regarding the effects on distribution are summarized below.

The survey revealed that most households (93 percent) had ration cards and that the four rationed commodities—sugar, oil, tea, rice—were obtained regularly (by 95 percent of the households). Households purchase additional quantities of these commodities on the open market. For instance, about 80 percent of the households buy sugar from other sources to supplement the rationed quantities. Thus the ration system mainly transfers income. Analysis shows that income transfers through the ration system have a clearly progressive effect on income distribution, but favor the urban population and the population in the Nile Delta.

Equity

The availability of subsidized bread from licensed bakeries and fixed-price flour—the two most important commodities in the system—differs throughout the country. Bread is usually available in the cities, and flour is available in most rural regions. As quotas are placed on bread or flour purchases only occasionally and as the income elasticities for some types of bread and flour are positive, the income transfers incorporated in these commodities increase as income does. Households in Upper Egypt and in urban areas in general benefit from this part of the system more than other households do. It should be noted, however, that rural households benefit significantly as consumers from depressed grain prices on the open market. These prices are low, in part, because of import subsidies (wheat, maize) and export taxes (rice). Together with the gains of rural households (farm producers) from livestock protection, the overall effect of subsidies and food price policy on distribution helps to equalize incomes and is biased against the urban population.

While subsidies provide a large part of the real income of the poor, this comes mainly through the subsidy on *balady* flour and bread and the ration system. Subsidies on goods sold by cooperatives, including frozen chicken, contribute little to the incomes of the poor. Similarly, subsidies on yellow maize and animal feed seldom reach small farmers and landless producers of meat and dairy products.

Food subsidies contribute to inflation to the extent that they increase the fiscal deficit. Because the prices for those food commodities that the poor spend a large share of their budget on are kept nominally stable through subsidies, a reduction of food subsidies might reduce inflation but it would shift more of the burden of inflation on the poor.

The system of subsidies and consumer prices in total—including both government outlets and open markets—favors the poorer groups of the population more than the upper income groups. But there are components of the system that favor the rich. These include the subsidies of commodities sold by cooperatives, and the subsidies on *fino* flour and *fino* bread. Therefore, the subsidies transferred through government outlets favor the urban population and are slightly regressive.

---

[64] The implications of the system for foreign trade were the subject of Grant M. Scobie, *Food Subsidies in Egypt: Their Impact on Foreign Exchange and Trade,* Research Report 40 (Washington, D.C.: International Food Policy Research Institute, 1983). The effects of the subsidies on agriculture were the subject of von Braun and de Haen, *Effects of Food Price and Subsidy Policies.*

Costs

When the demand for food at a given price exceeds the supply at that price, either the price rises or a local disequilibrium occurs. With many prices fixed in Egypt, goods are distributed at the margin either by fixed rations or through a willingness to wait. Rations entail little allocative inefficiency. In effect, they serve as an income transfer from government revenues to virtually all consumers. However, lines at cooperatives, which indicate shortages of certain commodities, have resource costs that are not captured by any segment of the economy; opportunity costs from waiting are not revenues for anyone. The resource cost of searching and waiting, then, should be subtracted from the transfer of more than LE 100 million to individuals through the cooperative system. The net benefits were probably much smaller than the income transfer. Similarly, a smaller resource cost should be subtracted from the transfer inherent in bread and flour, because shortages of bakeries and flour outlets reduced the average net gain to consumers from the subsidies on those items. As it can be shown that willingness to wait did not increase the proportion of goods going to the poor, such resource costs do not serve as a way of targeting commodities.

There is some concern in Egypt that subsidized food is wasted. A careful assessment of the use of bread and flour for animal consumption shows that about 6 percent of wheat supplies appears to be used as livestock feed. The costs to the economy from that are less than the subsidy because this use of bread and flour has an output effect as well, but the resources that go into processing and distributing those commodities are wasted.

Nutrition

Egyptian households acquire more food than households in most developing countries do, although malnutrition is moderate and child mortality remains high. It appears, then, that policies aimed at increasing purchases of food by households, particularly purchases of foods by children, are not the most effective tools for eliminating existing malnutrition. This is especially true for policies aimed at promoting expensive animal products.

On the other hand, income transfers from the subsidy system are an appreciable portion of the real purchasing power of many families. For example, more than half the families in Upper Egypt received transfers from government-distributed food that made up more than 10 percent of their expenditures. The figure in greater Cairo was nearly 40 percent. As elasticities for calories for the poorest rural and urban quartiles were 0.40 and 0.30, respectively, the loss of this transferred income would have reduced daily calorie consumption by 100-200 kilocalories per capita for these families. In addition, if marginal prices for breads, flours, and grain were changed, consumption, distinct from income effects, would be reduced. Depending on the form of the reduction in subsidy expenditures, then, such policy changes could appreciably affect nutrition.

Modifying the System

As the subsidy system is a complex system that includes several instruments and strives to achieve diverse goals, there is no need to consider all-or-nothing approaches to policy reformulation. It is surely possible to improve economic efficiency with little loss to the welfare of the poor by modifying only some prices or quotas or both. The data in this report, along with the estimated income and price parameters, can be used to do that.

Many of the costs of the system will be reduced equal to the fiscal savings in the overall bill no matter which commodities or marketing system the savings come from. The benefits, however, will vary considerably by goods and outlets. A pragmatic approach to modifying the system that considers such factors will be designed very differently from any approach based on a sweeping view of consumer subsidies as either undifferentiated costs or benefits.

APPENDIX 1: SURVEY DESIGN

A basic guideline for choosing the size of a sample can be derived from statistical theory. Assuming that the population is normal, the necessary sample size, N, can be determined by the following equation:

$$N = [f(Z) \, s/D \, \bar{x}]^2, \qquad (33)$$

where $f(Z)$ is the number of standard deviations that correspond to the confidence level Z, s is the standard deviation of the variable in question, $\bar{x}$ is its mean, and D is the desired precision of the estimation of the population mean. For any value of D, the required N can be calculated to have a probability of Z that the sample mean will be within the desired precision of the true value. This guideline, however, can only be indicative, for a number of reasons.

First, when a survey contains dozens of questions, it becomes unwieldy to manipulate the covariance between items in order to obtain the desired confidence level for the questionnaire. Furthermore, at best, only estimates of s and $\bar{x}$ are available. More often, it is precisely because certain information is unavailable that a survey is undertaken. Hence, frequently even estimates of s and $\bar{x}$ are unavailable. Finally, because of logistics and management constraints, it is reasonable to suppose that sampling error is an increasing function of N. Such a nonlinear relationship goes beyond traditional sampling theory and requires more information than is generally available at the time the survey is designed.

Using data published from the 1974/75 CAPMAS survey of household budgets, it was possible to get an indication of the relative sizes of the urban and rural samples and the relative gain in confidence obtainable from larger samples. Taking expenditure on cereals as an indicator variable, the ratio of the urban and rural samples would need to be 6:10 for equal confidence. Furthermore, if one assumes the 1974 estimates to be the true population parameters, 850 interviews would be sufficient to obtain an estimate of the urban mean that would be within 4 percent of the true value 99.7 percent of the time. An additional 670 families would be necessary to obtain this confidence interval for an estimate of the mean within 3 percent of the "true" value. Expenditures on maize or rice produced similar numbers. By analogous calculations, such a sample size would be within 2.5 percent of the true mean 95 percent of the time. This degree of confidence was considered adequate and would, it was predicted, pick up differences between upper- and lower-income groups in the share of their budgets allocated to cereals the size reported in the CAPMAS study with confidence levels greater than 90 percent. Given the lower costs of obtaining information in urban areas and the difficulty in obtaining price variations in a single cross-sectional survey, it was decided to increase the size of that round to give a greater degree of confidence than could be expected from the larger rural sample.

Once the size was determined, it was necessary to choose the frame. For practical considerations, some clustering was desired, although care was taken to maintain a representative sample. It was possible to obtain a confidence interval for village selection using a formula similar to that presented above and standardizing village means and deviations to account for different sizes. Unfortunately, the means and standard deviations of expenditures for villages are not available in published forms. Accordingly, results from the survey pretest were used as a rough guide to selecting the number of villages while maintaining the confidence interval chosen. In actuality, once clustering was chosen, the assumption of independence for the selection of the first stage was invalidated, although the procedure probably still gave an indication of the relative sizes of the urban and rural frames desired.

Having chosen the number of villages, a catalog of the villages in Egypt was ordered according to village size in subsamples for Upper and Lower Egypt. The first village selected was chosen from a table of random numbers. The rest were taken from the list of villages in equal intervals determined by dividing the total number of villages by the number of villages in the sample. Chi square tests were made to ascertain whether the distribution of the selection was significantly different from national figures for population groupings (four size brackets were used) and for the percentage of villages within each governorate. For each village, between 1 and 4 census tracts—depending on the size of the village—were selected, each containing approximately 250 families. A random selection of families was chosen from the census listings for these tracts so that each village had the same percentage of the sample as it had of the total population of villages selected. These names were used as markers in the field work. In order not to exclude families established since the 1976 census or families in new construction, supervisors were told to choose the house immediately to the right of the main door of the marker family.

The urban selection was based on a random drawing from four subsamples of urban census tracts. The subsamples were for Greater Cairo (44 percent), Alexandria-Port Said (16 percent), other Delta urban areas (26 percent), and Upper Egypt (14 percent). Each subsample was stratified by a variable for the average amount of schooling in 1976, in order to maintain socioeconomic representation. As urban populations were assumed to be more mobile than their rural counterparts, instead of marker families, an enumeration of every fifth household in each of the 50 census tracts was used. A random selection of these names was then chosen for the survey.

Lists of villages and census tracts can be obtained from the authors.

APPENDIX 2:
GLOSSARY OF VARIABLES

AGEHEAD	= the age of the head of the household.
ANI	= livestock feed (cereals) in kilograms per year.
BAK	= a dummy variable that equals 1 if there is a bakery in a village and 0 if there is not.
BF	= the budget share of food.
BREADAV	= the amount of bread available to a household.
BREAD LIMIT	= a dummy variable that equals 1 if there is no bakery or if there are reported shortages of bread and 0 otherwise.
CHL	= proportion of children in a household; the number of children 5 years or younger divided by the number of family members.
CITYGRT	= a dummy variable that equals 1 if a household is in Cairo, Giza, or Alexandria and 0 otherwise.
CITYSMAL	= a dummy variable that equals 1 if a household is in a city with fewer than 100,000 inhabitants and 0 otherwise.
CLASS 1	= a dummy variable that equals 1 if the household is in the lowest expenditure quartile and 0 otherwise.
CLASSTIME	= variable TIME multiplied by variable CLASS 1.
COT	= a dummy variable that is 1 for cotton producers and 0 for other producers.
CTX	= the logarithm of CITYGRT multiplied by LTX.
DELTA	= a dummy variable that is 1 if the household is in the delta and 0 otherwise.
DIS	= the distance to the governorate capital in kilometers. It is 0 for the urban sample.
EARNPERS	= the number of people earning income in a household divided by the number of people in the household.
EMPL	= dummy variable for employment groups, classified by the main occupation of the head of the household. EMPL 1: if self-employed, 1, if not, 0. EMPL 2: if farm worker, 1, if not, 0. EMPL 3: if nonagricultural worker, 1, if not, 0. EMPL 4: if unemployed or outside workforce, 1, if not, 0.
EQEX	= the equity share of a group based on its share of income (calculated as expenditures).
EQPOP	= the equity share of a group, based on its share in the population.

EXN	= expenditures per capita per month in piasters.
EXP	= the expenditures of a group according to survey results, grouped by the main occupation of the heads of household.
FHOUSLAB	= the amount of female adult labor available to a household.
FLAVAIL	= the amount of flour available to a household.
FLOUR LIMIT	= a dummy variable that equals 1 if flour is reported as not always available, and 0 otherwise.
FLSHOP	= a dummy variable that equals 1 if there is a flour shop in a village and 0 if there is not.
H1	= a dummy variable that equals 1 if the census tract is urban and rice consumption in it is high (25 percent of all census tracts) and 0 otherwise.
Home production	= a dummy variable that equals 1 if the product is produced at home and 0 if it is not.
HUM	= human consumption of cereals in a household per year in kilograms.
HUMN	= human consumption of cereals in kilograms per capita per year (using wheat grain equivalents).
IC	= expenditure in a household as actually observed (with subsidies).
$I_{i,k}$	= the input costs of farm household i for input k.
IWS	= per capita expenditure in a household in a hypothetical situation, without food subsidies or price distortions.
L1	= a dummy variable that equals 1 if the census tract is urban and rice consumption in it is low (25 percent of all census tracts) and 0 otherwise.
LAB	= the amount of male labor available in a farm household. Given in number of male adult equivalents; child labor is valued at 0.3 male adult equivalents.
LAN	= farm size in feddan, if the household cultivates land. If not, LAN equals 0.
LANPC	= land per capita in feddan.
LFX	= the log of the food expenditures of a household.
LIQ	= special liquidity requirements of the household during the observation periods (the shares of expenditures for weddings, funerals, and medical treatment, and of debt repayment in total expenditure).
LIV	= livestock on the farm in animal units (aggregated on the basis of starch requirements).
$LP_{dependent}$	= the logarithm of the price of the dependent variable.
LP_{rice}, LP_{tea}, and so forth	= the logarithm of the price of the commodity named.
LTX	= the logarithm of TXN.

LTX2	$= (LTX)^2.$
$LTIME_{dependent}$	= the logarithm of TIME for the dependent variable.
$LTIME_{rice}$	= the logarithm of TIME for the commodity named.
LSEARCH	= the logarithm of SEARCH.
$LWAIT_{bread}$	= the logarithm of WAIT for the commodity in the subscript.
Mills inverse	= 1/Mills ratio.
Mills ratio	= a transformation of the probability of purchasing the commodity; see Chapter 8.
NONPOOR	= a dummy variable that is 1 when the household is in the top three expenditure classes and 0 otherwise.
NORAT	= a dummy variable that is 1 if a household has no ration card and 0 otherwise.
NTX	= the variable NUM multiplied by LTX.
NUM	= the number of household members.
OWN_{cer}	= total grain available from a household's own production in kilograms per year.
OWN_{egg}	= total number of eggs available from a household's own production per month.
PCE	= the open market price of cereals.
P_{cj}	= the price of good j at a cooperative.
PCM	= the ratio of the cereal price to the milk price.
$PDF^s_{1,r}$	= the international farm-gate price of commodity s at location 1 and price r.
$PDC^s_{1,r}$	= the domestic consumer price of commodity s at location 1 and price tier r.
$P_{dependent}$	= the price per kilogram of the dependent variable.
P_{fish}, P_{tea}, and so forth	= the price per kilogram of the commodity named, except where noted otherwise.
PH^j_i	= the highest price observed during the preceding year for basic cereals (j) and household i.
PI^j_i	= the price instability coefficient observed during the preceding year for basic cereals (j) and household i.
PIC^s_1	= the equivalent international consumer price of commodity s at location 1.
PIF^s_1	= the domestic farm producer price of commodity s at location 1.
PL^j_i	= the lowest price observed during the preceding year for basic cereals (j) and household i.

POP $\qquad$ = the population of a group, according to survey results, grouped by the main occupation of the heads of household.

P_{oj} = the open market price of good j in piasters per kilogram.

Pr_{ci} = a dummy variable that is 1 if household i shops at a cooperative and 0 otherwise.

PRD = the production of cereals in kilograms per year (all cereals and cereal products are given in wheat grain equivalents).

P_{rj} = the ration price of good j.

Pr_{oi} = a dummy variable that is 1 if household i buys on the open market and 0 otherwise.

PRQ = the quantity of rice sold to the government (compulsory deliveries).

PSB = the instability of cereal prices. It is the sum of PI_i^j weighted by the shares of the crops in production.

PS_k = the subsidy rate on input k. This is calculated as the difference between the international and domestic prices of the input divided by its domestic price.

PUC = purchases from cooperatives.

PUO = purchases of cereals from the open market (including wage payments received) in kilograms per year of wheat grain equivalent.

PUOPEN = open market purchases of cooperative goods.

PUR = rationed purchases.

PUS = purchases of cereals from subsidized government outlets in kilograms per year of wheat grain equivalent.

PWS = the price of wheat straw (the village mean per bundle).

Q_{cj} = per capita quantity of good j purchased from a cooperative in grams.

$Q_{i,r}^s$ = quantity consumed in a year by household i of commodity s at price tier r.

$Q_{i,v}^s$ = the quantity consumed in a year by household i of commodity s produced by farm households in quantity v.

Q_j = the quantity consumed of good j.

Q_{oj} = the quantity of good j purchased on the open market in grams.

Q_{rj} = the demand for rations of good j in grams.

Q_{Tj} = total demand for good j.

RATION = a dummy variable defined as 1 if the household received the commodity as a ration in the preceding month, and 0 if it did not.

Rice Fdn = feddan of rice cultivation per capita.

RURAL = a dummy variable defined as 1 if the family lives in a village and 0 otherwise.

SAL   = the total sales of cereals on the open market, including wage payments in kind in kilograms.

SEARCH   = the time spent searching for a good at the cooperative, in minutes. This is defined as the reported time needed to reach the cooperative divided by the estimated probability that the good was available in the store.

SED   = seed and losses of cereals in kilograms per year.

SERVANT   = a dummy variable that is 1 if a household uses someone outside the household to purchase food and 0 otherwise.

SEX   = a dummy variable that is 1 if the head of household is female and 0 otherwise.

STR   = changes in cereal stocks during the period of observation in kilograms of wheat grain equivalent.

SUB   = acquisition of subsidized cereals per year in kilograms of wheat grain equivalent per household.

SUBN   = per capita acquisition of subsidized cereals per year in kilograms of wheat grain equivalent.

SUC   = a dummy variable that is 1 for sugar producers and 0 for other producers.

TC   = annual income transfers to or from a household on the consumption side in Egyptian pounds.

TCARD   = the number of ration cards held by a household.

TC_i^g = annual income transfers to or from households (i) through the commodity group or ration (g) in Egyptian pounds per capita.

$TIME_{bread}$, $TIME_{rice}$, and so forth   = for the good named; it is waiting time and time spent going to the cooperative divided by the open market price.

$TIME2_{bread}$, $TIME2_{rice}$, and so forth   = the square of TIME.

TN   = the total net income transfer to or from a household in a year in Egyptian pounds.

TP   = income transfers to or from a household in a year on the production side in Egyptian pounds. For urban households, TP is assumed to be 0.

TRANR   = the income transfer received by a group from government subsidized food. It is the per capita transfer multiplied by the number of people in the group.

TXN   = per capita monthly expenditures. Expenditures include the value of the transfer embodied in ration commodities.

TXP   = total household expenditure per capita per year in Egyptian pounds.

UPPER   = a dummy variable that equals 1 if a household is in Upper Egypt and 0 otherwise.

URBAN   = a dummy variable for the urban sample that equals 1 if a household is in an urban area and 0 otherwise.

URBMIG   = a dummy variable that equals 1 if the household migrated to an urban area and 0 if it did not.

VILSIZE   = the size of a household's village. The number of observations in a village is used as a proxy because the number of cases randomly drawn in each of the sample villages is a constant fraction of village size.

w   = the opportunity cost of time.

WAIT   = the time spent waiting for a good at a cooperative, in minutes.

$WAIT_{bread}$ = the time spent waiting for bread, in minutes.

WORCOP   = the number of workplace cooperatives in which the household is a member.

Y   = income.

YSB   = the instability of a farm's cereal yields as reported by farmers. It equals $\sum_j a_{ij} [(YH_{ij} - YL_{ij})/YL_{ij}]$, where a_{ij} equals the production share of crop j in the total cereal production of farm i, with j running from 1 to 3 (wheat, rice, and maize); YH is the highest yield during the preceding 5 years; and YL is the lowest yield during that time.

Z   = a group of regional and demographic variables, including the number of family members, the proportion of children in the family, and the degree of urbanization.

APPENDIX 3:
SUPPLEMENTARY TABLES

Table 43—Cropping pattern according to survey and comparison to national figures

Crop	Survey		National Data	
	(feddan)	(percent of seasonal area)	(1,000 feddan)	(percent of seasonal area)
Winter crops	1,641	100.0	5,063	100.0
Wheat	466	28.4	1,400	27.7
Pulses	99	6.0	250	4.9
Barley	28	1.7	91	1.8
Berseem[a]	904	55.1	2,777	54.8
Other winter crops	144	8.8	545	10.8
Summer crops[b]	1,628	100.0	5,215	100.0
Cotton	473	29.1	1,178	22.6
Rice	469	28.8	956	18.3
Maize	409	25.1	1,907	36.6
Sorghum	110	6.8	412	7.9
Other summer crops	167	10.3	762	14.6
Permanent crops	75	100.0	593	100.0
Sugarcane	39	52.0	251	42.3
Horticulture	36	48.0	342	57.7
Area not used	83	4.6[c]	. . .[d]	. . .[d]
Total area	1,799	. . .	. . .	. . .

Sources: The survey data are from the household survey made by the International Food Policy Research Institute and the Institute of National Planning, Cairo, 1981/82. The national data are from U.S. Department of Agriculture, Office of the Agricultural Attaché, Cairo, *Annual Agricultural Situation Report* (Cairo: U.S. Embassy, Office of the Agricultural Attaché, 1983); and data received from the Egyptian Ministry of Agriculture in 1982.

Notes: The figures from the survey are the sums of the area reported for 1980/81 seasons. The national data are for 1980/81.

[a] This includes both long and short season berseem.

[b] This includes the Nile season.

[c] This is the percentage of total area.

[d] No comparable data were available.

Table 44—Results from bread and flour entry equations for urban areas

Independent Variable	Bread		Flour	
	Balady	Fino	Balady	Fino
Constant	−1.123	−0.702	0.556	−0.970
TXN	−0.0036 (2.89)	0.0021 (1.90)	−0.0033 (1.90)	0.0019 (1.71)
NUM	−0.0008 (0.03)	0.069 (3.35)	...	...
FLAVAIL	−0.154 (1.42)	−0.166 (1.90)	0.313 (2.83)	0.272 (3.10)
BREADAV	0.368 (3.32)	0.052 (0.52)	−0.277 (2.42)	0.086 (0.86)
CITYGRT	0.543 (4.48)	0.305 (2.67)	−0.225 (1.88)	0.341 (3.07)
FHOUSLAB	−0.143 (2.14)	−0.155 (2.75)	0.168 (2.90)	−0.013 (0.26)
$WAIT_{bread}$	−0.0042 (3.10)	0.0019 (1.48)	−0.0009 (0.65)	0.0002 (0.17)
$WAIT2_{bread}$	−0.0023 (0.92)	−0.0086 (2.91)	0.0086 (3.69)	−0.0077 (3.29)
$TIME_{rice}$	0.0012 (1.12)	−0.0004 (0.68)	0.0005 (0.52)	0.0006 (0.69)
$TIME2_{rice}$	0.0010 (0.56)	−0.0015 (1.65)	...	...
P_{rice}	−0.0065 (0.52)	0.0013 (1.29)	−0.0070 (0.55)	0.0033 (0.31)
P_{balady}	0.277 (4.45)	0.0042 (0.08)	−0.455 (7.26)	0.115 (2.15)
P_{fino}	...	...	0.111 (1.94)	−0.034 (0.72)
P_{maize}	...	...	0.0054 (2.43)	0.0005 (0.24)
Mean	0.790	0.444	0.209	0.510

Source: Data from the household survey made by the International Food Policy Research Institute and the Institute of National Planning, Cairo, 1981/82.

Note: The independent variables are defined in Appendix 2.

Table 45—Results from bread and flour response equations for urban areas

Independent Variable	Bread		Flour	
	Balady	Fino	Balady	Fino
Constant	2.57	−1.76	−86.6	−2.34
LTX	0.205 (2.09)	0.337 (4.43)	5.85 (1.47)	3.10 (2.20)
LTX2	...	...	−0.803 (1.33)	−0.243 (1.50)
NTX	−0.022 (3.56)	−0.024 (4.56)	...	−0.169 (2.27)
CTX	−0.471 (6.31)	−0.203 (2.82)	...	−0.346 (2.28)
NUM	...	...	0.177 (0.85)	0.552 (2.14)
FLAVAIL	0.037 (0.38)	0.043 (0.49)	−0.237 (0.20)	0.321 (1.02)
BREADAV	0.112 (0.89)	−0.284 (3.07)	...	...
CITYGRT	...	...	−5.89 (5.15)	−2.38 (4.61)
FHOUSLAB	...	...	0.58 (0.87)	0.211 (1.59)
$LWAIT_{bread}$	0.165 (3.13)	0.167 (4.03)	0.185 (0.39)	0.046 (0.45)
$LWAIT_{bread} \times$ CLASS 1	−0.012 (0.25)	...	...	...
WORCOP	−0.378 (4.03)	−0.112 (1.43)	1.17[a] (0.74)	...
$LTIME_{rice}$	0.030 (0.66)	0.010 (0.22)	...	...
LP_{rice}	−0.179 (0.69)	0.158 (0.62)	...	...
LP_{balady}	−0.094 (0.16)	−1.02 (3.00)	11.16 (1.98)	0.743 (0.55)
LP_{noodle}	...	−0.111 (1.01)	13.63[b] (2.07)	0.481 (0.49)
LP_{wheat}	...	1.06 (2.53)	5.17 (1.02)	−1.01[c] (0.07)
Mills inverse	0.183 (0.223)	−0.577 (0.88)	6.68 (1.01)	−3.72 (1.22)
R^2	0.12	0.22	0.23	0.20
Number of observations	774	435	205	500
Mean	2.73	1.47	8.42	1.94

Source: Data from the household survey made by the International Food Policy Research Institute and the Institute of National Planning, Cairo, 1981/82.

Notes: The independent variables are defined in Appendix 2.

The R^2s are t-statistics from weighted regressions and R^2s from unweighted regressions, as the weighting procedure results in wide swings in the reported R^2 with little actual change in the equation.

[a] This is for UPPER.

[b] This is for LP_{fino}.

[c] This is for LP_{maize}.

Table 46—Results from cooperative entry equations for urban areas

Independent Variable	Sugar	Oil	Tea	Rice	Beans	Lentils	Frozen Meat	Frozen Chicken	Frozen Fish
Constant	0.497	−0.606	−0.883	0.366	−1.775	−1.497	−2.47	−0.345	0.881
TXN	0.0022 (1.63)	0.0027 (2.07)	0.009 (0.53)	−0.0005 (0.38)	0.0006 (0.39)	−0.0003 (0.25)	−0.0087 (3.55)	0.0006 (0.46)	−0.0050 (2.58)
NUM	0.0206 (1.08)	0.0405 (2.02)	0.0372 (1.38)	0.0129 (0.61)	0.0065 (0.21)	0.0464 (2.21)	−0.0152 (0.65)	0.0258 (1.25)	0.0546 (2.71)
CITYGRT	−0.004 (0.03)	0.359 (3.60)	−0.101 (0.73)	−0.2658 (1.58)	−0.193 (1.03)	0.165 (1.50)	0.959 (7.13)	0.389 (3.45)	0.322 (3.10)
DELTA	...	...	...	−0.299 (1.62)	...	...	...	...	...
WORCOP	0.368 (4.06)	0.027 (0.29)	0.250 (1.94)	0.596 (6.19)	0.227 (1.73)	0.365 (3.84)	0.301 (2.91)	0.123 (1.31)	0.065 (0.70)
RATION	0.011 (0.06)	−0.326 (2.04)	−0.461 (2.19)	−0.268 (1.69)	−0.009 (0.06)	−0.163 (1.03)	...	...	...
WAIT	−0.0091 (7.71)	−0.0078 (5.44)	...	−0.0063 (6.67)	...	...	−0.0058 (4.50)	−0.0141 (9.84)	−0.0094 (5.85)
WAIT × CLASS 1	−0.0002 (0.12)	−0.0010 (0.56)	...	−0.0023 (1.85)	...	0.0020 (1.46)	−0.0051 (1.78)	−0.0001 (0.03)	...
WAIT × SERVANT	−0.0009 (0.41)	0.0021 (0.89)	...	0.0034 (2.30)	...	...	−0.0070 (2.52)	−0.0067 (1.88)	−0.0079 (2.54)
SEARCH	−0.0060 (2.50)	−0.0014 (1.04)	−0.0153 (3.84)	−0.0028 (2.50)	−0.0279 (4.99)	−0.0048 (1.95)	−0.0042 (2.81)	−0.0074 (2.65)	−0.0067 (3.22)
SEARCH × CLASS 1	...	...	−0.0127 (1.71)	...	−0.0019 (0.23)	−0.0140 (2.56)	...	...	...
WAIT	...	...	...	−0.0005 (0.40)	...	...	...	...	...
P_{sugar}	−0.0011 (0.14)	...	...	...	...	...	...	...	...
P_{tea}	...	...	0.0002 (0.23)	...	...	...	...	...	...
P_{rice}	...	...	...	−0.0087 (0.77)	...	...	...	...	...
P_{fish}	...	...	...	...	...	...	...	...	−0.0030 (2.24)
$P_{chicken}$	...	...	...	...	...	...	...	0.0021 (0.97)	−0.0036 (1.51)
P_{meat}	...	...	...	...	...	...	0.0092 (4.24)	...	...
P_{oil}	...	0.0046 (1.13)	...	...	...	...	...	...	...
P_{beans}	...	...	...	...	0.0266 (1.60)	...	...	...	...
$P_{lentils}$	...	...	...	...	...	0.0062 (1.42)	...	...	...
Mean	0.554	0.288	0.82	0.265	0.075	0.202	0.239	0.315	0.330

Source: Data from the household survey made by the International Food Policy Research Institute and the Institute of National Planning, Cairo, 1981/82.

Note: The independent variables are defined in Appendix 2.

Table 47—Results from cooperative response equations for urban areas

Independent Variable	Sugar	Oil	Tea	Rice	Beans	Lentils	Frozen Meat	Frozen Chicken	Frozen Fish
Constant	2,609	353	−60	−2,450	2,200	157	3,853.54	−976	−68.25
LTX	−639.85	167.99	15.43	500.87	123.41	193.45	391.55	846.18	1,051.89
	(1.23)	(6.23)	(2.22)	(8.08)	(3.29)	(4.56)	(2.78)	(5.28)	(2.01)
LTX2	167.16	...	...	...	...	...	...	...	−106.70
	(2.62)								(1.64)
NTX	−43.88	−15.55	−2.13	−11.77	−11.83	9.05	−36.88	−69.25	−40.80
	(2.41)	(8.01)	(3.46)	(2.47)	(3.97)	(3.80)	(1.68)	(2.55)	(1.81)
CTX	−90.38	−18.05	...	...	−67.70	−69.17	...	−206.57	...
	(1.82)	(0.53)			(1.62)	(2.15)		(2.74)	
NUM	81.82	...	...	...	...	...	76.42	172.41	97.21
	(1.34)						(1.04)	(1.95)	(1.24)
CITYGRT	...	...	17.04	...	38.72	...	...	...	...
			(1.18)		(0.46)				
WORCOP	20.21	−101.18	−0.99	−602.0	...	...	50.23	−122.98	96.96
	(0.28)	(2.94)	(0.10)	(4.67)			(0.80)	(1.34)	(1.86)
LSEARCH	−36.06	−33.15	4.50	...	−81.22	−33.96	−15.23	−34.39	−52.22
	(0.96)	(1.53)	(0.49)		(1.87)	(1.30)	(0.56)	(0.49)	(1.38)
LWAIT	−42.52	−8.76	...	135.06	...	...	41.32	−47.46	−31.58
	(0.74)	(0.47)		(2.05)			(1.04)	(0.46)	(0.53)
PUR	−0.254	−0.113	−0.073	0.08	−0.049	−1.56	...	...	...
	(3.97)	(1.30)	(0.67)	(0.97)	(0.29)	(0.47)			
PUOPEN	−0.141	...	...	...	...	...			
	(1.87)								
$LWAIT_{bread}$	...	...	...	142.26	21.31	...	...	...	...
				(3.00)	(0.90)				
$LTIME_{rice}$	...	0.065	...	...	−81.23	...	...	−45.18	...
		(0.01)			(1.87)			(1.46)	
LP_{rice}	...	...	...	...	...	−61.99	−225.95	...	423.16
						(1.00)	(1.22)		(2.11)
LP_{sugar}	...	...	24.81	...	...	...	...	...	...
			(0.54)						
LP_{balady}	...	191.58	...	−618.06	−171.47	191.14	555.15	...	...
		(1.47)		(2.02)	(0.66)	(1.20)	(2.36)		
LP_{meat}	...	...	...	...	...	...	−942.35	...	...
							(1.93)		
LP_{noodle}	...	...	...	190.80	...	...	...	...	...
				(1.58)					
$LP_{chicken}$	...	...	...	...	...	...	−42.74	79.06	−35.24
							(0.12)	(0.18)	(0.11)
LP_{fish}	...	...	...	...	...	...	...	−63.5	−161.56
								(0.51)	(1.44)
SEX	...	...	−21.21	...	...	...	...	...	...
			(1.58)						
Mills inverse	−378.6	−0.75	10.71	2,388.01	1,040	−392.2	606.50	−138.43	−829.43
	(0.67)	(1.19)	(10.52)	(2.94)	(1.54)	(0.94)	(1.63)	(0.17)	(1.72)
R^2	0.32	0.34	0.28	0.37	0.56	0.37	0.28	0.25	0.37
Number of observations	543	282	80	260	74	198	234	309	323
Mean	1,011	537	47	1,261	521	438	752	1,085	811

Source: Data from the household survey made by the International Food Policy Research Institute and the Institute of National Planning, Cairo, 1981/82.

Notes: The independent variables are defined in Appendix 2.

The R^2s are t-statistics from weighted regressions and R^2 from unweighted regressions, as the weighting procedure results in wide swings in the reported R^2 with little actual change in the equation.

Table 48—Results from open market entry equations for urban areas

Independent Variable	Sugar	Oil	Tea	Rice	Beans	Lentils	Fresh Meat	Fresh Chicken	Fresh Fish
Constant	−0.690	−0.813	0.659	−0.811	−0.895	−1.75	2.65	−0.143	0.302
TXN	0.0011 (0.90)	0.0012 (0.99)	0.0024 (1.69)	0.0006 (0.49)	0.0023 (1.87)	0.0033 (2.61)	0.0135 (3.98)	0.0012 (0.98)	0.0021 (1.82)
NUM	0.0437 (2.02)	0.0481 (2.25)	0.0178 (0.93)	0.0034 (0.17)	0.0516 (2.50)	0.0774 (3.46)	0.0670 (2.62)	0.0651 (3.35)	0.0500 (2.61)
CITYGRT	−0.093 (0.70)	−0.402 (3.76)	−0.031 (0.35)	−0.1459 (1.13)	−0.773 (6.59)	−0.598 (4.91)	−0.416 (3.63)	−0.015 (0.16)	0.236 (2.52)
DELTA	...	...	...	0.3567 (2.28)	...	...	...	...	...
WORCOP	−0.488 (4.19)	−0.253 (2.31)	−0.0363 (0.41)	−0.270 (2.77)	0.183 (1.78)	−0.214 (1.78)	−0.318 (2.82)	−0.066 (0.75)	0.173 (1.94)
RATION	−0.091 (5.11)	−0.807 (5.02)	−0.466 (2.62)	−0.589 (3.90)	0.0057 (0.05)	0.0717 (0.43)	...	...	...
WAIT	0.0103 (8.43)	0.0045 (3.52)	...	0.0026 (3.27)	...	...	0.0023 (1.47)	0.0093 (5.37)	0.0003 (0.24)
WAIT × CLASS 1	−0.0023 (1.57)	−0.0042 (2.53)	...	−0.0010 (1.12)	...	...	−0.0038 (1.57)	0.0009 (0.31)	0.0051 (2.03)
WAIT × SERVANT	0.0063 (1.76)	0.0006 (0.25)	...	0.0004 (0.30)	...	...	−0.0006 (0.25)	−0.0060 (2.44)	−0.0022 (1.08)
SEARCH	0.0063 (2.45)	0.0005 (0.46)	0.0026 (1.62)	−0.0000 (0.05)	−0.0019 (1.32)	0.0008 (0.39)	0.0005 (0.43)	0.0013 (0.88)	0.0013 (1.36)
SEARCH × CLASS 1	...	...	−0.0063 (2.85)	...	−0.0025 (1.26)	−0.0016 (0.55)	...	...	...
$WAIT_{bread}$	...	...	...	−0.0005 (0.41)	...	...	...	...	...
P_{rice}	...	...	...	0.0327 (3.27)	...	...	...	...	...
P_{tea}	...	...	−0.0001 (0.01)	...	...	...	...	...	...
P_{sugar}	0.0005 (0.06)	...	...	...	...	...	...	...	...
P_{fish}	...	...	...	...	...	...	...	...	−0.0006 (0.53)
$P_{fish} \times$ CLASS 1	...	...	...	...	...	...	...	...	−0.0092 (5.96)
$P_{chicken}$	...	...	...	...	...	...	...	−0.0025 (1.23)	...
$P_{chicken} \times$ CLASS 1	...	...	...	...	...	...	...	−0.0038 (2.64)	...
P_{meat}	...	...	...	...	...	...	−0.0083 (3.29)	...	...
$P_{meat} \times$ CLASS 1	...	...	...	...	...	...	−0.0011 (1.37)	...	...
P_{oil}	...	0.0097 (2.31)	...	...	...	...	...	...	...
P_{beans}	...	...	...	...	0.0081 (0.09)	...	...	...	...
$P_{lentils}$	...	...	...	...	...	0.0055 (1.32)	...	...	...
Mean	0.265	0.186	0.648	0.309	0.178	0.116	0.843	0.597	0.533

Source: Data from the household survey made by the International Food Policy Research Institute and the Institute of National Planning, Cairo, 1981/82.

Note: The independent variables are defined in Appendix 2.

Table 49—Results from open market response equations for urban areas

Independent Variable	Sugar	Oil	Tea	Rice	Beans	Lentils	Fresh Meat	Fresh Chicken	Fresh Fish
Constant	−4,431	840	−102.85	−11,786	3,721	1,826	2,393	3,709	−3,031
LTX	1,371.96 (2.42)	193.93 (6.48)	61.41 (4.84)	4,391.54 (3.68)	206.65 (1.51)	127.94 (3.57)	1,115.44 (11.94)	1,224.54 (8.89)	378.23 (6.33)
LTX2	−107.27 (1.58)	...	...	−509.69 (3.28)	...	...	...	...	...
NTX	−58.97 (3.33)	−10.72 (4.56)	−6.69 (3.66)	...	−25.78 (3.40)	−6.82 (1.90)	−63.20 (4.38)	−123.06 (5.32)	−11.14 (3.12)
CTX	−150.47 (2.31)	−73.94 (1.89)	−16.41 (3.40)	−421.12 (3.02)	−120.49 (0.81)	...	−84.92 (1.86)	−47.20 (0.85)	−139.52 (2.83)
NUM	124.34 (2.07)	...	18.08 (2.86)	−83.68 (2.97)	...	...	176.83 (3.94)	386.11 (4.93)	...
CITYGRT	...	...	11.54 (1.48)	...	−522.31 (1.47)	−256.54 (2.64)	...	...	...
$LP_{dependent}$	166.93 (0.85)	−100.27 (1.21)	−23.90 (1.49)	−649.15 (1.90)	−8.71 (0.35)	−48.35 (0.61)	−553.21 (1.67)	−577.75 (2.95)	−214.67 (2.68)
$LP_{dependent} \times$ CLASS 1	16.2 (0.44)	...	...	226.97 (2.46)	...	...	−19.63 (2.10)	−33.09 (1.48)	−3.94 (0.30)
$DELTA \times LP_{rice}$	...	...	...	381.09 (4.25)	...	...	...	...	...
$LTIME_{dependent}$	...	...	...	...	...	...	...	135.01 (2.02)	48.38 (1.57)
PUR	−0.359 (4.96)	−0.070 (0.63)	0.188 (1.56)	−0.073 (1.02)	−0.178 (0.24)	−0.115 (0.31)	...	...	...
PUC	−0.054 (1.17)	...	...	...	...	...	−0.3823 (7.75)	−0.130 (2.67)	−0.0633 (0.91)
LP_{rice}	−155.0 (1.32)	−118.21 (1.82)	...	...	−775.16 (3.03)	−201.28 (2.26)	−27.43 (0.22)	223.51 (2.05)	...
LP_{sugar}	...	...	2.37 (0.112)	...	...	...	...	...	...
LP_{balady}	535.65 (1.94)	...	...	339.10 (0.55)	...	316.91 (1.36)	−85.60 (0.53)	−99.81 (0.43)	−770.74 (3.36)
LP_{meat}	286.89 (0.65)	−122.17[a] (0.81)	...	...	...	...	...	−727.08 (1.97)	686.71 (2.02)
LP_{noodle}	...	86.34[b] (0.64)	...	658.07 (1.89)	−305.69[c] (1.06)	−312.88[d] (1.90)	222.34[a] (0.96)	...	380.95 (1.58)
LP_{fish}	...	...	...	...	...	...	429.60 (7.74)	41.82 (0.45)	...
$LWAIT_{bread}$	...	...	...	...	118.34 (1.56)	...	...	66.15 (2.26)	33.77 (1.40)
$LTIME_{rice}$	...	...	...	...	...	...	13.55 (0.55)	25.28 (1.23)	...
Mills inverse	−71.29 (0.29)	5.19 (0.69)	118.97 (1.43)	4,311.02 (3.71)	356.81 (0.16)	−453.97 (0.61)	221.57 (0.70)	−776.07 (1.31)	−278.97 (0.75)
R^2	0.43	0.33	0.21	0.26	0.23	0.32	0.35	0.32	0.23
Number of observations	260	182	623	303	174	113	826	585	522
Mean	1,035	507	82	2,435	1,017	377	1,349	1,285	976

Source: Data from the household survey made by the International Food Policy Research Institute and the Institute of National Planning, Cairo, 1981/82.

Notes: The independent variables are defined in Appendix 2.

The R^2s are t-statistics from weighted regressions and R^2 from unweighted regressions, as the weighting procedure results in wide swings in the reported R^2 with little actual change in the equation.

[a] This is for $LP_{chicken}$. [b] This is for LP_{ghee}. [c] This is for LP_{lentil}. [d] This is for LP_{bean}.

Table 50—Results from other entry equations for urban areas

Independent Variable	Pasta	Eggs	Milk	Cheese
Constant	0.835	0.158	0.796	0.365
TXN	0.0043 (1.43)	0.0149 (6.79)	0.0078 (3.82)	0.0070 (3.55)
NUM	0.203 (5.82)	0.066 (2.99)	0.0075 (0.35)	0.0032 (0.16)
CITYGRT	0.313 (2.28)	−0.026 (0.23)	0.757 (6.78)	0.548 (5.37)
SEX	−0.067 (0.39)	−0.095 (0.71)	−0.075 (0.54)	−0.172 (1.38)
$TIME_{bread}$	−0.121 (0.78)	...	0.0003 (0.20)	−0.0003 (0.22)
$P_{dependent}$	−0.0047 (0.56)	0.0037 (0.14)	−0.016 (3.35)	0.0002 (0.18)
$P_{dependent} \times CLASS\ 1$	−0.042 (4.42)	...	...	−0.0051 (5.67)
$TIME_{rice}$	−0.0018 (4.95)	...	...	−0.0009 (2.02)
P_{cheese}	...	...	0.0004 (0.31)	...
OWN_{egg}	...	1.43 (12.67)	...	...
CHL	...	...	0.565 (1.76)	...
Mean	0.926	0.738	0.820	0.671

Source: Data from the household survey made by the International Food Policy Research Institute and the Institute of National Planning, Cairo, 1981/82.

Notes: The independent variables are defined in Appendix 2.

Table 51—Results from other response equations for urban areas

Independent Variable	Pasta	Eggs	Milk	Cheese
Constant	−1,082.2	−55.85	−7,495.2	−3,571.4
LTX	1,833.3 (3.58)	22.41 (9.24)	7,447.2 (5.32)	375.6 (1.29)
LTX2	−148.08 (2.57)	−1.75 (2.98)	−676.5 (4.24)	−61.83 (1.64)
NTX	−82.10 (3.59)	−0.908 (3.40)	−198.9 (3.16)	−7.72 (2.30)
CTX	51.11 (1.01)	...	216.0 (1.54)	108.54 (1.86)
NUM	216.85 (2.65)	2.37 (2.49)	47.64 (2.16)	...
$L P_{dependent}$	−444.06 (5.15)	−3.09 (1.80)	−917.7 (4.28)	51.70 (0.74)
$L P_{dependent} \times$ CLASS 1	−107.78 (1.27)	...	142.7 (1.54)	...
$L TIME_{rice}$	−56.73 (2.17)	...	...	...
$L TIME_{rice} \times$ CLASS 1	55.76 (1.12)	2.10 (2.14)	−381.2 (1.64)	...
OWN_{egg}	...	0.216 (1.82)	...	...
$L P_{rice}$	...	−2.52 (1.62)	−188.0 (1.33)	−205.0 (1.92)
$L TIME_{bread}$	29.94 (1.12)	−0.358 (1.04)	−122.9 (1.54)	−21.83 (0.92)
WORCOP	94.68 (1.61)	...	...	...
CITYGRT	...	−1.43 (1.55)	58.53 (0.28)	−515.89 (3.49)
Mills ratio	−320.53 (0.46)	12.82 (2.84)	...	3,283.6 (3.15)
R^2	0.15	0.27	0.21	0.12
Number of observations	908	723	804	658
Mean	1,227	10	3,031	529

Source: Data from the household survey made by the International Food Policy Research Institute and the Institute of National Planning, Cairo, 1981/82.

Notes: The independent variables are defined in Appendix 2.

The R^2s are t-statistics from weighted regressions and R^2 from unweighted regressions, as the weighting procedure results in wide swings in the reported R^2 with little actual change in the equation.

Table 52—Results from budget share equations for urban areas

Independent Variable	Cooked Beans	Tamiya	Fruit	Vegetables
Constant	0.224	0.056	−0.577	0.973
LTX	−0.046	−0.0058	0.144	0.072
	(4.91)	(6.17)	(5.83)	(2.34)
LTX2	0.0024	. . .	−0.0083	−0.0057 .
	(4.54)		(5.48)	(3.08)
NTX	−0.0006	0.0002	−0.0000	−0.0003
	(2.48)	(1.07)	(0.13)	(3.53)
CTX	−0.0001	−0.0000	0.0018	−0.0256
	(0.28)	(0.08)	(1.92)	(1.88)
SEX	−0.0013	−0.0020	−0.0033	−0.0046
	(1.18)	(2.46)	(0.95)	(1.01)
WORCOP	−0.0025	−0.0008	0.0025	0.0045
	(3.24)	(1.39)	(1.04)	(1.65)
CITYGRT	0.0015	0.0016	0.0005	0.0073
	(2.02)	(2.69)	(0.20)	(2.64)
FHOUSLAB	0.0002	0.0012	. . .	. . .
	(0.38)	(2.97)		
CHL	. . .	. . .	. . .	0.198
				(1.81)
R^2	0.25	0.14	0.06	0.14
Number of observations	980	980	980	980
Mean	0.011	0.007	0.042	0.072

Source: Data from the household survey made by the International Food Policy Research Institute and the Institute of National Planning, Cairo, 1981/82.

Notes: The independent variables are defined in Appendix 2.

The R^2s are t-statistics from weighted regressions and R^2 from unweighted regressions, as the weighting procedure results in wide swings in the reported R^2 with little actual change in the equation.

Table 53—Estimations of hours spent baking

Independent Variable	Probability of Baking	Hours Spent Baking if a Household Baked	
		Urban Areas	Rural Areas
Constant	0.352 (0.87)	42.39 (1.17)	26.9
BREADAV	−0.385 (3.39)	−5.02 (1.53)	−23.49 (8.27)
BREAD SHORT	. . .	. . .	9.31 (2.16)
CITYGRT	−1.36 (12.96)	−6.20 (0.74)	. . .
URBMIG	0.728 (1.30)	19.62 (2.47)	. . .
LTX	−0.240 (2.76)	−0.839 (0.40)	0.0015[a] (2.39)
NUM	0.067 (2.45)	−0.76 (1.50)	3.29 (5.70)
CHL	−0.042 (0.71)	−1.05 (1.19)	−33.07 (3.83)
FHOUSLAB	0.127 (1.92)	2.675 (2.20)	6.86 (5.97)
FLAVAIL	0.235 (2.17)	−2.41 (1.59)	4.24 (1.56)
$WAIT_{bread}$	0.002 (1.76)	−0.023 (1.45)	. . .
Mills ratio	. . .	−21.74 (0.81)	. . .
R^2	. . .	0.12	0.22
Number of observations	980	252	134.5

Source: Data from the household survey made by the International Food Policy Research Institute and the Institute of National Planning, Cairo, 1981/82.

Notes: The independent variables are defined in Appendix 2.

The R^2s are t-statistics from weighted regressions and R^2 from unweighted regressions, as the weighting procedure results in wide swings in the reported R^2 with little actual change in the equation.

[a] This is total expenditures in piasters.

Table 54—Results from bread and flour entry equations for rural areas

Independent Variable	Bread		Flour		Open Market Flour	Combined Open Market and Balady Flour
	Balady	Shami	Balady	Fino		
Constant	−0.538	−1.973	0.993	−1.061	−1.819	1.039
TXN	−0.0036 (1.30)	0.0064 (2.80)	−0.0008 (2.80)	0.0053 (0.28)	0.0023 (1.14)	−0.0008 (0.45)
NUM	0.0000 (0.0)	0.0006 (0.03)	0.0363 (2.94)	0.0136 (0.90)	0.0350 (3.14)	0.0476 (4.26)
UPPER	0.407 (3.36)	−0.815 (4.03)	0.653 (6.13)	−0.244 (2.30)	−0.230 (2.25)	0.167 (1.75)
FLAVAIL	−0.070 (0.67)	0.152 (1.08)	0.896 (8.58)	0.110 (0.95)	−0.323 (3.98)	0.234 (2.73)
FLOUR LIMIT	...	...	−1.269 (13.99)	−0.991 (9.88)	1.327 (12.48)	−0.292 (3.38)
BREADAV	1.74 (17.97)	1.24 (8.79)	−0.342 (3.52)	0.225 (2.14)	−0.137 (1.52)	−0.433 (5.17)
LANPC	−0.550 (0.62)	−0.135 (1.60)	−0.263 (1.86)	−0.399 (2.77)	−0.425 ...	−1.23 (3.16)
P_{fino}	...	0.0075 (1.69)	...	0.0046 (1.31)	...	−0.0211 (0.74)
P_{balady}	0.002 (0.67)	0.011 (3.65)	0.0013 (0.19)	0.0011 (0.15)	0.0035 (0.61)	0.0440 (1.81)
$P_{balady} \times$ CLASS 1	...	...	0.0027 (1.78)	...	−0.0033 (2.34)	−0.0005 (0.01)
$P_{open\ market\ flour}$	...	...	−0.0725 (2.62)	...	−0.011 (0.51)	...
P_{wheat}	0.0001 (0.73)	−0.0001 (0.56)	0.0000 (0.17)	−0.0004 (2.20)	0.0001 (0.83)	0.0001 (1.26)
P_{rice}	−0.0053 (0.50)	0.0076 (0.50)	−0.0020 (2.26)	...	0.0058 (0.67)	−0.0286 (3.50)
P_{maize}	0.0003 (2.20)	−0.0003 (1.39)	−0.0059 (3.91)	0.0003 (2.21)	0.0001 (0.07)	−0.0006 (4.75)
$P_{maize} \times$ CLASS 1	−0.0001 (1.32)	−0.0002 (1.39)	...	...	...	...
Mean	0.183	0.058	0.346	0.127	0.365	0.671

Source: Data from the household survey made by the International Food Policy Research Institute and the Institute of National Planning, Cairo, 1981/82.

Note: The independent variables are defined in Appendix 2.

Table 55—Results from bread and flour response equations for rural areas

Independent Variable	Bread		Flour		Open Market Flour	Combined Open Market and Balady Flour
	Balady	Fino	Balady	Fino		
Constant	−20.89	−1.90	−73,798	−42,802	−39,592	−46,521
LTX	0.426 (2.35)	0.249 (0.800)	5,125.8 (8.41)	9,547.5 (4.34)	2,850.2 (4.35)	7,767.9 (7.76)
NTX	−0.029 (4.42)	−0.058 (3.18)	−195.2 (6.53)	−857.2 (3.11)	−317.8 (6.10)	−524.7 (4.59)
CTX	−0.501 (2.55)	...	−575.1 (0.74)	...	...	−1,148.4 (1.88)
NUM	...	...	...	1,847.0 (2.34)	−111.4 (1.19)	925.86 (2.66)
UPPER	0.628 (2.12)	...	−2,849.4 (2.04)	3,600.8 (2.93)	...	...
FLAVAIL	0.099 (0.49)	...	−2,513.0 (1.46)	2,905.3 (1.59)	1,035.2 (4.15)	210.5 (0.30)
FLOUR LIMIT	...	...	−2,155.3 (3.26)	−3,190.9 (2.87)	28.09 (0.29)	948.6 (1.20)
LANPC	−0.049 (0.09)	0.875 (1.05)	247.6 (0.15)	3,315.9 (0.95)	7,698.5 (3.84)	389.7 (0.29)
$LP_{open\ market\ flour}$	...	...	−10,144.0 (4.42)	...	−14,636.1 (8.83)	−5,945.5 (3.48)
$LP_{flour} \times$ CLASS 1	...	...	...	...	...	−103.45 (0.26)
LP_{fino}	...	...	860.3 (0.31)	3,205.0 (0.78)	−3,144.8 (1.46)	−2,398.1 (1.26)
LP_{balady}	−0.837 (1.82)	−0.572 (0.85)	−3,545.2 (1.09)	−5,181.9 (1.42)	−5,223.6 (1.46)	...
LP_{wheat}	−1.45 (1.93)	...	4,026.0 (1.96)	−3,654.8 (1.13)	−3,230.7 (1.30)	4,739.9 (2.42)
LP_{maize}	2.092 (3.37)	0.606 (0.78)	6,252.7 (3.35)	5,139.8 (1.81)	3,339.9 (1.84)	1,284.6 (1.30)
LP_{rice}	−0.104 (0.23)	−0.40 (0.70)	...	48.61 (0.03)	2,946.9 (1.68)	524.9 (0.35)
LP_{meat}	2.79 (1.79)	...	...	9,860.9 (1.04)	7,165.0 (1.36)	...
Mills inverse	0.485 (0.88)	3.59 (1.31)	13,648.1 (2.32)	−3,670.3 (2.54)	56,983.6 (3.90)	14,559.3 (2.13)
R^2	0.24	0.25	0.36	0.30	0.38	0.30
Number of observations	255	81	480	177	507	932
Mean	2.43	1.68	13,877	9,489	12,662	14,807

Source: Data from the household survey made by the International Food Policy Research Institute and the Institute of National Planning, Cairo, 1981/82.

Notes: The independent variables are defined in Appendix 2.

The R^2s are t-statistics from weighted regressions and R^2 from unweighted regressions, as the weighting procedure results in wide swings in the reported R^2 with little actual change in the equation.

Table 56—Results from open market entry equations for rural areas

Independent Variable	Sugar	Oil	Tea	Rice	Beans	Lentils	Fresh Meat	Fresh Chicken	Fresh Fish	Frozen Fish from Cooperatives
Constant	0.65	−0.19	1.33	−3.87	−2.48	−2.76	0.469	0.545	−3.708	−2.109
TXN	0.0017 (0.90)	0.0020 (1.07)	0.0013 (0.68)	0.0002 (0.11)	0.0035 (1.91)	0.0028 (1.62)	0.0076 (3.14)	0.0001 (0.04)	0.0114 (4.51)	−0.0001 (0.04)
NUM	0.023 (2.11)	0.038 (3.37)	0.023 (2.05)	0.009 (0.87)	0.044 (3.94)	0.050 (4.61)	0.037 (2.62)	0.033 (2.87)	0.058 (5.31)	0.057 (3.78)
UPPER	0.202 (2.21)	−0.442 (4.93)	0.214 (2.63)	−0.03 (0.28)	−0.314 (3.59)	−0.198 (2.03)	1.001 (6.51)	−0.994 (8.64)	0.679 (6.07)	−0.955 (4.53)
Cooperative membership	...	...	...	...	...	...	−0.135 (1.39)	0.105 (1.15)	−0.409 (4.85)	0.520 (4.56)
Commodity available at co-operative	−1.88 (11.36)	−1.60 (5.46)	−1.50 (8.18)	−1.76 (4.31)	−0.719 (1.40)	−3.06 (2.03)	−0.0083 (1.97)	...	−0.0037 (2.28)	0.022 (12.14)
$P_{dependent}$	0.0109 (2.70)	0.0167 (4.64)	0.0003 (0.73)	0.0283 (3.53)	0.0144 (3.14)	0.0034 (1.42)	0.0008 (0.28)	0.0037 (1.67)	−0.0009 (0.80)	...
$P_{dependent} \times$ CLASS 1	−0.0114 (6.31)	−0.086 (4.07)	−0.0010 (5.68)	−0.0190 (4.73)	−0.0063 (2.41)	−0.0058 (3.95)	−0.0023 (5.64)	−0.0030 (4.03)	−0.0032 (3.41)	...
Own produce available	−0.94 (3.67)	−0.10 (1.08)	...	−3.49 (8.08)	−0.45 (2.66)	...	−0.065 (0.47)	0.465 (5.34)	...	...
P_{meat}	...	...	...	0.0082 (3.53)	...	...	...	−0.0059 (2.35)	0.0077 (3.34)	...
P_{beans}	...	...	...	...	...	...	−0.0076 (1.21)	−0.0011 (2.12)	0.0112 (2.52)	−0.0085 (0.97)
P_{rice}	...	...	...	...	...	...	−0.0029 (0.27)	0.348 (4.06)	−0.0080 (0.99)	...
P_{fish}	...	...	...	...	...	...	...	...	...	0.0008 (0.56)
P_{wheat}	...	...	...	...	...	...	−0.0002 (1.57)	...	...	...
P_{flour}	...	...	...	0.0180 (3.19)	0.180 (3.52)	...	...	0.0067 (1.16)	0.0158 (2.58)	...
$P_{noodles}$	...	...	...	0.0176 (1.79)	...	...	...	...	...	...
RATION	−0.87 (5.48)	−1.03 (8.10)	−0.810 (5.05)	−0.095 (0.99)	−0.206 (2.67)	−0.480 (5.39)	...	...	...	...
SEX	...	...	−0.25 (2.39)	...	...	...	...	...	...	...
BREAD LIMIT	...	...	...	...	−0.174 (1.92)	...	...	...	...	...
Mean	0.807	0.359	0.689	0.455	0.261	0.316	0.832	0.609	0.487	0.111

Source: Data from the household survey made by the International Food Policy Research Institute and the Institute of National Planning, Cairo, 1981/82.

Note: The independent variables are defined in Appendix 2.

Table 57—Results from open market response equations for rural areas

Independent Variable	Sugar	Oil	Tea	Rice	Beans	Lentils	Fresh Meat	Fresh Chicken	Fresh Fish	Frozen Fish from Cooperatives
Constant	−464	−125	35	921	−1,565	1,613	5,112	3,890	266	7,952
LTX	374.10 (12.28)	226.60 (4.48)	65.90 (8.35)	1,342.86 (4.04)	265.72 (2.38)	297.70 (3.94)	660.63 (9.91)	1,128.0 (10.60)	745.1 (8.74)	874.35 (3.20)
NTX	−10.5 (7.22)	−11.25 (1.87)	−4.26 (3.70)	−101.0 (1.22)	−20.0 (1.42)	−22.02 (2.50)	−11.23 (1.70)	−72.0 (4.39)	−62.8 (5.27)	−52.7 (1.65)
CTX	...	−56.70 (1.95)	−15.72 (3.23)	−308.0 (1.92)	...	...	−98.0 (2.93)	−199.2 (3.31)	−124.1 (2.68)	182.7 (1.47)
NUM	...	17.58 (1.00)	8.7 (2.50)	171.1 (1.22)	29.0 (0.68)	44.8 (1.59)	17.98 (0.87)	161.1 (3.21)	154.8 (4.17)	114.0 (1.22)
UPPER	132.9 (3.88)	5.28 (0.09)	19.3 (3.44)	−1,543.4 (6.69)	334.6 (0.74)	160.8 (2.36)	270.96 (3.00)	−223.0 (1.19)	...	1,674.8 (3.90)
$LP_{dependent}$	−66.83 (1.01)	−11.68 (0.23)	−25.65 (2.40)	187.2 (0.73)	−223.54 (2.31)	62.19 (1.12)	−985.0 (3.89)	−743.5 (2.97)	−48.4 (0.93)	...
$LP_{dependent} \times$ CLASS 1	...	...	...	...	...	...	12.50 (1.02)	−10.48 (0.44)	...	...
RATION	−0.067 (2.23)	−0.204 (3.34)	−0.539 (7.39)	−0.829 (4.94)	0.304 (1.30)	0.531 (2.73)	−142.6 (1.23)	−514.11 (3.45)	−234.5 (2.21)	...
Own produce available	96.51 (0.57)	−22.35 (0.66)	...	227.5 (0.51)	94.8 (0.74)	...	...	−120.36 (1.04)	...	...
LP_{ghee}	...	−90.69 (1.48)	...	...	...	...	...	...	...	...
LP_{rice}	...	...	...	...	29.36 (0.23)	215.3 (2.48)	39.07 (0.54)	353.46 (2.04)	−36.5 (0.37)	−268.0 (0.94)
$LP_{lentils}$	...	...	...	...	157.89 (1.54)	...	...	...	...	...
$LP_{chicken}$	...	...	...	...	702.57 (2.35)	181.6 (1.06)	...	...	−540.0 (2.77)	−2,413.0 (2.97)
LP_{meat}	...	...	...	939.2 (0.62)	−454.38 (0.83)	−648.8 (2.00)	...	−256.7 (0.49)	...	...
LP_{flour}	...	...	10.77 (0.83)	...	−9.53 (0.07)	71.88 (0.93)	−106.9 (1.19)	−176.09 (1.25)	205.1 (1.84)	...
LP_{noodle}	...	...	...	218.9 (0.45)	...	...	...	...	...	...
LP_{beans}	...	...	...	...	...	...	...	...	...	1,089.54 (2.37)
LP_{maize}	...	...	...	−1,067.2 (2.29)	...	...	...	...	...	...
LP_{fish}	...	...	...	...	...	...	73.50 (1.93)	−63.33 (0.83)	...	...
LP_{sugar}	...	...	−10.80 (0.79)	...	...	...	...	...	...	...
Mills inverse	349.9 (2.14)	598.44 (1.90)	52.62 (1.47)	−1,011.7 (0.78)	833.1 (1.72)	816.7 (2.69)	−481.5 (1.12)	−550.59 (0.97)	433.33 (1.88)	−897.3 (0.94)
R^2	0.29	0.24	0.25	0.29	0.20	0.25	0.28	0.36	0.31	0.28
Number of observations	839	499	958	632	362	439	1,156	846	676	154
Mean	963	466	64	4,122	661	483	887	1,209	759	776

Source: Data from the household survey made by the International Food Policy Research Institute and the Institute of National Planning, Cairo, 1981/82.

Notes: The independent variables are defined in Appendix 2.

The R^2s are t-statistics from weighted regressions and R^2 from unweighted regressions, as the weighting procedure results in wide swings in the reported R^2 with little actual change in the equation.

Table 58—Results from other entry equations for rural areas

Independent Variable	Pasta	Eggs	Milk	Cheese	Wheat	Maize
Constant	0.487	−0.805	−1.22	−1.95	−7.75	−3.22
TXN	0.0027 (1.45)	0.0054 (2.89)	0.0068 (3.01)	0.0096 (4.41)	0.0003 (0.09)	0.0009 (0.42)
NUM	0.083 (3.51)	0.033 (2.96)	0.023 (1.41)	0.038 (3.00)	0.003 (0.17)	−0.023 (1.89)
UPPER	−0.287 (2.97)	−0.391 (3.65)	−1.02 (8.80)	...	0.680 (4.77)	−0.478 (4.39)
$P_{dependent}$	−0.0012 (0.10)	0.065 (1.67)	−0.016 (3.02)	−0.0018 (1.53)	0.0002 (1.12)	0.0013 (1.07)
$P_{dependent} \times$ CLASS 1	−0.036 (6.57)	−0.076 (5.20)	−0.011 (2.80)	−0.0096 (5.56)	0.0003 (0.40)	...
P_{milk}	...	−0.0020 (0.49)	...	−0.016 (3.72)	...	...
P_{meat}	−0.0037 (1.59)	0.0016 (0.67)	0.0080 (2.62)	0.0046 (1.88)	0.0142 (4.05)	0.0071 (2.79)
P_{flour}	0.021 (0.94)	0.015 (0.70)	0.055 (2.10)	0.099 (4.58)	0.094 (3.27)	0.0065 (0.28)
P_{cheese}	...	...	−0.001 (0.10)	...	...	...
P_{beans}	...	...	−0.012 (1.90)	−0.0026 (0.58)	...	...
P_{maize}	0.0001 (0.52)	−0.0002 (1.70)	−0.0008 (5.50)	0.0007 (0.62)	0.0001 (0.52)	...
CIIL	...	0.357 (1.52)	0.970 (3.49)	−0.128 (0.53)	...	...
Own produce available	...	−0.927 (11.57)	−2.69 (6.94)	−1.92 (13.64)	−1.01 (3.03)	−1.04 (4.75)
P_{rice}	0.026 (3.07)	...	...	...	0.170 (1.50)	0.023 (2.59)
BREAD LIMIT	−0.094	...	...	...	0.092 (0.75)	0.081 (0.86)
FLOUR LIMIT	...	...	...	...	0.536 (4.02)	0.077 (0.87)
P_{wheat}	...	...	...	...	...	−0.0000 (0.03)
Mean	0.662	0.374	0.194	0.385	0.085	0.210

Source: Data from the household survey made by the International Food Policy Research Institute and the Institute of National Planning, Cairo, 1981/82.
Note: The independent variables are defined in Appendix 2.

Table 59—Results from other response equations for rural areas

Independent Variable	Pasta	Eggs	Milk	Cheese	Wheat	Maize
Constant	−89.74	9.15	−5,907.5	−9,788.6	26,385	140,710
LTX	745.95	7.38	2,207.42	−1,267.76	23,946.0	5,288.10
	(7.68)	(7.42)	(5.71)	(5.31)	(3.02)	(6.23)
LTX2	...	...	...	...	−2,723.51	...
					(2.17)	
NTX	−33.24	−0.511	−214.79	−66.99	...	−119.15
	(2.73)	(4.44)	(4.40)	(2.47)		(1.91)
CTX	...	−0.67	−203.26	−50.02	...	−1,313.06
		(1.58)	(0.91)	(0.53)		(1.32)
NUM	43.11	1.43	555.75	181.40	−619.73	...
	(1.31)	(3.57)	(2.81)	(2.10)	(1.96)	
UPPER	−93.06	−0.136	367.32	−315.43	4,889.39	10,672.8
	(1.26)	(0.15)	(0.81)	(0.96)	(2.28)	(4.89)
Own produce available	...	0.189	−582.85	−1,683.22	3,169.74	3,888.55
		(0.19)	(0.30)	(2.99)	(0.49)	(0.99)
LP_{milk}	...	1.44	−1,107.6	32.12	...	...
		(1.48)	(2.48)	(0.17)		
LP_{rice}	−15.65	...	...	...	...	...
	(0.11)					
LP_{cheese}	...	0.719	625.02	−688.33	...	...
		(1.38)	(2.75)	(6.70)		
LP_{eggs}	...	−3.52	...	...	...	...
		(1.86)				
LP_{wheat}	...	...	...	...	3,711.61	4,079.32
					(0.90)	(1.41)
LP_{pasta}	−298.80	...	...	...	...	...
	(2.10)					
LP_{maize}	...	...	...	...	−8,219.51	3,360.91
					(1.63)	(1.44)
LP_{flour}	0.517	−1.42	415.26	831.01	−6,139.75	2,988.89
	(0.30)	(0.99)	(0.62)	(2.80)	(1.36)	(1.09)
LP_{beans}	...	−1.36	232.49	...	...	...
		(1.09)	(0.36)			
$LP_{dependent} \times$ CLASS 1	...	...	...	34.80	...	...
				(0.76)		
FLSHOP	...	0.718	...	...	...	...
		(1.23)				
FLOUR LIMIT	...	...	...	...	1,190.52	...
					(0.86)	
BREAD LIMIT	1.61	...	...	...	1,953.36	507.21
	(0.04)				(1.05)	(0.42)
LP_{meat}	...	−3.74	...	2,127.67	...	−3,072.75
		(0.85)		(1.85)		(3.66)
Mills ratio	117.17	1.98	957.90	−3,530.89	−16,408.9	8,546.0
	(0.25)	(0.31)	(0.62)	(2.61)	(1.00)	(0.52)
R^2	0.23	0.26	0.29	0.19	0.29	0.32
Number of observations	919	520	270	535	118	292
Mean	1,140	4.13	1,870	990	11,258	8,867

Source: Data from the household survey made by the International Food Policy Research Institute and the Institute of National Planning, Cairo, 1981/82.
Notes: The independent variables are defined in Appendix 2.

The R^2s are t-statistics from weighted regressions and R^2 from unweighted regressions, as the weighting procedure results in wide swings in the reported R^2 with little actual change in the equation.

Table 60—Results from budget share equations for rural areas

Independent Variable	Cooked Beans	Tamiya	Fruit	Vegetables
Constant	0.049	0.086	0.281	−0.300
LTX	−0.0042 (4.56)	0.0250 (4.19)	0.0736 (4.89)	0.107 (4.19)
LTX2	...	−0.0016 (4.31)	−0.0044 (4.89)	−0.0076 (4.69)
NTX	0.0003 (1.89)	−0.00005 (4.76)	−0.0013 (4.28)	−0.0018 (3.43)
CTX	0.0000 (0.04)	0.00003 (0.15)	0.0006 (1.25)	0.0004 (0.44)
SEX	0.0000 (0.30)	0.0018 (2.13)	0.0043 (2.16)	0.0071 (2.09)
UPPER	0.0017 (2.74)	−0.0017 (3.04)	0.0057 (4.32)	−0.020 (8.93)
NUM	...	...	0.010 (4.05)	0.011 (2.76)
R^2	0.05	0.04	0.05	0.15
Number of observations	1,389	1,389	1,389	1,389
Mean	0.005	0.005	0.023	0.058

Source: Data from the household survey made by the International Food Policy Research Institute and the Institute of National Planning, Cairo, 1981/82.

Notes: The independent variables are defined in Appendix 2.

The R^2s are t-statistics from weighted regressions and R^2 from unweighted regressions, as the weighting procedure results in wide swings in the reported R^2 with little actual change in the equation.

BIBLIOGRAPHY

Alderman, Harold. "Allocation of Goods Through Non-price Mechanism: Implications of Rationing and Waiting Times in Egypt." Ph.D. dissertation, Harvard University, 1984.

__________. "Impact of Income and Food Price Changes on Food Acquisition by Low-Income Households: A Review of the Evidence." Report prepared for U.S. Agency for International Development, Office of Nutrition, Washington, D.C., July 1984.

Alderman, Harold; Braun, Joachim von; and Sakr, Sakr Ahmed. *Egypt's Food Subsidy and Rationing System: A Description.* Research Report 34. Washington, D.C.: International Food Policy Research Institute, 1982.

Barzel, Yoram. "A Theory of Rationing by Waiting." *Journal of Law and Economics* 17 (April 1974): 73-95.

Beaton, George H. "Energy in Human Nutrition: Perspectives and Problems." *Nutrition Review* 41 (1983): 325-340.

Becker, Gary Stanley. "A Theory of the Allocation of Time." *Economic Journal* 75 (September 1965): 493-517.

Braun, Joachim von. *Ernaehrungssicherungspolitik in Entwicklungslaendern—Oekonomische Analyse am Beispiel Aegyptens.* Kiel: Kieler Wissenschaftsverlag Vauk, 1984.

Braun, Joachim von and Haen, Hartwig de. *The Effects of Food Price and Subsidy Policies on Egyptian Agriculture.* Research Report 42. Washington, D.C.: International Food Policy Research Institute, 1983.

Deaton, Angus. "Inequality and Needs: Some Experimental Results from Sri Lanka." *Population and Development Review* 9 (1983): 35-49.

__________. "Theoretical and Empirical Approaches to Consumer Demand Under Rationing." In *Essays in the Theories and Measurement of Consumer Behavior in Honor of Sir Richard Stone,* pp. 55-72. Edited by Angus Deaton. Cambridge: Cambridge University Press, 1981.

__________. *Three Essays on a Sri Lankan Household Survey.* Living Standard Measurement Study, Working Paper 11. Washington, D.C.: World Bank, 1981.

el-Edel, M. Reda A. "Impact of Taxation on Income Distribution: An Exploratory Attempt to Estimate Tax Incidence in Egypt." In *The Political Economy of Income Distribution in Egypt.* Edited by Gouda Abdel-Khalek and Robert Tignor. New York: Holmes and Meier, 1982.

Egypt, Ministry of Health, Nutrition Institute. *Arab Republic of Egypt National Survey, 1978.* Washington, D.C.: U.S. Agency for International Development, 1978.

Griliches, Zvi; Hall, B.; Hausman, J. "Missing Data and Self-Selection in Large Panels." *Annales de l'INSEE* 30-31 (1978): 137-176.

Gronau, Reuben. "Leisure, Home Production and Work—The Theory of the Allocation of Time Revisited." *Journal of Political Economy* 85 (December 1977): 1099-1123.

Heckman, James J. "Sample Selection Bias as a Specification Error." *Econometrica* 47 (January 1979): 153-162.

Hussein, Mohamed Amr. "Protein Requirements of Egyptian Women." Paper presented at a symposium on protein requirements, University of California, Berkeley, Cal., 1981.

Janvry, Alain de; Siam, Gamal; and Gad, Osman. "The Impact of Forced Deliveries on Egyptian Agriculture." *American Journal of Agricultural Economics* 65 (August 1983): 493-501.

Kennedy, Eileen T. and Pinstrup-Andersen, Per. *Nutrition-Related Policies and Programs: Past Performances and Research Needs.* Washington, D.C.: International Food Policy Research Institute, 1983.

Korayem, Karima. *The Impact of the Elimination of Food Subsidies on the Cost of Living of the Urban Population in Egypt.* Geneva: International Labour Organisation, 1980.

Kornai, Janos. *The Economics of Shortage,* 2 vols. Amsterdam: North-Holland, 1980.

Lechtig, Aaron, et al. "The One-Day Recall Dietary Survey: A Review." *Archivos Latinoamericanos de Nutrición* 26 (1976).

el-Lozy, Mohammed; Field, J.; Roper, G.; and Burkhardt, R. *Childhood Malnutrition in Rural Egypt.* Health Care Delivery System Project Monograph 4. Cambridge, Mass.: Massachusetts Institute of Technology, 1980.

McDonald, John F. and Moffitt, Robert A. "The Uses of Tobit Analysis." *Review of Economics and Statistics* 62 (May 1980): 318-321.

Nichols, Donald A.; Smolensky, E.; and Tideman, T.N. "Discrimination by Wasting Time in Merit Goods." *American Economic Review* 61 (June 1971): 312-323.

Pekkasinen, M. "Methodology in the Collection of Food Consumption Data." *World Review of Nutrition and Dietetics* 12 (1970).

Pellett, P. and Shaderevian, S. *Food Composition Table for Use in the Middle East.* Beirut: American University, 1970.

Pitt, Mark M. "Food Preferences and Nutrition in Rural Bangladesh." *Review of Economics and Statistics* 65 (February 1983): 105-114.

Pollack, Robert A. and Wachter, Michael L. "The Relevance of the Household Production Function for the Allocation of Time." *Journal of Political Economy* 83 (April 1975): 255-277.

Pollack, Robert A. and Wales, Terence J. "Demographic Variables in Demand Analysis." *Econometrica* 49 (November 1981): 1533-1591.

Prais, S. J. and Houthakker, H.S. *The Analysis of Family Budgets.* Cambridge: Cambridge University Press, 1955.

Quandt, Richard E. "Economic Disequilibrium Models." *Econometric Reviews* 1 (No. 1, 1982): 1-65.

Radwan, Samir and Lee, Eddy. *The Anatomy of Rural Poverty: Egypt 1977.* Geneva: International Labour Office, 1980.

Soliman, Ibrahim; Fitch, James B.; and Aziz, N.A. "The Role of Livestock Production on the Egyptian Farm." Economics Working Paper 85, Agricultural Development Systems Project, Ministry of Agriculture, Cairo, and the University of California-Berkeley, Cairo, July 1982.

Telser, Lester G. "Iterative Estimation of a Set of Linear Regression Estimates." *Journal of the American Statistical Association* 59 (1964): 845-862.

Theil, Henri. *Principles of Econometrics.* New York: Wiley, 1971.

Tobin, James. "Estimation of Relationships for Limited Dependent Variables." *Econometrica* 26 (January 1958): 24-36.

__________. "A Survey of the Theory of Rationing." *Econometrica* 20 (October 1952): 521-553.

Treville, Diana de. "Food Processing and Distribution Systems in Rural Egypt: The Case of Grain and Bread." Working paper written for the International Food Policy Research Institute, Washington, D.C., n.d. (mimeographed).

U.S. Department of Agriculture, Office of the Agricultural Attaché, Cairo. *Annual Agricultural Situation Report.* Cairo: U.S. Embassy, Office of the Agricultural Attaché, 1983.